COLUMBIA RIVER GORGE

A Complete Guide

Edited by Philip N. Jones

6 5 4 3 2
5 4 3 2 1

Published by The Mountaineers
1011 SW Klickitat Way, Seattle, Washington 98134

Published simultaneously in Canada by Douglas & McIntyre, Ltd., 1615 Venables Street, Vancouver, B.C. V5L 2H1

Published simultaneously in Great Britain by Cordee, 3a DeMontfort Street, Leicester, England, LE1 7HD

Manufactured in the United States of America

Edited by Kris Fulsaas
Maps by Beth Duke
Cover photograph: Crown Point, by Kirkendall/Spring; inset photos (except center) by Kirkendall/Spring
All photographs by Philip N. Jones unless otherwise credited
Illustrations by Julie Kierstead Nelson
Cover design by Elizabeth Watson Design
Book design and layout by Barbara Bash

Title page: Saint Peters Dome

Library of Congress Cataloging in Publication Data
Columbia River Gorge : a complete guide / edited by Philip N. Jones.
     p.   cm.
     Includes bibliographical references and index.
     ISBN 0-89886-234-5
     1. Outdoor recreation—Columbia River Gorge (Or. and Wash.)—
Guidebooks. 2. Columbia River Gorge (Or. and Wash.)—Description and travel—Guidebooks. I. Jones, Philip N.
GV191.42.C63C65   1992
917.95′4—dc20   92-5998
                                                                       CIP

Printed on recycled paper

Contents

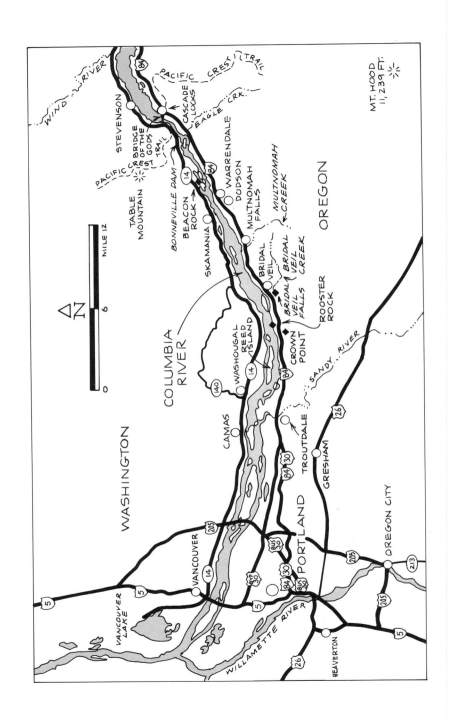

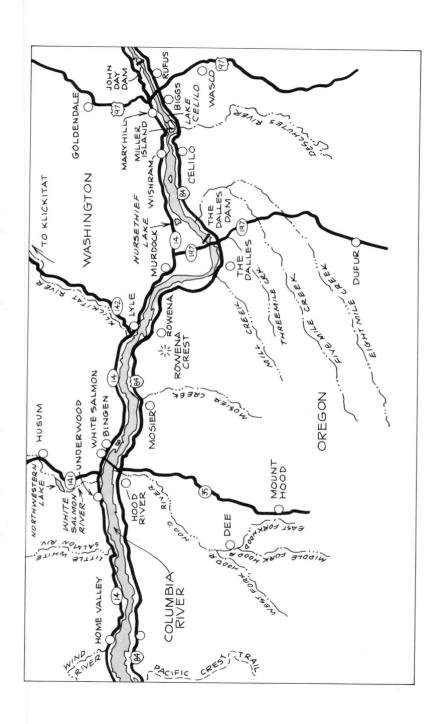

LEGEND

▬▬▬	MAJOR ROAD	→	DIRECTION
────	SECONDARY ROAD, PAVED	~···~	RIVER, STREAM, CREEK
= = =	GRAVEL OR ABANDONED ROAD	←	KAYAK PUT IN
• • • • • •	ROUTE- HIKING TRAIL	→	KAYAK TAKE OUT
━•━•━•	ROUTE FOLLOWING PAVED ROAD	☀	SUMMIT OR PEAK
─ ─ ─ ─	COLUMBIA WILDERNESS BOUNDARY	⊟	BRIDGE
		▼	VIEWPOINT
┼─┼─┼─	POWER LINES	⌇	WATERFALL
★	START AND/OR END OF ROUTE	◆	POINT OF INTEREST
Ⓟ	PARKING	▲	CAMPGROUND
		⬛	PICNIC SITE

SAFETY CONSIDERATIONS

Many of the outdoor activities described in this book involve certain inherent dangers. Participants in those activities must be constantly alert for their own safety, as no guidebook can be substituted for careful judgment, adequate training, and experience. Adverse weather conditions and changes in trails, roads, routes, and waterways cannot be anticipated by the authors, but must be taken into account by hikers, climbers, cyclists, paddlers, windsurfers, and other visitors to the Columbia Gorge. The inclusion of a particular trail or route in this guide is not a representation that the trail or route is safe for all parties. Readers assume responsibility for their own safety, as the authors, the editor, and the publisher will not be responsible for the safety of the users of this guide. The editor and the authors would appreciate receiving any corrections or suggestions from readers; please write to the editor in care of the publisher.

Introduction

The Columbia River Gorge is one of the most dramatic landscapes of the Pacific Northwest. Stretching for nearly ninety miles along the Washington–Oregon border, it is the only sea-level passage through the Cascade Range. Its towering walls are lined with basalt cliffs, remnants of ancient volcanoes, narrow side canyons, spectacular waterfalls, and breathtaking viewpoints. Its landscapes vary from rain forest to desert to alpine, its waters vary from tidal open reaches to steep mountain streams, and its flora and fauna vary from the common to the rare and endemic.

The Columbia, the great River of the West, not only flows through the Gorge, it created the Gorge over a period of several million years. Today, the Gorge can only be described as unique. Everything about the Gorge, from its geologic history to its weather, sets it apart as a special place, not just as a striking natural feature, but as a major economic, recreational, and aesthetic resource.

The purpose of this collaborative book is to provide an overview of the natural history of the Gorge and its recreational opportunities. No single author could competently describe the Gorge—its history, weather, geology, flora, and fauna—much less describe the opportunities available for hikers, climbers, cyclists, boaters, photographers, and campers. The fourteen authors who have contributed to this volume have each provided a chapter describing their special areas of interest and expertise. Through their contributions, it is our hope that this book will present, in a single volume, a summary of the natural history of the Gorge and the myriad recreational activities that have found a home there.

In each of the chapters, we have attempted to convey not just hard scientific facts about the Gorge or information on history and recreation, but also the elusive reasons why the Gorge is such a special place. Those reasons are not easily stated, but they are easily understood by those who have visited the Gorge, and we hope that those reasons will become even more evident as one learns more and more about the Gorge and the story it has to tell. It is a story of great geologic events, of Native American cultures, of fierce storms, of rare plant species, of the impact of transportation and commerce on a delicate landscape, of pioneer migrations, of railroad building, dam construction, and the designing and building of an historic scenic highway.

It is another story, as well. It is a story of windsurfers skimming across the Columbia, of hikers following trails into the side canyons and onto the ridgetops, of climbers struggling on the basalt cliffs, of cyclists pedaling the roadways of the Gorge, of kayakers and canoeists on the Columbia and its tributaries, and of campers, picnickers, and photographers marveling at the waterfalls.

Visitors should also be aware of the political struggles occurring in the Gorge. A brief history of the battle over land-use planning in the Gorge is given in the first chapter of this book, but keep in mind that the battle rages on. Even though the Columbia River Gorge National Scenic Area Act was passed in 1986, that act merely established the legal mechanism for implementation of regional land-use planning in the Gorge. The effectiveness of that legislation depends on its implementation, a never-ending process. As this book went to press, the Columbia Gorge Commission and the U.S. Forest Service were in the process of adopting an overall management plan for the Gorge, which will be followed by the adoption of individual plans by the six counties in the Gorge.

The process of adopting land-use plans for the Gorge will be a delicate one, as will the day-to-day implementation of those plans. At every step of the process, the forces of development will conflict with the forces of preservation as crucial decisions are made. The quality of the results depends on the people who participate in that process, and the quality of their ideas. Every regular visitor to the Gorge should feel obligated to participate in that process.

Visitors to the Gorge also owe a duty to leave the Gorge in as good (or better) condition as when they entered it. It is a fragile natural landscape that requires considerable care. All of the normal rules of wilderness ethics should be strictly followed: leave no litter, pick up the litter of others, stay on trails, and dispose of wastes properly. The Gorge deserves our very best treatment.

The authors hope this book encourages more people to hike, climb, windsurf, cycle, paddle, picnic, and camp in the Columbia Gorge, and to become students of its natural and cultural history. More importantly, however, we hope to instill in those visitors the same reverence we feel for the Gorge. If so, we will have told its story well.

P.N.J.

FURTHER READING

At the end of each chapter, we give suggestions for further reading on the particular subject covered in each chapter. On the general subject of the Columbia River Gorge, we suggest:

Friends of the Columbia Gorge. *Columbia River Gorge Guided Tour.* Cassette tapes, 1988.

Spranger, Michael S., ed. *The Columbia Gorge: A Unique American Treasure.* Washington State University, 1984.

Webber, Bert, and Margie Webber. *Oregon Covered Bridges.* Webber Research Group, 1991.

Shepperds Dell Bridge (Oregon Historical Society negative No. 52857)

PART I

◆

HISTORY

BY CHUCK WILLIAMS

The Columbia River Gorge is the only sea-level passage through the Cascade Range between Canada and California and, as such, for millennia has played—and continues to play—a major role in the human history of the Pacific Northwest.

Many traces of this important part of our common heritage have been erased—irreversibly—by "progress," especially the dams, railroads, and highways that continue the Gorge's tradition as the region's main transportation corridor. Fortunately, however, many fascinating historic sites and structures remain for visitors to explore.

The first residents of the Gorge most likely depended on big-game hunting for most of their subsistence, and the oldest artifacts found—thus far, at least—are bone spear points used to hunt the now-extinct mammoth. During the past few thousand years, residents increasingly settled in permanent villages along the river, and fishing became the primary food provider.

At the time that the United States was established, the Gorge was home for an exceptionally large American Indian population and had become the main trade-mart in the Northwest. The Columbia's waterfalls and rapids—before they were inundated by dams—provided exceptional fishing spots, and village after village lined the great river, which provided abundant salmon, steelhead, sturgeon, and smelt, as well as wapato, the native potato that once thrived in wetlands along the river.

The stretch of the river between the Long Narrows/Big Eddy (now the site of The Dalles Dam) and Celilo Falls was the cultural transition between the canoe people of the ocean and the more nomadic plateau tribes. Thousands of native people from miles around camped here along the river each summer, fishing, trading, and socializing with each other and the year-round residents.

The abundance of salmon, roots, and cedar allowed the Chinookan-speaking people of the lower Columbia (up to the Narrows east of The Dalles), including the Cascades, Wishrams, and Wascos in the Gorge, to build large permanent villages along the Columbia, their food provider and highway. The banks of the river were lined with huge longhouses, sometimes 200 feet long, built of cedar planks. These homes were usually sunk 2 to 6 feet into the ground and were occupied by extended families.

The Chinooks traveled seasonally to fish and gather roots and huckleberries, but most of their food came to them. Their main mode of transportation—huge canoes carved from cedar trees—could carry large loads and, combined with their strategic location and surplus of salmon, enabled these people to become important traders.

Some of the Sahaptian-speaking people of the eastern end of the Gorge, such as the Wyams at Celilo Falls, lived along the river in permanent structures. Most, however, were more migratory than the Chinooks, especially after obtaining horses in the early 1700s. In spring, small groups traveled to traditional gathering sites to dig roots. Summers were usually

She Who Watches

spent camped at fishing sites. During the fall, these people hunted and gathered huckleberries in the mountains, including at Indian Heaven, a plateau just north of the Gorge where a prehistoric racetrack is still visible. Winters were generally spent up sheltered tributary canyons, such as along the Klickitat and Deschutes rivers, in longhouses made of reed mats. Like the Chinooks, these tribes dried and stored salmon, meat, roots, and berries for winter, a time of much storytelling and religious activity, including dancing. Winter was also a time to manufacture baskets, clothing, tools, and similar items. Near the mouths of the White Salmon and Klickitat rivers, Sahaptian-speaking Klickitat Indians shared villages with the Chinooks.

To the Native Americans in the Columbia Gorge, their natural environment has always had religious significance, not just economic importance. These people believed in guardian spirits, and the spirit quest was an important ritual. Numerous spirit-quest sites, being at higher elevations, have survived, but most village sites, petroglyphs, cemeteries, and other prehistoric cultural sites have been destroyed by construction or buried beneath reservoirs.

In the early 1800s, more than 90 percent of the native residents of the western Gorge died from diseases, such as small pox and measles, brought by the white newcomers. Being more migratory, the Indians in the eastern end of the Gorge fared better. Most, however, were removed to reservations during the late 1850s, returning—when they could—to the Gorge to fish. Despite numerous efforts to take away this treaty right, enrolled members of the confederated Yakima, Warm Springs, Umatilla, and Nez Perce tribes continue to fish in the Columbia Gorge, although fishing methods have had to change due to the demise of Celilo Falls and other important fishing sites. Traditional dip-net fishing from platforms continues at some sites, such as below the Bridge of the Gods, along the lower Klickitat River, and near Sherars Falls on the Deschutes.

The first non-Indian explorer to enter the Columbia, the mythical "River of the West," was Bostonian Robert Gray, whose 1792 "discovery" in his ship *Columbia Rediviva* led to the river's present name and the United States' claim to the region. Later the same year, English Lieutenant William Broughton of Captain George Vancouver's expedition sailed up the Columbia to the mouth of the Gorge, gave Mount Hood its present name, and on Reed Island (now a state park) claimed the region for England, leading to years of conflicts with the expanding United States.

The Lewis and Clark expedition, the first non-Indians to travel through the Gorge and return, entered the deep crevice from the east in 1805 and gave detailed descriptions of the people then living in the Gorge. However, the people they found, especially downriver, were already being decimated by the exotic diseases brought by European fur traders, who began obtaining sea otter and beaver pelts from Indians at the mouth of the Columbia in the late 1700s. Lewis and Clark, having traded their horses for dugout canoes upriver, floated into the Gorge. They had to portage around Celilo Falls but, using ropes, were able to float their heavy boats through the Long Narrows, which Clark described as an "agitated gut swelling, boiling, and whorling in every direction." Even though it was autumn and most of the seasonal residents had already left, the riverbanks were lined with racks of salmon drying in the sun. Lewis and Clark estimated that the permanent residents of the Narrows had 10,000 pounds of salmon drying in the sun, to be used during the winter and traded to other tribes.

In the western end of the Gorge, the expedition again found game to complement their fish diet; they observed numerous swans, condors, and other birdlife. In fact, the waterfowl were so plentiful and loud that Lewis and Clark had trouble sleeping at night.

The next non-Indian explorer, David Thompson, was a fur trader with the Canadian North West Company. He traveled through the Gorge in 1811 and established a good relationship with the natives living at the Great Cascades (five miles of rapids), the location of the portage that was crucial to the expansion of the fur trade. When he reached the mouth of the Columbia, Thompson found Americans building Fort Astoria, a trading post taken over by the British during the War of 1812. The Hudson's Bay Company took over the fur trade in the Pacific Northwest and in 1824 moved its headquarters to Fort Vancouver (now a National Historic site) just downriver of the Gorge.

In the 1840s, a mass migration of pioneers followed the Oregon Trail to its overland terminus west of The Dalles. From here—until the Barlow Road was built around Mount Hood to Oregon City (1845–46)—the newcomers had to float through the Gorge on rafts, a treacherous ending to a long journey. In 1842, a wagon road was built around The Cascades on the north bank. As conflicts grew between the Indians and the pioneers, a major fort was built at The Dalles between 1850 and 1867.

The 1850 Donation Land Claims Act allowed pioneers to claim up to 320 acres of land per person (640 for married couples), and Francis Chenoweth filed a claim on the north bank at The Cascades of the Columbia. When steamboat travel began on the mid-Columbia the following year, Chenoweth built a wooden-railed, mule-drawn portage tramway— the first railroad in Washington—around the rapids. A competing portage railroad was built on the south bank, and cutting cord wood for steamboats became the main source of income for the growing pioneer population at The Cascades. Another portage railroad was built to bypass the Long Narrows and Celilo Falls, so passengers traveling upriver had to change boats at The Cascades and again east of The Dalles.

As a result of the growing friction between Indians and settlers, in 1855 the major tribes were pressured into signing treaties that established reservations. In the Yakima, Warm Springs, and Grand Ronde (Willamette Valley) treaties, the tribes gave up title to the vast majority of their lands in the Gorge and elsewhere, but reserved many rights, including fishing, hunting, picking berries, and gathering roots at traditional sites within the lands they ceded to the U.S. government.

However, violations, especially by white newcomers coveting remaining Indian lands and minerals, soon led to a series of skirmishes generally referred to as the Yakima War of 1856. A major battle took place at The Cascades of the Columbia, where Yakima and Klickitat Indians attacked the Fort Rains blockhouse and nearby pioneer settlements. U.S. Army soldiers led by Lieutenant Phil Sheridan came upriver from Fort Vancouver, finally drove off the attackers, and hanged some apparently innocent local Indian leaders. New forts were soon built at each end of the rapids.

After the war fizzled out and most local Indians had been sent to the reservations, development again boomed. Towns at The Cascades and The Dalles were among the largest in the Northwest, and improved transportation helped commercial agriculture, fishing, and logging become important industries. Large canneries were built, and fish wheels increased the commercial catch of salmon and steelhead. Incline railroads and flumes were often used to bring logs to the Columbia.

In 1862 the Oregon Steam Navigation Company began using the Oregon Pony, the first locomotive in the Northwest, to haul passengers around The Cascades portage. In 1896, the U.S. Army Corps of Engineers completed construction of locks to enable boats to bypass The Cascades rapids. An eight-mile-long canal around the Narrows and Celilo Falls was completed in 1915, but the era of the stern-wheelers had already come to an end, due to the completion of the first railroad through the Gorge in 1883.

The railroad through the Gorge accelerated settlement and allowed more commercial farming, including the orchards now famous for their spring blossoms. The Oregon Railway and Navigation Company held a firm monopoly on Gorge transportation for many years, but a competing railway was constructed along the north bank in 1908. The railroads have continued to play an important role in the Gorge, but it was highway construction that opened the Gorge for development and recreation.

The Columbia River Highway (now often referred to as the old scenic highway), begun in 1913, was the first major paved road in the Northwest. Not only does the road traverse a beautiful place, but the highway itself is scenic, built with a concern for the landscape that is unheard-of today. The story of its design and construction is told in the next chapter.

The Columbia River Highway also led to the first preservation efforts in the Columbia Gorge. In 1915, at the urging of the Portland Chamber of Commerce and others, the U.S. Forest Service protected 14,000 acres on the Oregon side.

Across the river, the family of Henry Biddle, who, in 1915, had bought Beacon Rock to build a trail to the top, tried to donate the rock to

Barn at Dodson, built circa 1870

the state of Washington to prevent its demolition by the Corps of Engineers, who wanted to blow it up for rock to build a jetty at the mouth of the river. Washington's governor refused the gift, however, so the Biddle family offered the rock to the state of Oregon—as an Oregon state park in Washington. Washington state was finally embarrassed into accepting the gift.

The completion of Bonneville Dam in 1938 and The Dalles Dam in 1957 flooded the Columbia's rapids and waterfalls, including famous Celilo Falls, as well as most petroglyphs and other archaeological sites. The dams also further devastated the once-great fishery, but made Lewiston, Idaho, a seaport.

The runs of anadromous fish (those that migrate to the ocean, then return to fresh water to spawn), prior to development on the Columbia, once numbered upwards of 16 million salmon and steelhead each year, according to the most comprehensive study ever done. Now only about 2.5 million fish return annually, and about three-fourths of the loss is due to hydroelectric development and operation.

To help compensate for the damage done by the dams, Congress passed the Mitchell Act in 1938 to provide mitigation monies for hatcheries. The states, however, placed almost all of the hatcheries below Bonneville Dam, where non-Indian commercial fishermen would get the fish, instead of above Bonneville, where the fish runs were devastated (and where the Indians fish).

Fortunately, the "fish wars" of the 1960s, pitting Indians against non-Indians and commercial against sport fishermen, have waned, and in-

Tooth Rock viaducts, circa 1916 (Oregon Historical Society negative No. 71161)

creased cooperation has resulted in improved fish runs and more emphasis on upriver runs. Some runs, such as spring chinook, are still in trouble, but other runs, especially fall chinook and steelhead, are rebounding quite dramatically. While native fishing sites, such as Celilo Falls—which was an essential part of Indian life—are gone for now, at least the once-great fish runs are beginning to return.

The Columbia Gorge's stunning beauty has long been recognized; naturalist John Muir even compared it to his beloved Yosemite Valley. But the Gorge's role as the Northwest's main transportation corridor and its great capacity for hydroelectric-power generation doomed its chances of becoming a national park, a designation that the Gorge obviously deserves. Efforts to protect the Columbia Gorge blossomed periodically during this century, but each time faded away after a few more places—those imminently threatened—were put into public ownership.

The construction of Bonneville Dam in the late 1930s sparked the area's first real environmental battle—but not over the dam itself, which provided needed jobs during the Great Depression. "Cheap" electricity from the dam lured outside industrialists, who envisioned the Gorge as "the Pittsburgh of the West" and tried to construct steel mills and other polluting industrial plants.

Gorge lovers were appalled, and a federal commission was established to study the situation. Led by John Yeon, the commission released a comprehensive study in 1937 (one of the country's first environmental impact statements) calling for establishment of a recreation area. World War II sidetracked protection efforts, but the commission helped block the planned steel mills and standardize electrical rates throughout the Northwest so that industries would not have a financial incentive to locate in the Gorge.

Extensive clear-cutting around unprotected waterfalls in the 1950s brought renewed battles. In a campaign led by the Portland Women's Forum, many threatened areas on the Oregon side were put into public ownership, often through trades. This effort, however, also faded without protecting the Gorge as a whole. Each state did establish a Columbia River Gorge Commission, with members appointed by the governors, but the commissions never had regulatory powers, enough staff, or the means to purchase threatened lands. The counties, for the most part, ignored the advisory commissions' recommendations and routinely approved projects opposed by the commissions. Three decades later, the two commissions were replaced by a single bistate commission.

The battle over Gorge protection heated up again in the mid-1970s, but with two new twists: port districts, armed with millions of dollars of federal economic-development funds, embarked on a vigorous drive to bring heavy industry to the Gorge; and local residents began to organize and lead the fights against overdevelopment of their home. Friends of the White Salmon River formed to fight seven dams planned for that stream by the local public utility. Mid-Columbia Concerned Citizens formed because a polluting zirconium plant was approved at Dallesport. And the local chapter of the Audubon Society fought industrialization of the Steigerwald Lake wetlands at the western entrance to the Gorge.

In 1979 the leaders of these groups formed the Columbia Gorge Coalition and made the first public proposal for a Columbia Gorge National Scenic Area, with the National Park Service as the lead agency and with protection for the lower tributary canyons. In 1981, the Friends of the Columbia Gorge formed and joined in the battle for federal legislation.

Finally, in November 1986, after years of bitter debates and increasing local polarization, Congress passed and the president signed legislation establishing a Columbia River Gorge National Scenic Area, as well as giving Wild and Scenic River designation to segments of the lower White Salmon and Klickitat rivers. The legislation exempts established cities and towns and divides the rest of the Gorge into two categories: "special management areas" administered by the Forest Service, and agricultural areas managed by a bistate commission made up of twelve people appointed by the counties and governors. Much of the actual administration is left up to the local governments, with considerable economic development grants available if they cooperate.

The final bill enacted by Congress was a compromise among the various elements fighting for or against passage of the bill. To some environmental groups, the bill was clearly not strong enough. To some residents of the Gorge, the bill was an unfair and unneeded restriction on their property rights. To other elements, it was, like most other legislation, the best compromise that could be worked out. The battle over development continues, and it remains to be seen how effective the legislation will be, or what effect it will have on the landscape of the Columbia River Gorge, as the history of the Gorge continues to unfold.

FURTHER READING

Attwell, Jim. *Columbia River Gorge History.* Vols. 1 and 2. Tahlkie Books, 1974 and 1975.

Bullard, Oral. *Konapee's Eden: Historic and Scenic Handbook of the Columbia River Gorge.* TMS Book Service, 1985.

Williams, Chuck. *Bridge of the Gods, Mountains of Fire: A Return to the Columbia Gorge.* Friends of the Earth and Elephant Mountain Arts, 1980.

Desert shooting star
(Dodecatheon
conjugens)

◆

THE COLUMBIA RIVER HIGHWAY

BY RICHARD N. ROSS

Following the path of Lewis and Clark after 1805, a trickle of explorers, traders, and trappers became a flood of American settlers traveling west along the Oregon Trail through the Columbia River Gorge in the 1840s. After 2,000 miles of wagon travel, progress was stopped by steep basalt cliffs and towering mountains at several places in the Gorge, requiring weary emigrants to strap their belongings to makeshift rafts and pray they would make it through the boiling Cascades rapids of the Gorge.

In 1872, the Oregon legislature appropriated $50,000 to build a rugged wagon road from Troutdale to The Dalles. The resulting road was steep, narrow, twisting, and short-lived. Fragments of the wagon road can be found today crossing the lower slopes of Shellrock Mountain and above Tooth Rock.

Between the 1850s and the 1880s, other transportation advances improved the Gorge traveler's lot and reduced the Pacific Northwest's isolation. First, portage roads and railways were built around The Cascades and the Long Narrows, east of The Dalles. Steamboats plied the Columbia after the 1850s, and between 1878 and 1896 a canal around The Cascades was slowly constructed by the Army Corps of Engineers at Cascade Locks. In 1883, the first transcontinental railroad to the Northwest was built through the Gorge to reach Portland. Unfortunately, the new railroad wiped out portions of the just-completed wagon road through the Gorge.

As the twentieth century began, the westward movement through the Gorge had advanced from log rafts to Pullman rail cars, but road travel remained impossible.

The automobile, first seen as a rich man's toy, took on increasing speed and popularity. Auto enthusiasts fueled a powerful national movement for hard-surfaced roads; their rallying cry was "Good Roads." At the same time, a new conservation movement worked to protect natural resources through the establishment of new national forests, parks, and wildlife refuges.

Meanwhile, the City Beautiful movement struggled to end slums and build model park systems, boulevards, and neighborhoods. Landscape design and engineering were joined as a new art form. The Craftsman

Footbridge near Latourell Falls, circa 1920 (Oregon Historical Society negative No. Gi817)

movement took hold among architects and builders, extolling simple hand-hewn structures, rustic designs, and the use of natural materials. All of these national influences were to merge in the building of the Columbia River Highway.

A remarkable group of civic-minded men joined in the effort to build a great American road in the Columbia River Gorge. The prime mover was Sam Hill of Seattle, attorney for the Great Northern Railway and son-in-law of rail mogul James J. Hill. Sam Hill brought together civil engineer Sam Lancaster, lumber barons Simon Benson and John B. Yeon, publisher Sam Jackson, Portland's leading retailer, Julius Meier, and Multnomah County Commissioner Rufus Holman. This influential group moved Oregon very quickly in 1912–13 to begin the Columbia River Highway.

Sam Hill was a seasoned world traveler and a tireless Good Roads promoter. Hill owned a 7,000-acre ranch at Maryhill, Washington, in the east end of the Gorge, which he then hoped to promote as a Quaker agricultural colony. Samuel C. Lancaster of Mississippi, an expert road builder fresh from building the Seattle boulevard system (1907–09), toured Europe with Hill, where they were impressed with well-built mountain roads in Italy, Switzerland, and Germany. The terraced vineyards along the Rhine River reminded them of the eastern end of the Gorge. Along Lake Lucerne in the Swiss Alps, they were inspired by the Axenstrasse road tunnel, a 300-foot tunnel with rock "windows" and beautiful arched stone guardrails, built in the 1860s.

In 1909, Hill hired Lancaster to build a model road system on Hill's Maryhill Ranch. Lancaster's Maryhill Loops wound gently up Maryhill Canyon from the Columbia River, like the Swiss alpine roads. The Maryhill roads were the first paved rural roads in the state of Washington. Today, the loops can be found running up Maryhill Canyon, above the Stonehenge Memorial, northeast of the junction of US 97 and Washington State Highway 14. Hill's road-building demonstration and lobbying efforts failed to convince the state of Washington to build a road through the Gorge, so he turned his attention to Oregon.

In 1912, lumber-baron-turned-hotel-builder Simon Benson donated $10,000 to Oregon Governor Oswald West, so that convicts from the state prison could begin grading a new Columbia River road at the base of Shellrock Mountain, then, as now, a formidable barrier. John B. Yeon, a millionaire lumberman, also turned his interests to Good Roads. He was to serve, without pay, as Multnomah County's roadmaster from 1913 to

The builders of the Columbia River Highway

1918, supervising the entire construction of the Columbia River Highway in Multnomah County. The election of progressive Republican Rufus Holman to the Multnomah County Commission in 1913 changed the commission to favor Good Roads projects. Meanwhile, Julius Meier, later governor of Oregon from 1930 to 1934, led the newly formed Columbia River Highway Association to promote a Columbia river road across Oregon from Pendleton to Astoria.

Hill raised the curtain with a flair. In February 1913, he wined and dined the entire 1913 Oregon legislature on his private excursion train through the Gorge to his Maryhill Ranch. The lawmakers were impressed by Hill's model road system and his hospitality. More importantly, Hill's astounding lobbying convinced the legislature to create a State Highway Commission and Department. By August 1913, Sam Lancaster was hired as assistant state highway engineer, and as consulting engineer to Multnomah County, to supervise the design and construction of the Columbia River Highway through the Gorge. In October 1913, location surveys had begun.

Lancaster's experience convinced him that great boulevards should be built in harmony with the landscape. He laid out the highway to connect the "beauty spots" of the Gorge, but he maintained that "the highway was so built that not one tree was felled, not one fern crushed, unnecessarily."

Lancaster's design emulated the timeless hand-hewn qualities of the great mountain roads of Europe. Consequently, he hired skilled Italian-American stonemasons to craft the masonry retaining walls, guardrails, and scenic observatories of his Columbia River Highway. The Craftsman style of the highway influenced a generation of lodges, hotels, homes, campgrounds, parks, and trails throughout the Gorge. Two decades later, some of these stonemasons were to build Mount Hood's Timberline Lodge.

All of the highway's structures and its gentle, curving alignment were closely tied to the landscape of the Gorge, to help the traveler appreciate what "God had put there." Lancaster and his immigrant stonemasons created a road that later generations would acclaim as a "poem in stone."

Not only was the highway an aesthetic marvel, the design was state-of-the-art engineering. For the seventy-four miles from Troutdale to Chenoweth Creek Bridge just west of The Dalles, Lancaster and state engineers established a 24-foot-wide roadbed with a maximum 5 percent grade and a minimum curve radius of 100 feet.

Significant obstacles stood in the path of this advanced road design. Rockslides and cliffs bordered the river throughout the Gorge, with barely room for the railroad at river level. Every few miles there were mountain barriers, major streams, and ravines needing structures. Although Lancaster supervised the design and location of the highway only in Multnomah County and at Mitchell Point in Hood River County, his design standards were carried throughout the remainder of the Gorge to The Dalles.

The new road was open from Troutdale to the city of Hood River in July 1915. Paving and finish work on that section followed in stages until 1920. Construction of the eastern section from Hood River to The Dalles took place from 1918 to 1922, resulting in a road that was paved continuously for 202 miles (except for 1 mile) from The Dalles to the Pacific. The Oregon Highway Commission, in its biennial report for 1922, proudly declared, "The Columbia River Highway is considered to be one of the finest and most scenic highways in existence. . . . Excellent camping places have been developed at convenient intervals and nothing has been left undone that would contribute to the comfort and pleasure of the traveler."

Between 1914 and 1922 Oregon built a series of bridges, tunnels, viaducts, and highway sections in the Gorge unequaled by any mountain highway in the United States. From 1915 to the mid-1920s, the Columbia River Highway was in the international spotlight. *The London News* crowned it the "King of Roads." In August 1915, *Sunset* magazine declared, "The dream of a century . . . most certainly will become one of the noted scenic automobile boulevards of the world."

On June 7, 1916, the highway was dedicated in an elaborate pageant at Multnomah Falls. Later in the same day, the highway's builders toasted themselves at Crown Point with loganberry juice, a temperance drink, while cannons roared and President Wilson pushed a button at the White House that automatically raised the American flag on Crown Point. Governor James Withecombe proclaimed, "The people of the Oregon Country greet you and thank you for unfurling the flag of freedom on Crown Point, Columbia River Highway, as we dedicate to the world the greatest highway ever built." The new highway was an immense source of pride for the road builders, and indeed for all Oregonians.

The Vista House at Crown Point was the most spectacular parks structure built along the Columbia River Highway. Sam Lancaster suggested Crown Point as a fitting site for a great observatory from which the Gorge "could be viewed in silent communion with the infinite" and for a memorial to "the trials and hardships of those who had come into the Oregon Country." Multnomah County built Vista House during 1916–18 at the grand cost of $100,000, eight times its original estimate. This lavish memorial to the pioneers is faced with ashlar sandstone, fitted out with stained-glass windows, marble floors, and brass handrails, and originally had a terra-cotta tile roof. Critics dubbed it the "$100,000 outhouse." It is the Columbia River Highway's grandest observatory and Oregon's first Art Nouveau building.

Vista House was designed by Edgar Lazarus, whose poet sister, Emma, wrote the tribute to American immigrants inscribed "beside the golden door" of the Statue of Liberty. Like the Statue of Liberty, the Vista House today marks the emigrants' gateway to the "promised land" at the end of the Oregon Trail. Today, Vista House is restored as a visitor and interpretive center.

Vista House at Crown Point, circa 1925 (Oregon Historical Society negative No. 58430)

From 1913 on, the Gorge experienced rapid development of rustic roadhouses, auto camps, and lodges. Roadhouses or inns could be found at Troutdale, Crown Point, Latourell Falls, Bridal Veil, Multnomah Falls, Bonneville, Lindsey Creek, and Mitchell Point. Auto camps could be found on Sandy Boulevard in Portland, and at Cascade Locks, Mitchell Point, Hood River, Mosier, Rowena, and The Dalles. In 1925 the Mount Hood Loop Highway joined the Columbia River Highway, creating a loop from Portland through Hood River that became one of America's most popular highway tours.

Two notable rustic lodges in the national park tradition were built at Bonneville in 1922 and at Multnomah Falls in 1925. Multnomah Falls Lodge, built of stone by the Portland Parks Bureau, has survived well, and now—with more than 2 million visitors a year—is the most popular scenic site in Oregon and in the national forest system. Lancaster's Lodge at Bonneville was a seventy-two-acre resort complete with a log dining hall and tent cabins. Sam Lancaster intended his lodge, located above Tooth Rock, to be the first in a system of lodges and camps in the Gorge, modeled on what he had seen in the Swiss Alps. Unfortunately, the lodge burned in the late 1920s and Lancaster did not have the funds to rebuild.

In 1921 Simon Benson, who opened Portland's Benson Hotel in

1913, built the Columbia Gorge Hotel on the bluffs at Wah-Gwin-Gwin Falls in West Hood River. It was a lavishly landscaped $400,000 tourist palace in the Mediterranean style, the highway's most impressive accommodation. Benson hoped it would become a model for tourist hotels throughout Oregon. Unfortunately, it closed with the Depression and became a retirement home for nearly fifty years. In the late 1970s, Benson's grand hotel was reborn and rehabilitated, to again serve travelers in the Gorge.

Although the highway was beloved by all and built to endure, within a single generation it fell victim to onrushing progress. The relentless growth of truck and auto traffic in the 1930s was more than the narrow old road could safely handle. The scenic Tooth Rock viaducts near Bonneville Dam were bypassed by a highway tunnel and abandoned in the late 1930s when the dam was built. By the late 1940s, the state was building a new high-speed river-level road, the future Interstate 84, through the Gorge to replace the old highway. When the first section of the new route, from Troutdale to Bridal Veil, was dedicated in 1949, Governor Douglas McKay assured those assembled that the old highway would be maintained as a parkway, "perpetuating the scenic beauties for which it is justly renowned." The state kept its promise for the Crown Point section and the Rowena Crest scenic loops. For the middle of the Gorge, however, progress in the form of a new road meant isolation, abandonment, and destruction for the old highway.

By 1953, the entire middle section of the old highway from Warrendale to Mosier, thirty-four miles of the original seventy-four-mile road, was abandoned and broken into fragments by new road construction. Most mid-Gorge fragments of the old road were neither used nor maintained, except through the towns of Hood River and Cascade Locks. Citing safety concerns, the state Highway Division closed the Mitchell Point Tunnel, the Oneonta Tunnel, and the Mosier Twin Tunnels, and filled them with rubble. As the original stone guardrails deteriorated, they were replaced with modern steel railings, thus sacrificing much of the beauty of the old highway. Through the middle of the Gorge, ten state parks and waysides, several notable bridges, and the world-famous Mitchell Point Tunnel were left abandoned and mostly inaccessible when the new river-level road was completed in the 1950s. Along the entire length of the old highway, inns and roadhouses closed and tourist facilities deteriorated as most of the traffic took the faster water-level route.

The old highway's darkest hour came in early 1966, when blasting crews demolished the entombed Mitchell Point Tunnel, in order to control rockfall off of the point. History does not record what the road builders who crafted the Columbia River Highway thought of the tunnel's short life; none of them lived to see this scenic and engineering marvel destroyed in the name of progress. The daughter of John A. Elliott, the tunnel's designer, approved the demolition of her father's masterwork, stating

Mitchell Point Tunnel, demolished in 1966 (Oregon Historical Society negative No. 3587)

the prevailing belief of the times: "If he were alive today, I feel certain that he would, like the engineers who have ordered the demolition, feel that sentiment must give way to progress and public safety."

The turning point in the Columbia River Highway's long slide into oblivion came in the summer of 1981, when the National Park Service conducted a field survey and a reuse study of the old road. The Park Service survey documented the highway's remaining features, its historic values, and possible recreational opportunities on the abandoned sections.

Eventually the state of Oregon reconsidered its policy toward the Columbia River Highway in light of the increased public interest in preservation. In 1983 the Columbia River Highway Historic District was nominated to the National Register of Historic Places, and the Oregon Transportation Commission adopted a new policy calling for the restoration and preservation of the highway. The Oregon Highway Division then began several years of long-deferred bridge restoration and rebuilding of original rock guardrails and walls along the Crown Point and Rowena Crest scenic routes. In 1984, the American Society of Civil Engineers recognized the highway as a National Historic Engineering Landmark.

A critical event for the highway's rebirth came in 1986, when Congress passed the Columbia River Gorge National Scenic Area Act, which was closely followed by action taken by the Oregon legislature, pursuant to which the Oregon Department of Transportation has developed a master plan for restoring the remaining abandoned segments of the old highway as a continuous recreation trail. In 1991, the seventy-fifth anniversary of the completion of the Columbia River Highway, the Oregon Highway Division installed reproductions of the concrete mileposts that originally lined the highway. After three-fourths of a century, only three of the original mileposts were still standing. (Milepost 14 still stands near Wood Village, milepost 58 can be seen along the trail between Starvation Creek State Park and Viento State Park, and milepost 70 is between Hood River and the Mosier Twin Tunnels.)

Today, approximately fifty-seven miles of the original seventy-four-mile roadway remain between Troutdale and The Dalles. Although it may not be practical to restore the broken sections of the road for auto traffic again, bicycles and hikers will soon enjoy restored use of and access to many sections of the old road from Warrendale to Mosier. One exciting opportunity is the highly scenic and long-abandoned road between Hood River and Mosier, where 6.5 miles of fully intact road are blocked only by the rubble-filled Mosier Twin Tunnels.

Sam Hill and Sam Lancaster's greatest gift to Oregon and to the world is a highway that, for three-quarters of a century, has lifted the spirits of all who travel it. After nearly four decades of obsolescence and neglect, the historic Columbia River Highway's future again looks bright for rediscovery.

ABANDONED SECTIONS OF THE COLUMBIA RIVER HIGHWAY

When Bonneville Dam was built in the 1930s, and when the river-level highway that eventually became Interstate 84 was built in the 1940s and 1950s, much of the Columbia River Highway was destroyed. In a few cases, however, sections were merely cut off from maintained roadways and abandoned, covered by the mosses and ferns of the Gorge. Listed below are some of the more notable sections of the highway that are abandoned but still in existence. In a few cases, the old roadway is still in use as part of maintained trails. In most cases, the abandoned sections of the highway can be hiked or biked safely, but some are moderately dangerous due to missing guardrails and other hazards. Visit these sections of the

highway at your own risk. The highway sections listed below are described from west to east.

Moffett Creek Bridge. This dramatic bridge is still intact, even though it was abandoned in 1950. Its unusually shallow arch is known as a flat arch; when it was built in 1915, it was the longest flat-arched bridge in the country, and the longest three-hinged concrete span in the world. Westbound on I-84 at milepost 39.25, watch for an opportunity to pull off the freeway onto a section of the old highway. Park your car, then walk west along the old road a short distance to the bridge.

Tanner Creek Bridge. Just south and west of Bonneville Dam exit 40 from I-84, Gorge Trail 400 crosses the original Tanner Creek Bridge, built in 1915, and then follows the old roadbed west for a short distance.

Tooth Rock Viaducts. From the south side of Bonneville Dam exit 40, follow a dirt road east to an electrical substation. Park your car, then continue walking east on the old roadbed to a viaduct that leads to Tooth Rock. Another shorter viaduct is just east of Tooth Rock. Beneath the viaducts, the I-84 tunnel was built in 1936 during the construction of Bonneville Dam. On your way back to the car, watch for an even older roadbed that leaves the Columbia River Highway on the south side. The older roadbed is said to be the 1856 portage road and the 1872 wagon road.

Eagle Creek to Cascade Locks. Follow Gorge Trail 400 from Eagle Creek Campground to Cascade Locks, about two miles. Shortly after leaving the Eagle Creek area, the trail follows the old roadbed, crossing Ruckel Creek on one of the original bridges built for the highway.

Starvation Creek to Viento. This section of the Columbia River Highway is now an official trail, and is described in the chapter on hiking, in the second part of this book. Another short section of the highway can be visited by hiking west from Starvation Creek State Park on Trail 413.

Wygant Trail. Part of the first half-mile of the Wygant Trail (see the hiking chapter) follows the Columbia River Highway west from Mitchell Point.

Mitchell Point. Just east of exit 58, the original roadbed and a fragment of a stone railing of the highway can be seen high above the freeway. (The fragment of the 1915 railing should not be confused with a new stone wall installed to catch rockfall.) This was the location of the legendary

Shepperds Dell Bridge, built in 1914;
inset: concrete pillars for railings

Mitchell Point Tunnel, which included five "windows" overlooking the Columbia. The tunnel was closed in 1954 and destroyed in 1966. Although some fragments of the highway remain on a ledge on Mitchell Point, the area is not safe to visit.

Ruthton Point. At milepost 60.4 of eastbound I-84, fragments of the Columbia River Highway can be seen on the north side of two small hills immediately north of the freeway. Both segments can be walked, but the western segment is the more interesting of the two, since a section of railing and a short viaduct are still present.

Mosier Twin Tunnels. From downtown Hood River, follow State Street east, cross Hood River on a bridge, then cross Highway 35 and follow "Old Columbia River Road" (the Columbia River Highway) to the east on the graceful Hood River loops similar to the loops east of Crown Point and east of Rowena Crest. After 1.5 miles, the old highway is gated, but the road can be hiked or biked as far as the Mosier Twin Tunnels, which were abandoned and filled with rubble in the 1950s. The highway can also be followed from Mosier to the east end of the tunnels, but a portion of the roadway has fallen into private hands. From I-84, the tunnels can be seen from just south of Eighteenmile Island.

FURTHER READING

Bullard, Oral. *Lancaster's Road: The Historic Columbia River Scenic Highway*. TMS Book Service, 1982.

Historic Preservation League of Oregon. *Discover the Historic Columbia River Highway* (map and driving guide; Oregon Routes of Explorations Series), 1991.

Smith, Dwight A. *Columbia River Highway Historic District*. Oregon Department of Transportation, 1984.

Smith, Dwight A., et al. *Historic Highway Bridges of Oregon*. 2d ed. Oregon Historical Society Press, 1989.

Tuhy, John E. *Sam Hill: The Prince of Castle Nowhere*. Timber Press, 1983.

◆
GEOLOGY

BY JOHN ELIOT ALLEN

The geologic evolution of the Columbia River Gorge, although primarily a record of volcanic activity, also involves repeated changes in the course of the valley: erosion and sedimentation, faulting, folding, uplift and subsidence, a period of cataclysmic flooding, and, finally, extensive landsliding. It thus exhibits a remarkable diversity of geologic events, matched in few places in North America.

In order to understand these events and recognize the features in the Gorge that tell the story, our discussion must range far to the east into eastern Oregon and Washington, Idaho, Montana, and even British Columbia. The story begins more than 40 million years ago, as we begin a geologic countdown.

A SHIFTING COASTLINE

Countdown, 40 Million Years Ago. Western Oregon was covered by a shallow sea, dotted with volcanic islands and lapping against a shoreline located at approximately the eastern edge of the present Willamette Valley. During a period of 36 million years, debris from giant explosive volcanoes farther east built up a pile of mudflows, lava, and ash beds more than three miles thick.

That debris is the rock (several formations) that makes up the main mass of the western Cascade Range. The Ohanapecosh Formation is exposed in the Gorge mostly on the north side of the present valley, especially in the great southwest-sloping ridge rising northeast of Stevenson. Outcrops along the highway east of Stevenson have greenish colors, indicative of their deep burial resulting in new metamorphic minerals. Buried hills of these oldest rocks also appear just west of Camas and, on the south side of the Gorge, just east of Crown Point.

Even then, an ancestral Columbia River flowed from the northeast through the older volcanic Cascade Range in a broad gentle valley that existed beneath present-day Mount Hood, continuing on a southwesterly course into the sea in the vicinity of Salem.

During this period, the coastline gradually retreated to near its present position, filled with debris from the volcanic outbursts carried in by the Columbia and other streams. The present Coast Range then consisted of a few low hills, with broad intervening plains underlain by soft unconsolidated muds and sands.

Countdown, 20 Million Years Ago. Mudflows (the Eagle Creek Formation), containing petrified wood and leaves, piled up to attain a thickness of nearly 1,000 feet, and are now exposed in the layered cliffs beneath Table Mountain and Greenleaf Peak, and in places along the Columbia River Highway between Warrendale and Shellrock Mountain.

During the long period of time between the deposition of the older rocks and these mudflows, a thick red weathering product called "paleosoil" formed upon the older rocks, which can be seen on the slopes of the ridge above Stevenson. In the far future, this slippery clay would give rise to many landslides on both sides of the Gorge.

REGIONAL LAVA FLOWS (THE COLUMBIA RIVER BASALT GROUP)

Countdown, 15 Million Years Ago. Far to the east, near the Idaho border with Oregon and Washington, tensional forces pulled apart the North American Plate, producing deep north–south-trending cracks in the crust, through which welled fantastic floods of basaltic lavas that spread out eventually to cover 60,000 square miles of eastern Washington and northeastern Oregon.

During a period of 3 million years at least 300 such flows poured out, a volume of rock that has been estimated at more than 40,000 cubic miles. Some individual flows contained nearly 150 cubic miles, although they averaged between 2 and 7 cubic miles each.

Most of the flows consisted of two parts—a basal "colonnade" made up of columns of basalt, and an "entablature" composed of basalt irregularly broken by joints into fragments the size of half a brick, locally called "brickbat basalt." As rock climbers in the Gorge are well aware, the columnar basalt is relatively stable and often safe for climbing, while the brickbat basalt is nightmarishly loose. Compare, for example, the stable columns on the south face of Beacon Rock with the loose brickbat of the Pillars of Hercules or Crown Point.

The contact between individual flows below the colonnade frequently contains a soil zone, consisting of weathered basalt formed during the thousands, or hundreds of thousands, of years between outpourings of lava. At Oneonta Gorge, such a zone is seen about 10 feet above the level of the Columbia River Highway. In this zone between the highway and the falls one can find sixty-five holes, from 6 inches to 3 feet in diameter, most of them extending in a northwest direction. Some of the holes contain bits of charcoal. The holes represent the tree casts of a forest over-

Lava flows near Hood River

whelmed 14 million years ago by the west-flowing upper lava flow.

The lava was so voluminous and so hot that the flows were able to pour for hundreds of miles before they cooled and solidified. In eastern Washington they shoved the Columbia River northwest to its present course around the "Big Bend," and coursed down the ancestral Columbia River valley through the Cascade Range into the retreating sea west of Salem, filling the valley and shoving the river dozens of miles to the north.

During the long, quiet intervals between the outpouring of lavas, the river had time to cut new channels along the northern edge of each previous flow. These valleys in turn were filled and the river moved north again. Each of the spectacular promontories that now accentuate the scenery along the northern Oregon coast is now thought to represent a valley of the ancestral Columbia filled with lava.

During this period, the rocks were formed that now compose the majestic cliffs that line the Gorge. The lava flows abutted the older rocks only a mile or so north of the present valley, and flowed up tributary canyons. The tops of Table Mountain, Greenleaf Peak, and Archer Mountain are capped by the basalt, resting in narrow, V-shaped valleys carved in the older rocks, and the lava only extends for a mile or so north of the cliffs. Hamilton Mountain north of Beacon Rock is capped by lava that, 14 million years ago, flowed up into and filled a side valley of the ancestral channel of the Columbia River, which then lay south of the present Gorge.

The amphitheater of Multnomah Falls is an excellent place to view these lava flows. Of the six layers of basalt evident at Multnomah Falls, the one next to the top is pillow lava, formed when the lava flowed into a lake, while the uppermost flow is a basal colonnade of columnar basalt.

The cliffs east of Bridal Veil, containing up to sixteen different lava flows, were built during this same time period. St. Peters Dome, a dramatically eroded pinnacle above Dodson east of Ainsworth State Park, is composed of at least ten flows of basalt. Although the summit of the dome has been reached by climbers, the loose basalt makes the climb extremely dangerous.

A SHIFTING RIVER

Countdown, 14 Million Years Ago. We do not yet know how many old channels of the Columbia River existed, but we do have a record in the Gorge of two of them, which intersect the present Gorge at Crown Point and at Bridal Veil. Crown Point is composed of a lava flow filling a channel that has been traced through the upper Bull Run area almost to Mount Hood and then northeast to near The Dalles. Beneath the great cliff of Crown Point lie volcanic sediments that filled the lower part of the channel. The east wall of the channel was cut in one of the hills of older lavas mentioned earlier.

Many lakes were formed along the edges of the lava flows, where tributary valleys were dammed by them. When the lava poured into these lakes, they produced "pillow basalt." When a lobe of liquid lava enters water, it immediately freezes and crusts over. As pressure continues, the liquid again breaks out and forms a "pillow." These events continue until a pile of pillows are produced, such as those shown in a road cut on the Columbia River Highway half a mile east of Crown Point. Another fine Columbia River example appears in the road cut at the highway intersection south of The Dalles Bridge across the Columbia (US 197).

Countdown, 12 Million Years Ago. Folding of the basalts began to warp the land into a series of arches and basins. The Portland–Vancouver Basin, the Hood River Basin, the Mosier Basin, and The

Hills on the Washington side, near Wishram

Dalles Basin were formed, with intervening uplifts or "anticlines."
    During the same time a new, deep, narrow Columbia River canyon
was again cut north of the Crown Point canyon, parallel to, and about ten
miles to the south of the present Gorge. At Bridal Veil, where it intersects
the Gorge, this fossil canyon goes far below present sea level. It was first
partly filled with a lava flow, which was mostly cut away again, and then
refilled to the brim during a 10 million-year period during which more
than a thousand feet of silts and quartzitic gravels (the Sandy River Mud-
stone and Troutdale Formation) accumulated in the valley. The filling was
the result of a period of intense mountain-making activity in the Rockies
far to the northeast. During the spring floods, excess debris poured down
the great river from the rising ranges. The abundant quartzite pebbles that
are now found in the Gorge undoubtedly came from British Columbia.
    Bridal Veil canyon has been traced to the east along a line about ten
miles south of the present Gorge. Only the northern edges of the gravel fill

can be found; the main valley is buried beneath the later lavas of the Cascade Range. These patches of gravel have since been uplifted, and now appear at an elevation of more than 2,000 feet in the center of the Cascade arch before they drop down again to be seen above Mitchell Point and at river level in the Hood River Valley.

In the eastern part of the Gorge the quartzitic gravels filled the Hood River Basin, where they can be seen below the east abutment of the railroad bridge on the south side of the river and at the mouth of the Little White Salmon River on the north side. In the Mosier and The Dalles basins farther east, volcanic sediments of the same age as the gravels filled the basins to a depth of more than 500 feet. West of the Gorge, a 1,000-foot thickness of these gravels and underlying silts filled the Portland–Vancouver Basin to overflowing, to an elevation several hundred feet higher than today. They are best exposed along the Scenic Highway on the Sandy River south of Troutdale, but they can also be seen in Portland's West Hills in an old quarry just south of the entrance to the Cornell Road tunnel. Here many quartzite pebbles have been found along with other exotic rocks such as granite, rhyolite, and a schist.

These gravels also make up the upper parts of Mount Tabor and Kelly Butte. The gravels along the Sandy River contain a few quartzite pebbles and foreset beds that dip to the west, showing the direction of flow of the old river. Toward the end of this period, the Sandy River swung in a series of meanders along the eastern edge of the gravel-filled Portland–Vancouver plain. Subsequent uplift caused the incision of the loops and formed the present "incised meanders."

Uplift and warping of the Cascade Range continued during much of this time, and was also accompanied late in the period by faulting. The east side of the Hood River Valley was raised nearly 3,000 feet along a series of north–south faults. The broken rock adjacent to the faults is "pre-crushed" rock that for many years has been mined for road material in a quarry above the highway on the east side of Hood River.

During this same period, the Portland Hills rose at least 500 feet west of another fault at their base, which extends in a ruler-straight line for sixteen miles and adds to the height of the fold that forms the hills.

LOCAL VOLCANOES AND LAVA FLOWS (CASCADE AND BORING LAVAS)

Countdown, 6 Million Years Ago. After deposition of most of the gravels, a third period of volcanism broke out—this time from local vents rather than from faraway fissures. More than fifty volcanoes began to dot the area in and around Portland. The lava that came from these small cinder cones, unlike the dense black basalt of the previous volcanic period, is gray-colored and porous, containing many minute gas bubbles and cavities. In building the stone walls of the lodge at Multnomah Falls, the perceptive Italian stonemasons used many of these porous rocks. The black glassy basalt is appropriately predominant, but the gray porous lava is also well represented, as are fragments of petrified wood and opal boulders from the older formations, and quartzite pebbles and cobbles from the overlying gravels.

A group of twelve of these little volcanoes, consisting of gray lava and cinders, cluster around the town of Boring. In Portland they appear on the west side of Mount Tabor (well exposed in a quarry halfway up the butte) and in Kelly Butte, Rocky Butte, Mount Scott, Chamberlain Hill above the bluff east of Troutdale, and Swede Hill and others north of Sylvan.

Mount Sylvania, which underlies Portland Community College southwest of Portland, is a large shield volcano of the same age, as is Highland Butte southeast of Oregon City. Fortunately for Portland, all of these volcanoes are more than 2 million years old and are considered to be extinct.

North of the Columbia River, Prune Hill volcano, composed of quartzite-bearing gravels, lies on the west slope of Prune Hill northwest of Camas. The volcano produced the lava that has been mined for jetty rock for many years in the Fisher Quarries west of Camas. Farther to the east, the uplands west of Cape Horn are covered with lava from Mount Pleasant and Mount Zion cinder cones, which cap the gravels above Cape Horn viewpoint. In the Cascade Range, gray lava of the same age formed the great shields of Larch Mountain, Mount Defiance, and many others. It was during this last 5 million-year period before the Ice Age that the Cascade volcanic uplands were formed by flows from these and hundreds of other volcanoes.

Countdown, 4 Million Years Ago. These same volcanoes helped to again shove the river north to its present position. As the Cascade Range uplift continued, and the modern Columbia River canyon deepened to keep pace with the arching, the river cut down through the flanks of the volcanoes and even exposed the internal plumbing of several of them. The meandering Sandy River also began to cut down, eventually to form its present deep, winding canyon.

The internal volcanic plumbing exposed by the erosion can be seen throughout the Gorge. Beacon Rock, for example, is the central neck of a former volcano, consisting of lava frozen in the throat of a volcano. The volcano was worn away by the river and the floods, leaving only its core. Contrary to popular belief, it is not a "monolith," since it is broken by many columnar joints. The best columns appear on the south side of the rock, where rock climbers have found them to be a welcome relief from the normally unstable rock found elsewhere in the Gorge.

Wind Mountain and Shellrock Mountain are the frozen deep-seated magma chambers that once lay beneath two volcanoes now split by the river. They are intrusions of fine-grained granitoid rock, now exhumed by river erosion and the giant floods.

East of Wind Mountain lies Dog Mountain, a down-dropped block of basalt whose lava flows have been folded on an arch. Similar effects can be seen at the Ortley fold (anticline) two miles east of Lyle, where the basalt flows have been crushed and squeezed out into vertical ridges as the arch was folded and faulted. The west side of the fold dropped down about 500 feet, while the east side arched up.

High on the south Gorge wall across the river from Beacon Rock, Nesmith Point is the dissected south half of a volcano similar to Wind Mountain and Shellrock Mountain. In the saddle behind Shellrock Mountain, a baked contact with the intruded basalt is evident.

Another deep-seated intrusion can be seen in a road cut on Interstate 84 just south of Cascade Locks. It was a dome-shaped intrusion, as testified by the fanlike arrangement of the columnar joints that formed when the intruding magma cooled, shrank, and cracked.

Columns always form at right angles to the surface of cooling, at the edge of the intrusion or at the base of the lava flow. Still another intrusion (with massive angular jointing like that in Wind Mountain and Shellrock Mountain, rather than columnar jointing) forms Government Island east of Cascade Locks, which was mined for jetty rock for many years.

THE ICE AGE

Countdown, 2 Million Years Ago. The onset of the Ice Age severely affected the Northwest. The Cordilleran ice sheet came down out of Canada, filled Puget Sound as far south as Tacoma and beyond, and covered most of eastern Washington north of the present Columbia River.

During advances and retreats of the ice, sea level was repeatedly lowered as much as 600 feet, producing twenty-five-mile-wide coastal plains, and raised again up to 50 and perhaps 100 feet above present sea level, when the terraces upon which most of the coastal towns now rest were carved out by the ocean waves.

During periods of low sea level, the Columbia River Gorge, then a narrow, V-shaped canyon, was cut hundreds of feet below its present depth. During high periods, this deep gorge was filled and the Portland–Vancouver Basin was again covered by gravels and sands coming down the river from the ice fronts far to the northeast.

Countdown, 700,000 Years Ago. As the sea level fluctuated, terraces along the Sandy River at 800, 600, and 500 feet elevation were successively carved out of the meandering walls of the valley, mantled with mudflows from Mount Hood far upstream, and then cut partly away to the next lower level of the river. Similar terraces formed at lower elevations across east Portland.

The majestic high peaks that now punctuate the summit of the Cascade Range began to grow, and their glaciers advanced down the valleys around them. From Mount Hood, the combined Sandy and Zigzag glaciers extended down the valley as far west as Cherryville, and Ladd Glacier came down the west fork of Hood River almost to the Hood River Valley.

Small mountain glaciers formed on the uplands as low as 3,000 feet elevation. One such glacier cut into the north side of Larch Mountain to expose its core. Another scoured out the basin of Bull Run Lake. Numerous small glaciers cut into the northeast sides of other peaks, and into the east edges of the high plateau surfaces, as at Benson Plateau.

Countdown, 340,000 Years Ago. The Columbia River was dammed by lava flows coming down side valleys in at least three places. Trout Creek Hill, ten miles up Wind River, poured out lava that formed a dam 500 feet high across the river. The town of Carson now rests on the surface of that flow, and the high bench east of Cascade Locks and Herman Creek is a southside remnant.

Lavas from Red Mountain and Big Lava Flow Crater, fifteen miles up the Little White Salmon River, also dammed the river. The flat surface just east of the river mouth at 850 feet elevation is the surface of this flow.

Underwood Mountain to the west and White Salmon volcano to the east of the White Salmon River mouth both formed shields of lava that may have crossed the river to help build dams hundreds of feet high. Liquid lava pouring into the lake behind the dam produced lava pillows and brilliant yellow outcrops of shattered and altered lava that can be seen on Interstate 84 at Ruthton Point, just west of Hood River.

THE CATASTROPHIC FLOODS

Countdown, 15,000 Years Ago. The approaching end of the Ice Age brought on the greatest series of catastrophes to affect the Pacific Northwest since the lava floods. During the last advance of the ice, the Pend Oreille Lake lobe of the Cordilleran ice sheet came down out of British Columbia across the present site of the lake, and flowed up the lower course of the Clark Fork River for about ten miles, producing an ice dam 2,500 feet high.

Water piled up behind the dam to form a great lake, now known as Lake Missoula, since it covered the present site of that city. The terraces caused by waves in that lake can been seen more than 1,000 feet up on the slopes east of the town. The lake spread to cover 3,000 square miles in the intermontane valleys of Montana and contained 500 cubic miles of water, a fifth the volume of Lake Michigan.

When the water reached a depth of 2,000 feet east of the dam, it broke through, or floated the ice and the shattered jumble of rock-laden icebergs and water cascaded down through the future site of Spokane and across eastern Washington, carving out the multitude of now-dry channels and coulees now known as the "Channeled Scablands."

This deluge has been estimated to have flowed at a rate of 9.5 cubic miles of water per hour for forty hours, ten times the flow of all the rivers of the world and sixty times that of the Amazon River. It covered more than 16,000 square miles of the Pacific Northwest, forming temporary lakes above the Wallula Gap as it entered Oregon (Lake Lewis), in Oregon east of The Dalles (Lake Condon), and in the Willamette Valley (Lake Allison).

This was only the beginning. After the dam broke and the water poured out, the ice lobe inexorably shoved its way up the Clark Fork again and formed a new dam and a new Lake Missoula. Most geologists now believe that the lake refilled and broke out again and again at least forty times during a period of a little more than 2,000 years. The interval between the floods averaged 55 years. There is even some evidence of as many as 100 ice-age floods.

At The Dalles, the water reached an elevation of more than 1,000 feet, and the scars left by the high-water marks can be seen on the hillside northwest of town. The water overtopped Mayer State Park by 200 feet and Crown Point by 50 feet, where it reached an elevation of about 700 feet. Within the then-narrow, V-shaped Gorge, the floods stripped away the canyon walls and widened the river, cutting away the spurs and lower parts of the tributary stream courses to produce the U-shaped valley and waterfalls that now decorate the canyon walls.

As the floods spread out over the Portland–Vancouver Basin, the water fell to an elevation of about 400 feet. Today such a flood would leave only the upper couple of hundred feet of Mount Tabor, Rocky Butte, and the forty-story bank towers above the water.

Restricted by the narrows near Kalama, the water surged south up the Willamette River and up the Tualatin River, which then flowed east at Lake Oswego. It scoured out the lake basin and built up a large gravel bar west of the present lake, diverting the Tualatin River to its present southward course.

Continuing south from the Tualatin Basin, it crossed a low divide a number of places, eroding out channels and leaving many small lakes around the hamlet of Tonquin (near Sherwood), the only extensive scablands in western Oregon. Farther south it deposited another "expansion bar," forming the gravel plain around Wilsonville.

The main currents continued south up the Willamette past Oregon City, cut away the walls of the valley to form the cliffs that divide the city, eroded further scabland channels north of Peach Cove at the west bend of the river, and dropped a third great gravel bar upon which the town of Canby rests.

Direct evidence for the floods south of Canby lies mostly in the widespread occurrence of groups of glacial "erratics" in some 350 localities around the edges of the Willamette Valley. The erratics are rocks up to ten feet in diameter of a type unknown in western Oregon; they obviously came frozen in icebergs carried by the floods from British Columbia.

These erratics lie scattered along the course of the floods from Spokane to Eugene. More than thirty-five have been located around the shores of Lake Condon in eastern Oregon, several lie up tributary streams south of the river (one was carried up the Metolius River as far south as Maupin), and many have been found in the Portland area. They were first mapped in 1935 by Ira Allison of Oregon State College, hence the name Lake Allison for this ephemeral series of lakes.

All the erratics in the Willamette Valley were found below an elevation of 400 feet. The largest of them lies at 302 feet elevation on a spur north of Highway 99W between Sheridan and McMinnville, in the smallest state park in Oregon. In 1950 it weighed 160 tons, but "tourist attrition" has now reduced it to 90 tons.

Saint Peters Dome

Another even more important erratic is the "Willamette Meteorite," weighing 4,814 pounds, the largest ever found in the United States. It was discovered in 1902 at an elevation of 330 feet on a spur a mile or so up the Tualatin Valley northwest of West Linn. Recently other gneiss and granite erratics have been found within a few feet of the locality, proving that the meteorite was carried down from British Columbia, frozen in an iceberg, which stranded and melted on the spur. It now resides in the American Museum of Natural History in New York City.

EROSION AND LANDSLIDES

Countdown, 12,800 Years Ago. Since the last flood, many of the waterfalls in the Gorge have retreated several hundred feet from the original cliff fronts, and lie within amphitheaters several hundred feet wide. The combination of northern exposures and deep amphitheaters have always plagued photographers by keeping the sun well away from the beauty of the various falls.

For many years it was a puzzle to imagine how such small streams could cut such wide reentrants in the cliff walls. A visit to the falls during a prolonged bitter-cold spell solved the problem. Spray from the falls is blown back and forth by the frigid winds, freezing in the cracks on the brickbat faces of the cliffs and popping out the blocks of basalt. Five hundred feet of retreat, divided by 10,000 years of bitter winter freezes, gives a rate of only a little more than half an inch per year.

Countdown, circa 5000 B.C. The Parkdale lava flow came out from the base of a small cinder cone in the upper Hood River Valley west of Parkdale.

Countdown, A.D. 1270. The Cascades of the Columbia, for which the mountain range was named, resulted from a gigantic series of landslides, probably triggered by an earthquake, which came down from the cliffs of Table Mountain and Greenleaf Peak. The landslides cover fourteen square miles and forced the river a mile to the south, forming a 200-foot-high dam below Cascade Locks.

This dam, four times the height of Bonneville Dam, undoubtedly gave rise to the Indian legend of "The Bridge of the Gods." It probably took several years for the water to fill the lake behind the dam and then overflow, producing The Cascades. Since the Indians did not build bridges, and they had no word for bridge in their language, their account of being able to walk across dry-shod is thought to have been misinterpreted to mean a bridge.

The lake behind the dam lasted long enough to kill the forests on either side of the river as far east as Hood River. More than 3,000 pale gray tree stumps lined the river for miles when they were first described by Lewis and Clark in 1805–6. These stumps were mapped many years ago (*Mazama*, 1958), and a specimen of the wood was dated by radioactive carbon-14 methods as being about 700 years old.

Many other older and younger landslides are found in the Gorge, mostly on the north side, where the area east of Cape Horn is landslide terrane for miles along the river. Rooster Rock, for example, is a landslide block that originated in the draw between Crown Point and Chanticleer Point (Portland Women's Forum State Park). Another example is Phoca Rock. Now standing in the middle of the Columbia north of Bridal Veil, it originated high in the cliffs of Cape Horn on the Washington side of the Gorge. Aldrich Butte, just north of North Bonneville on the Washington side of the Gorge, is a landslide block of mudflow material. In all, a total of more than fifty square miles along the Columbia is underlain by landslide.

Countdown, A.D. 1935. The most active of the slides is the Collins Point landslide, three miles long and a mile wide, located between Wind Mountain and Dog Mountain. When the power line from Bonneville Dam was built across this slide, the line had to be relocated several times, and finally was moved up and over the hill behind the bluffs at the head of the slide.

The movement of the slide was measured, and near its head the slide was found to move at a rate of up to thirty-five feet per year. At the toe of the slide, where it pushes out into the river, the movement is only about six inches per year, but the highway and railroad have to be repaired every few years. The cabins of a Girl Scout camp located on the slide have to be jacked up and releveled each year. Their water-supply line is on the surface and contains several zigzag bends to take up the slack as the land moves, evidence that geologic processes are still active in the Gorge!

FURTHER READING

Allen, John Eliot. *The Magnificent Gateway: A Layman's Guide to the Geology of the Columbia River Gorge.* Timber Press, 1979; 2d ed., 1984.

Allen, John Eliot, Marjorie Burns, and Sam C. Sargent. *Cataclysms on the Columbia.* 2d ed. Timber Press, 1986; paperback, 1991.

Williams, Ira A. *Geologic History of the Columbia River Gorge.* 3d ed. Oregon Historical Society Press, 1991.

WEATHER

BY BILL WANTZ

The Columbia Gorge presents a wide array of weather conditions. The extremes of Gorge weather vary not only from day to day and from season to season, but also from one end of the Gorge to the other. In winter, the central Gorge is often an icy freezer, while nearby Portland merely experiences cold rain. In summer, the eastern end of the Gorge can be very hot and arid, while the central section of the Gorge remains damp and cool.

TEMPERATURE EXTREMES

Temperature variations are illustrative of the weather extremes that occur in the Gorge. Because of the moderating influence of the Pacific Ocean, western Oregon and Washington experience only moderate temperature changes from season to season and day to day, while temperatures in eastern Oregon and Washington are more extreme. Compared to the western region, the eastern region experiences lower winter temperatures and higher summer temperatures. The differences are caused by marine air, which readily flows into western Oregon and Washington, but only manages to penetrate east of the Cascade Range with difficulty.

Another temperature effect is the long warm-up from winter to summer, compared to the relatively short time that temperatures take to drop in autumn. The winter rainy season comes on very quickly, while the summer dryness remains a long-awaited event. That dichotomy occurs throughout the temperate zone and is not unique to the Northwest or the Gorge, but is due to the fact that summer storms are usually pushed just north of the Pacific Northwest, while winter storms easily descend as far south as northern California.

CLOUDS AND RAIN

Spring cloudiness in the Gorge follows the gradual spring warming, decreasing slowly as summer approaches. For much of the intermountain region, winter and spring are the wettest times of the year. During those seasons, showers and thundershowers spread north from the Gulf of California and, due to their vigor, even affect eastern Oregon and Washington. During the rest of the year, little storm activity manages to penetrate inland past the two major mountain ranges, the Coast Range and the Cascade Range.

The result is reflected in cloudiness statistics recorded at Portland and The Dalles. The highest percentage of cloudiness can be found in Portland in December, when the sky is cloudy 85 percent of the time, while the lowest can be found in The Dalles in July, when the skies are cloudy only 19 percent of the time.

Portland and The Dalles even display different cloudiness factors on an hourly basis. The Dalles is most likely to be cloudy in early afternoon, which reflects the building of afternoon clouds associated with showers. In Portland, clouds are most likely to be found during late morning hours, reflecting the prevalence of morning cloudiness that burns off by midday much of the year.

WINDS FOR WINDSURFERS

Wind blows through the Columbia Gorge and blasts into Portland as though someone left the back door open. The winds are cold, dry winds in January and hot, dry, savanna winds in August. They are both omnipresent and fickle. They tend to bring cold continental air on the heels of snow and freezing rain, or raise clouds of dust across the plains above Arlington.

Pressure differences control the winds that flow through the Gorge. If the pressure is greater on the west than on the east, air moves through the Gorge from west to east, and vice versa. A mere one-tenth of an inch of pressure difference can result in winds of twenty-five miles per hour at the receiving end. At times, sudden changes in pressure can spell sudden shifts in wind direction. Within a period of three or four days, pressures can begin higher in the east than in the west, resulting in strong easterly winds, only to be followed by a reversal of air pressures and equally strong winds flowing the opposite direction.

Some of those pressure changes are caused by new storms that move into the Northwest, but pressure changes can take place exclusive of storm movement. Behind every storm is a region of higher pressure. Particularly during fall months, these small migratory high-pressure areas drift inland a day or two after a storm passes through. When those high-pressure areas settle in over the northern Rockies, winds in the Gorge immediately become easterly. In the fall, those easterly winds are known as Indian summer.

Those episodes of east winds also indicate that a storm is off the coast, since east winds always blow *from* high-pressure areas *toward* low-pressure areas. Eventually, the offshore low-pressure area approaches the coast and spreads increasing cirrostratus clouds over the area. Rain follows within a day.

As windsurfers know, daily variation of winds follows a typical pattern during the warm season. At night, winds are very light and remain low even after sunrise. About 10:00 A.M., the winds pick up rather abruptly. All day the winds blow steadily, peaking at about 4:00 or 5:00 P.M. After sunset, the winds die off suddenly, and by dusk it is calm. Day after day this pattern prevails. Only when changes are oncoming will the winds remain strong overnight. The time of start-up in the morning is related to the eventual strength of the afternoon winds; stronger winds begin sooner.

This daily variation occurs due to nighttime temperature inversions that form during clear weather. In the evening, the ground radiates heat back to the sky. This loss of heat cools the immediate surface, which by conduction cools the air layer in contact with it. Being a little cooler and denser, this surface layer clings to the ground and resists scouring by wind. All night long, the cool surface layer grows deeper. By morning it will be 800 feet thick. Above, the winds blow stronger than ever, but below, it is calm.

Sunrise comes. Ridgetop winds are at their peak now, but surface winds are calm. The sun begins to heat the surface, warming it and the air in immediate contact with it. Slowly, the inversion layer is destroyed from the ground up. The surface winds remain light, however, until the entire inversion is gone, when winds suddenly break through, full force, to the surface. The breakthrough is so sudden it can occur in just a couple of minutes.

The winds in the Gorge accelerate from one end of the Gorge to the other. West winds may start out in Portland at eight miles per hour, but upon reaching The Dalles they are gusting to twenty-five or thirty miles per hour. East winds are similar. The acceleration occurs because of the force of the high pressure in the west acting upon the air over a period of time. As the wind moves through the Gorge, the pressure keeps pushing it along, moving it faster and faster.

In the Columbia Gorge, east winds are usually very dry winds. There are several reasons for the dryness. Air east of the Cascade Range is usually dry to begin with. Although it began as moist marine air, the moisture was diminished by precipitation when the air passed over the Cascade Range. Consequently, most of the air flowing back through the Gorge with east winds is dry air from eastern Washington and Oregon.

There is another factor that causes the east winds to be dry. Not all air flowing across the Cascade Range during an east wind originated at the surface. Mixed in with the surface air is air from higher elevations. As the higher air descends the west slopes of the Cascade Range, it dries out and warms at a rate of five degrees for every thousand feet of elevation loss. By the time it reaches sea level in the west, it is warm and dry.

That same warming also explains why east winds are always warm in the summer. The air starts out at eighty-five degrees at 3,000 feet in eastern Oregon and Washington. It warms about fifteen feet in its descent to sea level in the west. The same effect occurs in winter, but the results are much different. The air may start out at zero degrees in eastern Oregon, and warm fifteen degrees in its descent to the west, but that fifteen-degree air will be much colder than the air over the western end of the Gorge. Since winter temperatures east of the Cascade Range can dip well below zero at times, the air brought over the mountains and through the Gorge during the winter can be intensely cold.

Columbia Gorge winds are very persistent. During the summer, west winds blow at The Dalles nearly 90 percent of the time. Because of the persistence of the winds, much of the vegetation in the Gorge displays permanent bending and deformation, known as wind flagging. The amount of flagging is directly related to the average annual wind speed. Mild forms of flagging show deformed branches growing on all sides of the tree, while severe flagging bends the entire tree to the point that it becomes a shrub growing along the ground.

Examples of flagging exist throughout the Gorge. Every exposed hill or ridge in the Gorge has trees that are flagged by the wind. Most flagging results from winds blowing consistently from one direction. Strong winds blowing from several directions produce a type of flagging known as bottlebrush flagging, which results from wind so strong that the ends of the branches are broken off.

The persistent winds have another effect: they make possible an entire industry and culture that have sprung up around windsurfing in the Gorge, particularly in the central and east portions of the Gorge. The consistent west winds that blow past Hood River and The Dalles combine with the westbound current of the Columbia to produce the swells sought after by acrobatic windsurfers.

Other visitors to the Gorge need to be careful of the winds. Kayakers and canoeists on the Columbia must be prepared for rough water at any time, and cyclists planning a long pedal through the Gorge usually plan to travel west to east in order to take advantage of the consistent west winds.

DRY EAST, WET WEST

Of all weather parameters, precipitation is perhaps the most readily understood. Within the Gorge and its environs, tremendous differences occur in precipitation patterns. Moving east from Portland, average annual rainfall increases from thirty-seven inches at Portland to forty-five inches at Troutdale, the mouth of the Gorge. That increase is due to an increase in elevation, even though Portland and Troutdale are at the same elevation. As air masses move in from the Pacific, they rise up over the Cascade Range. As the air rises, it cools. Cool air can hold less moisture than warm air, and the excess is rained out. Due to strong, persistent air flows from the Pacific, considerable moisture is rained out on the west slopes of the Cascade Range (and the western end of the Gorge) each year.

Continuing east along the Columbia River, average annual rainfall rises to about 65 inches at Bridal Veil and peaks at 72 inches at Cascade Locks. This central area is the wettest in the Gorge—at river level. In the mountains just to the south, however, precipitation is about twice as great—nearly 200 inches of rain fall each year in the Mount Defiance–Larch Mountain area. Because of favorable topography, that area is the wettest in northwestern Oregon.

East of Cascade Locks, precipitation drops to only thirty-one inches at Hood River and twelve inches in The Dalles, due to what is commonly called the rain-shadow effect. After the cross-Cascades airflows reach the crest, they descend the lee slopes, following the terrain. The descending air warms, its humidity level decreases, and the rainfall is consequently much less. If rainfall does occur, it often evaporates before it reaches the ground.

These annual rainfall patterns bear on the variability of individual storms. As thundershowers approach the crest of the Cascade Range, they increase in intensity. Intensification means that the size of the storm increases, the height of the top of the cloud rises, the amount of rainfall increases, and hail is more likely. As a result, higher elevations receive more rain from a storm than lower elevations.

Thunderstorms are commonly caused by updrafts from hills. These updrafts begin rising in the morning, increase as the day progresses, and eventually rise high enough so that clouds form from the resulting cooling. Heat is then released by condensation of water vapor, which gives an added boost to the rising air currents. Some of these clouds reach 30,000 feet and will cause lightning, intense rains, and small hail. The lifetime of most single thunderstorm cells is about one hour. Because additional thunderstorm cells form in the same place, however, thunderstorms often appear to last for several hours.

Before a thunderstorm reaches its greatest elevation, rainfall peaks and lightning and hail are most severe. Soon, the updrafts are cut off in the lower part of the storm and the storm begins to die, or perhaps the storm drifts into the lee of a ridge. In either event, the rainfall tapers off and the storm ends. In all, the storm will have traveled less than twenty miles.

Precipitation falling as showers is visible—rainfall can be seen approaching. Watch the sky to the south and southwest; gray rain streaks begin creeping down from the bases of cumulus clouds and soon reach the ground. Intense showers obscure the terrain behind the cloud. Winds pick up as the thunderstorm approaches; first they blow lightly toward the storm, then switch abruptly and blow strongly away from it. The point where they switch is a gust front. Rain follows very quickly. Winds commonly gust to thirty-five miles per hour but will occasionally hit sixty miles per hour.

Major storms that spread inland across the region cause widespread weather effects. In summer, these storms spread solid altostratus and cirrostratus clouds into the west end of the Gorge, while at the east end only thickening cirrus are seen. Within six to twelve hours, rain begins in the west, while the east slowly clouds over. As the storm front comes through, only a little rain spreads through The Dalles for an hour or two, while at Cascade Locks rain has been falling for six hours.

Weak summer storms are called marine pushes. They develop in the same manner as storms, but usually are so weak that they do not bring rain. A marine push brings marine air from off the coast into western Oregon and Washington and then, if it is a strong push, through the Gorge and east of the Cascade Range.

Marine pushes develop first with west or southwest winds. These winds are especially brisk after several days of light winds. Watch for these winds; they are your clues to a change in the weather. Within a few hours, clouds spread into the western Gorge. Overnight skies in the west stay cloudy with clearing late the next day. In the east, perhaps the only difference is ten to fifteen degrees of cooling.

WINTER STORMS

Occasionally, cold arctic air masses descend on the Pacific Northwest from Alaska and Canada, bringing with them extended periods of subfreezing weather throughout the region. If the freezing weather is of sufficient duration and intensity, it turns the Gorge into a veritable freezer, with small streams and waterfalls freezing solid. The onset of such weather is followed immediately by a small but hardy band of ice climbers, who (realizing that such conditions are present perhaps only three or four times each decade) are quick to take advantage of the opportunity to sharpen their ice axes and crampons for an attempt to climb the waterfalls of the Gorge. Of course, the larger falls have never frozen solid, but even the smaller or seasonal falls are desirable goals of ice climbers.

The one weather event that typifies the Columbia Gorge more than any other is freezing rain, defined as rain that falls into a subfreezing layer of air. Remarkably common, freezing rain occurs every winter—often more than once in a season.

The stage is often set for freezing rain when cold arctic air pushes south out of Canada. This intensely cold air spreads throughout Washington and Oregon, overwhelming the region. Subfreezing temperatures prevail for a few days—often all the way to the coast—with clear skies and cold east winds.

Eventually a storm approaches the coast. Coming up out of the southwest, it first spreads wisps of cirrus over the region—forerunners of the rain to soon follow. The east winds blow even stronger as these clouds destroy the surface inversion. Moisture and upper-level warming spread over the

Eastern end of the Gorge in winter

area in a deep layer that settles like a blanket, both east and west of the Cascade Range, while the surface layer remains cold. Precipitation begins to fall, often in the form of snow.

As the storm proceeds toward the coast, it gradually displaces the cold arctic air mass with warmer air spreading up from the south. Eventually the only area with temperatures remaining below freezing is the Gorge. Cold air is trapped east of the Cascade Range and flows westward at low levels. Overhead, much warmer air has spread in with temperatures well above freezing.

The sequence of events with this type of storm is quite predictable. At first, snow falls, light and fluffy. The snow starts off very fine, with the flakes gradually becoming larger. As the warm air spreads in aloft, the snow begins to fall through a layer of above-freezing air. It melts into rain, only to fall into the deep layer of freezing air next to the ground. The rain freezes into ice pellets—sleet—that tinkle as they hit cars.

Slowly the warm air becomes thicker, and the cold layer near the ground grows thinner and thinner. The sleet changes to freezing rain—

rain that falls in liquid form but freezes when it hits the ground. Freezing rain will continue until the surface of the ground rises above the freezing point.

Traveling west to east through the Gorge during such an episode displays a variety of weather. Portland may have warmed above freezing and may be experiencing rain. Cascade Locks could have twenty-seven degrees with sleet and freezing rain mixed, while Hood River may have snow. As the storm shifts east, this patterns of events shifts along with it. Eventually the freezing rain retreats to Hood River, where it may linger for several hours. Finally the mild air spreads east and eliminates all of the freezing rain in the Gorge.

Because the cold air has depth, air 500 to 1,000 feet above the surface may be colder than air at river level, which explains why freezing rain may linger at higher elevations in the Camas–Washougal area even after it has ended at river level. As long as the tongue of subfreezing air exists, freezing rain will continue. These tongues often extend into Portland and affect Mount Tabor and the West Hills for several hours after warming has spread to lower points. Eventually, the colder air is dissipated and the wet, moderate weather typical of a Portland winter dominates the area, waiting for the next chapter in the weather story.

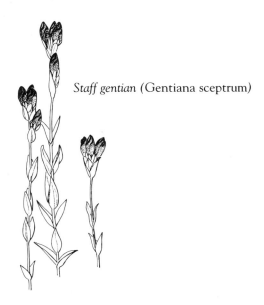

Staff gentian (Gentiana sceptrum)

WILDLIFE

By Mike Houck

If your objective is to explore as many habitat types and see as diverse an array of animals as possible in one day's outing, it would be difficult to beat the Columbia River Gorge. The Gorge's diversity of plant and animal life, geologic and scenic features, and topographic variety offer amateur and professional naturalists a limitless laboratory and playground within a few hours of the Portland–Vancouver metropolitan area.

This chapter focuses on the rich fauna and their associated habitats of the Gorge, to pique the reader's interest in general natural history. Hopefully, relationships among animals and their associated plant communities will become the objective of many days afield in the Columbia River Gorge.

A discussion of wildlife is not possible without reference to their "home" or habitat. All wildlife, whether the ephemeral Melissa blue butterfly or hearty mule deer, have the same basic life requirements: food, water, and cover. The key to successful wildlife viewing is knowing which habitat(s) a species or animal community prefers.

Some species have a tremendously broad range of habitat requirements that make them ubiquitous. For example, you could reliably expect to see robins, starlings, coyotes, and tree frogs throughout the Gorge. By contrast, if you want to see Lewis' woodpeckers, western bluebirds, and white-breasted nuthatches, your best bet is to look in the Oregon white oak and ponderosa pine communities that appear near Hood River and extend past The Dalles. Another habitat specialist is the pika (also known as rock rabbit), a small rabbitlike mammal. It is found only in talus slopes in the cooler Douglas fir–dominated forests. As you might expect, ospreys, bald eagles, and other fish-eating birds are most often seen feeding, roosting, and nesting near the extensive riparian habitats (black cottonwood, Oregon ash, and willow) associated with the Columbia River, including its islands and tributaries. John Muir's favorite bird, the American dipper, is specialized to nest and feed in and around fast-moving streams (especially those with waterfalls) on either side of the Gorge.

As one travels along the Oregon shore from the mouth of the Sandy River at the western end of the Scenic Area to the Deschutes River at the eastern boundary, the most obvious aspects are the subtle (and sometimes not so subtle) changes in plant species from moist, temperate forests to xeric (dry) shrub and grassland communities. On the south-facing slopes of the Washington side, this transition is more abrupt and occurs farther west. Microclimates, changes in topography, and soils differences have resulted in a complex mosaic of habitats throughout the Gorge.

There is no substitute for an aerial view of the Columbia River Gorge to fully appreciate the west–east and north–south contrasts in landform, vegetative patterns, and topographic variability. However, even the land-based traveler cannot miss the striking changes that occur during a trip through the Gorge. The following is a description of both the Oregon and Washington sides as one travels from the Sandy River delta in Oregon and from Washougal, Washington, to the eastern end of the Columbia River Gorge Scenic Area. These descriptions are very broad habitat descriptions to aid the reader in knowing where to begin looking for particular mammals, herptiles (amphibians and reptiles), birds, and butterflies. Over the next few years, a comprehensive, detailed vegetative mapping will occur as a function of Columbia River Gorge Commission activities.

Habitats

OREGON SIDE

Columbia River Riparian Zone. From the Sandy River to Hood River, the riparian habitat consists of black cottonwood, Pacific willow, red alder, creek dogwood, reed canarygrass, and stinging nettle. This is typical for the Portland–Vancouver metropolitan area lowlands. As black cottonwood drops out, the dominant trees become peachleaf willow and Columbia River willow (Hood River to The Dalles). Beyond The Dalles, willows continue to dominate, with some locust. Willow and alder are the dominant species to the west of the Deschutes River, and willow and white poplar are the most obvious species east of the Deschutes.

Mixed Conifer and Deciduous Forest Zone. As you travel from the confluence of the Sandy and Columbia rivers and proceed east, the dominant upland vegetation is typical temperate, mixed coniferous and deciduous forest. The dominant trees are Douglas fir and western hemlock mixed with the deciduous bigleaf maple. This habitat type extends from the Sandy to near Starvation Creek, between Cascade Locks and Hood River.

Transition Zone. From Starvation Creek to just past Hood River, Douglas fir becomes less robust and abundant and ponderosa pine and Oregon white oak become the dominant species, along with a more xeric understory. The forests are more open and scattered in this zone; the Hood

Rowena Plateau (photo by Joe Walicki)

River Valley is primarily orchard land, a change in vegetation that is especially striking from the air.

Ponderosa Pine and Oregon White Oak Zone. From the Rowena Plateau to The Dalles, ponderosa pine and Oregon white oak form the dominant overstory. Oregon white oak is found on the drier hillsides and a mix of oak and pine on the moister sites. (Poison oak often forms dense understory in this zone!) Extensive nonforested grasslands are found in this zone, which might provide a basis for referring to it as the oak–savanna zone.

Cliff and Grassland Zone. Steep cliffs with predominantly grassy vegetation replace the forest in this zone. The dominant grasses are the introduced, weedy cheatgrass (difficult to pick out of wool socks), Sandberg's bluegrass, bluebunch wheatgrass, and Idaho fescue. Gray rabbitbrush dominates between the cliffs and Columbia River riparian zone.

Cliff and Plateau Zone. Plateaus are dominated by gray rabbitbrush and scattered big sagebrush, ceanothus, and bitterbrush. Steep slopes are grassy with predominantly cheatgrass and Sandberg's bluegrass.

Rock Cliff and Talus Slope Zone. High rock cliffs form a steep wall to the Gorge. The slopes are covered primarily with Sandberg's bluegrass, cheatgrass, needlegrass, and bluebunch wheatgrass.

WASHINGTON SIDE

Columbia River Riparian Zone. As in the state of Oregon, a variety of riparian zones are found as one travels from east to west. Low-lying black cottonwood, willow, and alder dominate from the Washougal lowlands to near Archer Mountain west of Beacon Rock. From Archer Mountain to just east of Dog Mountain, steep cliffs dominate the landscape and willows form the primary tree species, with black cottonwood being restricted to more stable, less flooded sites. A long stretch of river between Dog Mountain and Dallesport consists of peachleaf willow, Pacific willow, and scattered locust. From Dallesport to near Maryhill, the riverine vegetation is primarily sparse red alder, black cottonwood, and willow. In the immediate vicinity of Maryhill there is extensive riprapping (artificial rock) of the riverbank which has reduced the vegetation dramatically.

Mixed Farming and Open Fields Zone. From Washougal to just east of Dog Mountain, farmlands and Douglas fir and bigleaf maple forest dominate the landscape. Oregon white oak occurs on the drier and south-facing slopes. Oaks appear much earlier on the Washington side than in Oregon, an indication of the drier south-facing slopes.

Transition Zone. As on the Oregon side of the Columbia, the moister mixed coniferous and deciduous forest is gradually replaced by xeric oak and ponderosa pine forest. In Washington, however, this transition begins much closer to the western end of the Gorge, due to the drier, south-facing slopes. The transition zone in Washington extends to Catherine and Major creeks (near Rowland Lake, east of White Salmon), where Oregon white oak and ponderosa pine dominate the overstory and poison oak forms dense understory growth.

Arid Grassland and Shrub Zone. The dominant grass is cheatgrass with some Sandberg's wheatgrass and bluebunch wheatgrass. As elsewhere in eastern Oregon and Washington, the weedy, introduced cheatgrass now dominates the native bunchgrasses, primarily due to overgrazing of once-rich grasslands. Gray rabbit-brush is the dominant shrub in this zone, which extends east to Dallesport.

Cliff, Talus Slopes, and Shrub Zone. Beyond Dallesport to the east of Horsethief Butte, shrub-dominated cliffs and talus slopes form the dominant vegetation. Ceanothus and bittercherry, as well as gray and green rabbit-brush, are the dominant shrubs.

Gently Sloped Grassland Zone. There is a short stretch of gentle slopes dominated by mixed grasses, balsamroot, and lupine.

Cliff and Grassland Zone. This is another short zone dominated by steep cliffs and rolling grasslands with few shrubs. The area has been heavily grazed.

Rock Cliff and Shrub Zone. This last zone, occurring around Maryhill State Park, has many steep cliffs and talus slopes. Gray rabbit-brush dominates the rocky areas and cheatgrass occurs on steep slopes and plateaus.

Common Gorge Wildlife

The following is a general description of major animal groups represented in the Columbia River Gorge. Many are common to both Oregon and Washington, a few have interesting distributional patterns within the Gorge, and one, the Larch Mountain salamander, is found nowhere else in the world. This introduction to general Gorge fauna is followed by a site-specific guide to viewing wildlife throughout the Gorge.

MAMMALS

One of the most visible mammals occurring throughout the Gorge are two races of mule deer, the western black-tailed deer and the "true" mule deer, which can be found east from near The Dalles throughout eastern Oregon and Washington. These two deer can be distinguished by both their preferred habitats and physical characteristics. The black-tailed deer prefers moister, coniferous forests typical west of The Dalles and has a striking black upper tail. The big-eared mule deer prefers drier ponderosa pine forests and sagebrush habitats east of The Dalles. As races of the same species (*Odocoileus hemionus*), they interbreed in the moist–dry transition zone around The Dalles.

Like the California condor and peregrine falcon, the white-tailed deer have been extirpated from the Gorge. While the peregrine is likely to be successfully reintroduced, it seems unlikely that the dramatic habitat changes wrought by dams and development will allow for reintroduction of the white-tailed deer. They are now restricted to islands in the lower Columbia River and the Umpqua Valley in southeastern Oregon.

Other mammals you can expect to see if you are in the right habitat are opossum, raccoon, striped and spotted skunk, gray and red fox, bobcat, coyote, black bear, porcupine, cougar, yellow-bellied marmot, badger, beaver, mink, nutria, muskrat, river otter, northern flying squirrel, northern pocket gopher, long-tailed vole, deer mouse, vagrant shrew, Townsend's vole, Nuttall's cottontail rabbit, western harvest mouse, Great Basin pocket mouse, Ord's kangaroo rat, white-tailed jackrabbit, and bats such as little brown myotis, yuma myotis, big brown, small-footed myotis, western pipistrelle, and pallid.

BIRDS

Birds, being highly mobile, are found seasonally, nesting or simply passing through the Gorge during migration. No avian species are found only in the Gorge nor do any birds have special distributional patterns like the mammals, amphibians, and reptiles. The best thing about birds, however, is that they are easy to find, often colorful, and frequently habitat-specific. They are not nocturnal like many mammals and do not hide under rocks and logs or in streams, as do many reptiles and amphibians. More than 200 species of birds have been observed within the Gorge, which makes them the premier choice for wildlife viewing. For this reason, many of the site descriptions focus primarily on the area's avifauna.

WATERFOWL

Waterfowl (ducks, geese, and swans) are concentrated primarily in the Columbia itself, in adjacent wetlands, or along its tributaries. By far the greatest concentrations of waterfowl are located outside the Scenic Area itself: Oregon's Sauvie Island and Washington's Ridgefield National Wildlife Refuge host more than 50 percent of waterfowl on the Columbia River from the Pacific Ocean to near Umatilla. Most of the remaining waterfowl can be found at the Umatilla National Wildlife Refuge. Still, an abundance of ducks, geese, and swans can be observed within the Scenic Area and many of the habitats (islands, wetlands, and riparian areas) are critical to these species.

INVERTEBRATES

As usual, the animals that lack backbones and are not "cute," or are popularly known as "bugs," are little studied. One group, however, is represented by spectacularly colored and much-loved critters . . . the butterflies. Butterflies represent a group to which amateurs can make significant contributions in recording range extensions. The reader is encouraged to keep county records and report them to the Xerces Society, 10 SW Ash, Portland, Oregon 97204. The Xerces Society is dedicated to conservation of invertebrates, including butterflies. They hold an annual July butterfly count and the public is encouraged to participate.

Also highly recommended is the National Audubon Society's *Field Guide to North American Butterflies*, by Robert Michael Pyle.

Wildlife Viewing Sites

The remainder of this chapter provides a biogeographical tour of the Columbia Gorge from west to east, focusing on the Columbia River and associated uplands within the Gorge. Adjacent upland habitats are also highlighted when they provide good viewing opportunities. The wildlife viewing areas were chosen because of personal familiarity or on the recommendation of several individuals who graciously provided suggestions, including David Anderson's Hood River County site guide in *Oregon Birds*, Wilson Cady of Washougal, Jeff Gilligan of Portland, Geoff Pampush of the Oregon chapter of The Nature Conservancy, and the staff of the Oregon Department of Fish and Wildlife. Additional suggestions are welcome and will be incorporated into an updated listing as the Gorge becomes better known and visited.

OREGON SIDE

Gary and Flag Islands (Rivermile 124). These two islands, owned by Multnomah County Parks, have dense vegetation (willow and black cottonwood) that provides habitat for beaver and many migratory and nesting birds. Osprey use the islands and adjacent Coast Guard beacon towers for nesting and feeding.

Multnomah Falls (Rivermile 136). This is the first of several locations where the American dipper (water ouzel) can be seen. This plumpish, gray, robin-sized bird is generally associated with fast-running high-mountain streams. In the Gorge it can be seen plying stream margins, flipping over rocks in search of its dietary mainstay, aquatic insects. The dipper also plunges into the stream (summer or winter!) to search out insects, fish eggs, and occasionally fish fry. Look for the dipper at the base of the falls or anywhere along the stream as it passes by the parking lot. Its gray color makes it easy to miss so look for its characteristic "dipping" as it stands on a rock or log at the water's edge.

Oneonta Gorge and Loop Trail (Rivermile 138). American dipper are commonly found in Oneonta Creek and near Horsetail Falls. The coniferous forest along the Oneonta loop trail is excellent habitat for warblers, flycatchers, red-breasted nuthatches, and woodpeckers.

This is the best place to see and hear the pika or rock rabbit (same order as the true rabbits and hares). This guinea pig–sized, almost tailless

Multnomah Falls in winter

mammal inhabits the talus slopes formed from the eroding basalt cliffs.
Their numerous burrows can be seen as you traverse the open talus fields
along the loop trail. The best way to "look" for the shy pika is to sit quietly

and listen for its sharp "eenk" call. If your voice is high-pitched enough (and if you are both quiet and patient), it is possible to entice them to venture within a few feet. Also look for their "hay mounds," small caches of dried vegetation they harvest and allow to dry in the entrance to their burrows before storing it underground for the winter.

Bonneville Dam (Rivermile 146). Osprey, common goldeneye, common merganser, belted kingfisher, and numerous waterfowl can be observed in the lake immediately behind the visitor center. The dock that serves tourist boats is an excellent platform for viewing these species. Peregrine falcons can be observed on occasion feeding on rock doves (domestic pigeons) near the dam.

Eagle Creek and Cascade Fish Hatchery (Rivermile 146.5). The Oregon Department of Fish and Wildlife's fish hatchery at the mouth of Eagle Creek and the creek itself are one of the best bird viewing areas in the Gorge. Every year an osprey pair nests high in a snag along the west bank of Eagle Creek, and American dippers nest under a footbridge about one mile from the hatchery. Winter is the best season to observe the dippers, since upstream freezing forces them to utilize the lower reaches of the stream to feed. They are unusual in that their complex, wrenlike song can be heard all winter. The dipper can be seen anywhere along Eagle Creek. A drive down a dead-end road to Overlook Park provides another view of "Bonneville Lake" and its waterfowl.

Herman and Lindsey Creeks (Rivermiles 151 and 159). The confluence of Herman Creek and the Columbia River, just west of a large log storage operation, is an excellent winter waterfowl viewing area and osprey nest nearby during the summer. Lindsey Creek, upstream several miles (east of Shellrock Mountain), also offers good waterfowl viewing during the winter months.

Starvation Creek Rest Area (Rivermile 160). One of the best rufous hummingbird viewing areas in Oregon is at this rest stop. An abundance of red-flowering currant (*Ribes sanguineum*) and a dense population of aggressive male hummers ensures a worthwhile stop regardless of your need for the facilities. The dense mixed deciduous and coniferous forest and plantings around the parking area provide good habitat for a variety of other birds such as cedar waxwing, Wilson's warbler, varied thrush, and MacGillivray's warbler.

Wells Island (Rivermile 167). Just west of Hood River is Wells Island. A small stand of black cottonwood surrounded by large willows constitutes the predominant habitat. Great blue heron nest communally on the west end of the island and can be seen either from the river or from the nearby Columbia Gorge Hotel. Canada geese nest on Wells Island as well.

Hood River (Rivermile 168). A comprehensive bird list for the city of Hood River and Hood River County appears in the spring 1987 issue of *Oregon Birds*. The following are highlights of bird viewing in the immediate vicinity of Hood River, along the Columbia River.

As many as 240 redhead ducks can be seen in the boat basin at the west end of town during winter months. Other waterfowl include American wigeon, coot, gadwall, wood duck, western grebe, pied-billed grebe, and horned grebe (red-necked, eared, and Clark's grebes can also be seen in fall migration).

The mouth of the Hood River is excellent habitat for gulls and shorebirds (dowitcher, sanderling, and sandpiper). South of the Hood River powerhouse, along the Hood River (Panorama Point), affords a beautiful view of Hood River Valley and Mount Hood as well as upland species such as western bluebird, chipping sparrow, purple finch, and western meadowlark.

Mosier and Rowena Loops (Rivermiles 175 to 182). East of Hood River is one of the best wildflower and wildlife viewing areas in the Gorge. Beginning at the town of Rowena there is a long climb west onto the Rowena Plateau. The road winds through orchards, Oregon white oak, and open grassy fields. Look for western bluebird, Lewis' woodpecker, yellow-bellied marmot, and badger. The southern slopes have lots of poison oak!

Rowena Overlook and Rowena Plateau (Rivermile 181). From the Rowena overlook there is a fantastic view of the Gorge and an unparalleled opportunity to look *down* on violet-green swallows, turkey vultures, and red-tailed hawks as they ride the currents rising off the Rowena bluff. The Tom McCall Preserve, known primarily for its April wildflower display, also hosts a variety of birds, including canyon wren, western bluebird, horned lark, western meadowlark, and white-throated swift. Two small ponds provide marsh and open-water habitat for pied-billed grebe and red-winged blackbird. The oaks (and poison oak) surrounding the ponds harbor a host of warblers during spring and fall.

The Tom McCall Preserve also provides an excellent vantage point to observe Caspian terns and gulls on the Klickitat River mudflats near Lyle, Washington. Bald eagles can also be seen on the Columbia below the Rowena Plateau.

Mayer State Park and the Columbia River (Rivermile 181). This is a good area for wintering waterfowl.

The Dalles and Vicinity (Rivermile 191). The open ponderosa pine and oak community surrounding The Dalles offers excellent habitat for western bluebird, Lewis' woodpecker, California quail, and house wren. Badger and marmot are two mammals likely to be seen.

Dunes (Rivermile 197). Just east of The Dalles is a large sand dune system that gave the Oregon Department of Transportation fits for years as the sand drifted across I-84, so they covered it with crushed rock. A spring surrounded by willow at the western end of the dunes is an excellent wildlife viewing area. Milkweed, host to monarch butterflies, grows along the northern edge of the dunes.

Just east of the dunes you encounter bitterbrush and gray rabbitbrush, indicators of an increasingly arid climate and a clue to begin looking for black-billed magpie, a species common to the Great Basin Desert. Magpies can be seen at Celilo Village and bald eagles roost near a downstream picnic area. A large population of diving ducks occurs here during the winter months.

Deschutes River Canyon (Rivermile 204). A short hike up the east side of the Deschutes River yields views of black-billed magpie, northern (bullocks) oriole, loggerhead shrike (summer), northern shrike (winter), marmot, and badger. Along the river one can view common merganser, common goldeneye, belted kingfisher, great blue heron (there's a rookery in the Columbia), spotted sandpiper, lazuli bunting, yellow-breasted chat, and red-winged blackbird.

Miller Island/Columbia River (Rivermile 205). A great blue heron rookery (communal nesting area), a large gull rookery, and a Canada goose nesting area make Miller Island an excellent site to view wildlife (from a distance, since nesting birds are susceptible to human intrusion).

WASHINGTON SIDE

Steigerwald Lake National Wildlife Refuge (Rivermile 125). As part of an effort to mitigate for loss of wildlife habitat due to construction associated with Bonneville Dam, the Steigerwald Lake area is in the process of habitat improvements. Approximately 700 acres have been transferred to the U.S. Fish and Wildlife Service. The land is currently agricultural with adjacent stands of black cottonwood and willow. More than 100 species of birds have been seen by Vancouver Audubon Society members, including tundra swan, bald eagle, and rough-legged hawk (winter); American bittern, wood duck, Virginia rail, and sora. A few yellow-headed blackbirds nest at Steigerwald Lake (the nearest colony is Bybee–Howell marsh on Sauvie Island). Great blue heron utilize this as a feeding area for their nearby Reed Island nesting colony. Rarer species that have been seen in the Steigerwald area include snowy owl, peregrine falcon, black-shouldered kite, great egret, cattle egret, Wilson's phalarope, western kingbird, and tufted duck. Purple martins can be seen nesting in nest boxes on Columbia River pilings.

Reed Island (Rivermile 126). Like other Columbia River islands, Reed Island provides important wildlife habitat more or less isolated from human disturbance. The island is predominantly black cottonwood stands surrounded by willow, gravel bars, and sandy beaches.

Franz and Arthur Lakes (Rivermile 138). This property was recently acquired by the Trust for Public Land. Franz is a large, shallow lake with abundant wapato (*Sagittaria latifolia*) and other wetland plant species. The lakes are bounded on the north by mixed deciduous and conifer forest, and on the Columbia River side by large willow forests. This important wetland system supports an abundance of waterfowl, birds of prey, tundra swans, bald eagles and snow geese in the winter months.

Pierce and Ives Islands (Rivermile 142). Pierce Island consists of two "islands," with large black cottonwoods surrounded by low willows and forbs. Ives Island also has a large stand of cottonwood with adjacent willows. Another great blue heron rookery is on Pierce Island and heron can be observed feeding along either shore of the Columbia during nesting season (February through July).

Beacon Rock State Park and Hamilton Mountain (Rivermile 142). North of Beacon Rock are trails that leave the Columbia River bottomlands and enter mixed conifer and deciduous forests where Swainson thrush—with their melodic, upscale, flutelike call—can be heard during summer months. Ruffed grouse, band-tailed pigeon, and lazuli bunting can be seen as well. Hamilton Mountain is well known for wildflowers and is a fantastic area to see numerous warblers during migration and nesting season. Canyon wrens greet those who climb high enough onto Hamilton Mountain to get near the sheer cliffs that this melodic songbird inhabits. This is one species that typically lives in eastern Oregon and Washington canyon country. The canyon wren's series of staccato, downscale notes is familiar to anyone who has rafted eastside rivers.

Aldrich Butte and Greenleaf Slough (Rivermile 144). Just north of the town of North Bonneville are Greenleaf Slough and Aldrich Butte. The slough and many small ponds have heavy deciduous forest around them. This is especially rich warbler and waterfowl habitat. Hooded merganser, osprey, MacGillivray's warbler, and red-eyed vireo can be seen here. A walk up Aldrich Butte passes through deciduous and coniferous forest; hairy and pileated woodpecker and black-throated gray warbler are common.

Rock Creek and Stevenson (Rivermile 150). Rock Creek empties into a large lagoon (Rock Cove) just west of Stevenson that pro-

The Hamilton Mountain Trail;
inset: glacier lily (inset photo by Joe Walicki)

vides nesting habitat for Canada goose and a favored feeding area for osprey, wintering bald eagle, and waterfowl such as canvasback, ring-necked duck, common goldeneye, bufflehead, ruddy duck, common loon, and western and pied-billed grebe.

Dog Mountain (Rivermile 159). A 3,000-foot elevation gain encompasses diverse plant communities and consequently represents a rich array of birds. The Dog Mountain trail provides an excellent birding outing. Lazuli bunting, turkey vulture, and numerous warblers (during spring migration) make Dog Mountain both an excellent wildflower and wildlife outing.

Burdoin Mountain (Rivermile 172). The eastside influence is definitely evident, with open oak savanna and ponderosa pine habitat predominating. The avifauna reflects this transition with golden eagle, prairie falcon, and ferruginous hawk representing the raptor community. Turkey, mountain quail, lazuli bunting, canyon wren, rock wren, ash-throated flycatcher, and Lewis' woodpecker are other drier-habitat species one can expect to see at nearby Locke and Rowland lakes, an oak (*Quercus garrayana*)-dominated habitat.

Major and Catherine Creeks (Rivermile 177). Between Burdoin Mountain and the Klickitat River, two streams—Major and Catherine creeks—flow into the Columbia River. This is an excellent area to hike in (watch out for poison oak!) and to look for rattlesnakes. The oak woodland and ponderosa pine habitat is also excellent for Lewis' woodpecker and western bluebird.

Klickitat River and Lyle (Rivermile 180). Gulls and Caspian tern can be seen on the mudflats at the mouth of the Klickitat River. In the river canyon about three-quarters of a mile upstream from the Columbia are nesting lesser goldfinch, lazuli bunting, mountain quail, Lewis' woodpecker, and wild turkey.

Dallesport (Rivermile 191). The flat, rolling, open grasslands attract nesting long-billed curlew, common nighthawk, occasional sandhill crane, yellow-bellied marmot, and other typical "eastern" Washington species. The cranes are probably individuals from the nearby Conboy National Wildlife Refuge near Mount Adams, Washington. Caspian tern nest at nearby Spearfish Lake (Rivermile 192).

Horsethief Lake State Park (Rivermile 194). This area offers diverse habitats for wildlife viewing. There are oak woodlands, Horsethief Lake, open scablands, small vernal pools, and sheer cliffs, which attract rock climbers as well as wildlife.

In oak forests there are great horned owl, lazuli bunting, mourning dove, and an array of perching birds. Gopher snakes, which often perfectly mimic rattlesnakes, are the most common snake in the area.

Look for introduced chukar and gray partridge on the cliffs around Horsethief Lake State Park. Chukar can often be heard during spring and summer uttering their loud "chuk, chuk, chuk" calls from a prominent rock near the top of the cliffs.

At Horsethief Lake look for grebes (western and pied-billed) and waterfowl (bufflehead, scaup, canvasback, and ring-necked duck).

On top of Horsethief Butte, where the Bretz floods scoured the area thousands of years ago, is dry, exposed basalt grassland. Western meadowlark, horned lark, rock wren, California quail, and chukar are the most common birds. The small vernal pools that dot the scablands have nesting cinnamon teal and wood duck. Marmot, badger, and ground squirrel can be seen on the butte as well.

Horsethief Lake State Park to Maryhill Museum (Rivermile 207). The cliffs and talus slopes are open and grassy and home to bobcat and marmot. Chukar and long-billed curlew have been seen in the open grassy fields. Goldeneye, Canada goose, scaup, and eared grebe can be seen around Brown's Island in the Columbia River.

Maryhill State Park (Rivermile 209). This is best known for the Maryhill Museum but is also a good viewing area for wildlife. Long-billed curlew and ring-necked pheasant are seen here. Burrowing owls have been reported to nest here as well.

Species of Special Interest

REPTILES AND AMPHIBIANS

There are several species of "herptiles" (amphibians and reptiles) that are of special interest or concern due to spotty distribution within the Columbia Gorge. A number of Gorge herptiles are listed by the state of Oregon as species of concern to the Oregon Department of Fish and Wildlife. These include the Oregon slender salamander (found in Douglas fir forests) and the sharptail snake (found in moist rotting logs and stable talus slopes).

Another species of interest, but which is not on either the Oregon state or federal list of species of concern, is the California mountain kingsnake. It resembles coral snakes in its bright banding and has been reported in the drier habitats in the Gorge near Lyle. The black snout, white neck collar, and alternating bands of red, black, and white make it distinctive in the Pacific Northwest. Any sighting of this species should be reported to fish and wildlife biologists in either state.

Larch Mountain Salamander. This is the only endemic animal species in the Gorge. Unlike the abundance of wildflowers that occur nowhere else in the world (endemics), this salamander represents the only vertebrate species that calls the Columbia Gorge its only home. A small two-inch (fifty-two-millimeter) amphibian, it has a chestnut or reddish dorsal stripe and a pinkish belly. Its habitat is talus slopes, under rocks in wet weather but deeper in cold and dry weather. The most significant habitat consideration for this species seems to be the distribution of talus slopes, which are patchier in Washington than in Oregon. The Oregon populations seem to be more continuous due to the contiguous, moist talus slopes that stretch far to the east. The Larch Mountain salamander is a federally listed "candidate" species, meaning additional information is needed prior to being listed as threatened or endangered.

BIRDS

Two species of birds are on the federal list: peregrine falcon and bald eagle. Peregrines are being introduced into the Gorge, which makes the preservation of their prime nesting habitat—sheer cliffs—critically important. Bald eagles nest and have winter roosts in old-growth forest within the Gorge Scenic Area and elsewhere along the Columbia system. (A fairly large winter roost is to the west of Sauvie Island near Portland.)

Other species of interest that are on the federal candidate list or on state threatened or endangered lists include western yellow-billed cuckoo (requires river-bottom black cottonwood and willow habitat and may occur in the Gorge), long-billed curlew (nests in the vicinity of The Dalles, Maryhill, and Umatilla), northern spotted owl (requires old-growth coniferous forest, which is extremely limited in the Gorge and a rare habitat type elsewhere in the Northwest), harlequin duck (nests in fast-moving tributaries and winters along the coast), northern goshawk, burrowing owl, ring-necked duck, bufflehead, barrow's goldeneye, greater sandhill crane, purple martin, and Lewis' woodpecker.

FURTHER READING

Mathews, Daniel. *Cascade–Olympic Natural History*. Raven Editions, 1988.

Nehls, Harry B. *Familiar Birds of the Northwest*. Portland Audubon Society, 1981.

Pyle, Robert Michael. *Field Guide to North American Butterflies*. National Audubon Society, 1981.

Whitney, Stephen R. *A Field Guide to the Cascades and Olympics*. The Mountaineers Books, 1983.

◆

WILDFLOWERS

BY RUSS JOLLEY AND JULIE KIERSTEAD NELSON
ILLUSTRATIONS BY JULIE KIERSTEAD NELSON

The Columbia Gorge is a natural wildflower garden of mighty dimensions. The numerous combinations of aspect and elevation along its length, from the rain-drenched west end to the arid east end, make every niche and recess of the Gorge unique in some way. Exploring all its corners could scarcely be done in a lifetime; the possibility of new discoveries could never be exhausted. In the pages that follow, there is no intention to consider all of the flowering plants that grow in the Gorge. Rather, the aim is to lightly sample the wildflowers, give a quick look into some of the typical floral habitats, and encourage the reader to do some exploring on his or her own.

Some 800 species of native wildflowers and flowering shrubs, almost a quarter of the total in Oregon, find a home in the Columbia River Gorge between the Sandy River at the west end and Biggs on the east. Some of these flowers are so small that they are scarcely visible without a magnifying glass. Others appear as specks of color on the ground, and the rest form a progression through every gradation of size and color to the showy species and masses of color that impress casual travelers. Gold-stars (*Crocidium multicaule*), common in the eastern Gorge in early spring, are not impressive singly, but millions in bloom can touch a hillside with yellow bright enough to be seen from across the Columbia River. In May, lupines bring a blue tinge to the brown hillsides near The Dalles.

A distance of only fifty miles spans the extremes from temperate rain forest near Bonneville Dam, through pine and oak woodlands near Mosier, to sagebrush desert at Celilo. This sea-level pass through the Cascade Range has such variety not only because the broad range of topography and climate provides a vast array of ecological niches, but also because events of geologic history have brought into the Gorge many species that originated in distant areas.

The probable origins of the Columbia Gorge flora are understood, at least in broad outline. Not surprisingly, many species are those typical of the Willamette Valley and Puget Trough, and even the coast. Other plants have apparently reached the Gorge by migrating north or south along the axis of the Cascade Range. Another group migrated to the Gorge all the way from the Rogue River Valley in southern Oregon. Still another group consists of plant species that normally grow only at high elevations but that are found at low elevations in the Gorge, evidently the result of an ancient downhill migration. Finally, there is a small number of endemic species, plants found only in the Columbia Gorge and vicinity and that may, in fact, have evolved there.

In addition to the native plants that arrived in the Gorge by natural processes, there are some of exotic origin, primarily from Europe or Asia, introduced by the white man. Many of these plants came with farm animals, agricultural seed supplies, and ship ballast; the rest were brought in deliberately as farm or range crops or as garden flowers. Introduced plants are seldom found in undisturbed areas of the Gorge, but are common along roads and railroads, and in pastures and other disturbed ground. Some are abundant, including field mustard (*Brassica campestris*), honesty (*Lunaria annua*), cornflower (*Centaurea cyanus*), and ox-eye daisy (*Chrysanthemum leucanthemum*). Some are serious pests, especially for the farmer and rancher, and the gradual weed invasion threatens some of our best wildflower spots as well.

Lupine plant (lower left) in Bridal Veil Falls State Park

The Great Columbia Gorge Flower Show

Each year the Columbia Gorge puts on a flower show. In fact, one might say that there are many shows, all different. At Latourell Falls, on the Columbia River Highway, the show opens with *Trillium ovatum* in March and closes with *Angelica genuflexa* in August, but many other wild-flower species come into bloom and fade away during the five-month interval. It is good to remember that the mix of species in bloom at any one time will change as the season progresses. Therefore, to see all the flowers that bloom at a particular place in the Gorge, one must visit it several times during the blooming season.

On the steep Dog Mountain Trail, the main flower show lasts from mid-May to late July. In mid-April, when the oaks along the lower trail are just beginning to leaf out, the electric blue flowers of hound's-tongue (*Cynoglossum grande*) are fully opened. In mid-June, phantom orchids (*Eburophyton austiniae*), pale leafless ghosts, rise from the duff of Douglas fir woods halfway up the mountain. In mid-July, it is worth the hard hike just to see the clumps of blue daisies (*Erigeron subtrinervis*) scattered over the grassy expanse near Dog Mountain's top. The epilogue of leafy aster (*Aster foliaceus*) and Hall's goldenweed (*Haplopappus hallii*) comes in September, also in the open meadow near the top.

FORESTS, LOW AND HIGH

Even in the dense forest of the western Gorge, where little direct sunlight reaches the forest floor, many wildflowers thrive. In early spring, trilliums (*Trillium ovatum*) are common, each with three petals at first pure white, gradually turning purple with age; wild heliotrope (*Valeriana scouleri*), hemispheric clusters of tiny pale pink flowers; wood sorrel (*Oxalis oregana*), often called "sour grass" because its cloverlike leaves have an acid taste; and wild bleeding heart (*Dicentra formosa*). Low Oregon grape (*Berberis nervosa*), a low, prickly leaved shrub, is often the main ground cover in Douglas fir forests. Its spikes of yellow flowers are followed by extremely sour-tasting blue berries in the fall. The deer's-head orchid or fairy slipper (*Calypso bulbosa*) also blooms in early spring, usually under Douglas fir trees and often where there is little ground cover except for moss.

Later on in spring, wild ginger (*Asarum caudatum*) produces strange, dark red flowers that lie on the ground, often concealed by forest litter. Vanilla leaf (*Achlys triphylla*) has thin spikes of pale flowers that bloom for only a short time, but the overlapping leaves of adjacent stems can hide the forest floor until fall, when the drying leaves give off a faint scent of vanilla. In late spring, the windflower (*Anemone deltoidea*) makes its appearance. Its three stem leaves have a triangular (deltoid) arrangement.

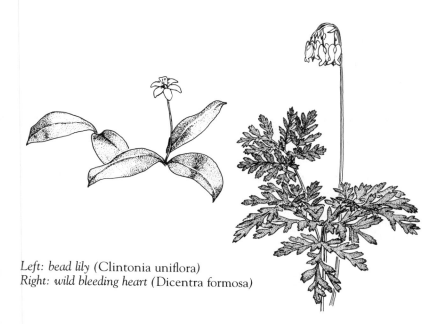

Left: bead lily (Clintonia uniflora)
Right: wild bleeding heart (Dicentra formosa)

About the same time, perfect six-pointed starflowers (*Trientalis latifolia*) can be found in coniferous forests of the Gorge from the Sandy River to the outskirts of The Dalles. All these forest flowers can be seen at Ainsworth State Park and Latourell Falls, and on many of the forest trails in the western Gorge.

In the Upper Multnomah Basin, directly below the Larch Mountain viewpoint, a network of Forest Service trails provides easy access to the largest remnant of old-growth forest—complete with spotted owls—left in the Gorge. A common wildflower here is bunchberry (*Cornus canadensis*), sometimes called Canadian dogwood, since the flower resembles that of its tree cousin, the Pacific dogwood. Its flowers are followed in autumn by clusters of bright red berries, and the leaves also turn red. Foamflower (*Tiarella trifoliata*) is also common in upper-elevation woods. Its delicate panicle of tiny white flowers is seen throughout the summer and well into fall. Other wildflowers you will see are trailing raspberry (*Rubus lasiococcus*) and bead lily (*Clintonia uniflora*), whose white six-petaled flower is followed by a single startlingly blue, beadlike berry at the top of the erect stem. In July, Mertens' coral root (*Corallorhiza mertensiana*), an orchid with no leaves and no chlorophyll, can frequently be seen in the deep woods along the trail. Pink rhododendrons (*Rhododendron macrophyllum*) light up the somber forest at elevations over 3,000 feet in the western Gorge, blooming in late June.

Some plants prefer streamsides and other damp places in the western Gorge. Tanner Creek Road, near Bonneville Dam, is a good place to see them. The quarter-mile-long road is gated to automobile traffic, so it is ideal for a short walk. In early April, pinkish flowers of coltsfoot (*Petasites frigidus*) and shocking pink flowers of salmonberry (*Rubus spectabilis*) are abundant along the road, both appearing while the stems are still leafless. By the first of May, luxuriant stands of pink-flowered *Corydalis scouleri* have taken over much of the roadside. A month later, giant cow-parsnip (*Heracleum lanatum*), up to six feet tall, is the most noticeable plant along Tanner Creek, as it is in most of the western Gorge. Then, in early July, the purple-red flowers of hedge-nettle (*Stachys cooleyae*) appear. This ill-scented plant is not really a nettle at all, but a member of the mint family. Two other wet-loving plants, yellow monkey flower (*Mimulus guttatus*) and pink or white Siberian lettuce (*Montia sibirica*), keep on blooming along Tanner Creek until late summer.

Typical open coniferous woods of the western Gorge are found along the Hamilton Mountain Trail. Try a hike in the first week of June. By then, the blue flowers of *Anemone oregana* will already have faded, but beside the trail you will find pink sea-blush (*Plectritis congesta*); the white or pinkish woodland star (*Lithophragma parviflora*); deep yellow wallflower (*Erysimum asperum*), fragrant as well; Solomon plume (*Smilacina racemosa*), a lily with a long spray of tiny white flowers; wild strawberry (*Fragaria vesca*); large-flowered blue-eyed Mary (*Collinsia grandiflora*); scarlet paintbrush (*Castilleja hispida*); bluish-purple leafy pea (*Lathyrus polyphyllus*); red-and-yellow columbine (*Aquilegia formosa*), a relative of the buttercups; Nootka rose (*Rosa nutkana*), with sweet-smelling flowers three inches across; and, in late spring, clumps of brightest yellow Oregon sunshine (*Eriophyllum lanatum*). The arrival of summer brings the tiger lily (*Lilium columbianum*), with shining orange petals spotted with red—more like a leopard than a tiger!

A number of flowering shrubs grace the open woods of the Gorge. One of the showiest is the red-flowering currant (*Ribes sanguineum*), which can be seen here and there along Interstate 84 from the Sandy River eastward. One can't help noticing it around the first of April, when the flowers are fully out but the bushes still have no leaves, nor can the hummingbirds, who viciously defend the bushes from interlopers. Serviceberry (*Amelanchier alnifolia*) is sometimes a large shrub, often a small tree, and is found throughout the Gorge west of The Dalles. Its white flowers brighten the often dreary days of early spring. In mid-April, a good display of serviceberry is seen at Rooster Rock State Park. About a month later, dazzling white shrubs can be seen along the highways on both sides of the river, especially between Cascade Locks and Hood River. This is buckbrush (*Ceanothus sanguineus*), its short panicles of fragrant white flowers standing erect on the stem like candles. Buckbrush has a short blooming season; by the end of May it has melted back into the forest background.

Clockwise from top: Oregon anemone (Anemone oregana), *marsh paintbrush* (Castilleja hispida), *coltsfoot* (Petasites palmatus frigidus)

Later on, around the first of June, deer brush (*Ceanothus integerrimus*) comes into full bloom a little farther east in the Gorge. Its cascades of white to deep blue flowers are a common sight on the Washington side between Dog Mountain and Bingen, and in Oregon on Highway 30 as it winds through Mayer State Park. In July, the cliffs and rocky places above Interstate 84 in the western Gorge are festooned with the white flowers of yet another shrub, *Holodiscus discolor,* aptly called ocean spray. Like serviceberry, it is a member of the rose family. About the same time that ocean spray is blooming on the cliffs, brilliant pink patches of fireweed (*Epilobium angustifolium*) appear along all the highways of the Gorge.

Perhaps the showiest flowering tree of the Gorge is the Pacific dogwood (*Cornus nuttallii*). An abundance of large white flowers makes the tree stand out against the dark evergreens. Around May 1, it blooms along low-elevation highways, especially Interstate 84 from Cascade Locks east to Hood River. Dogwood trees often bloom a second time in late summer or early fall.

CLIFFS AND WATERFALLS

Paleobotanist Leroy Detling, curator of the herbarium at the University of Oregon for 30 years before his death in 1967, postulated that many unusual features of Columbia Gorge flora resulted from past Ice Ages, during which high-elevation plants were pushed from their homes by the intense cold and ice. These boreal species were driven farther south and to lower elevations such as the nearly sea-level floor of the Gorge. When the ice retreated and the climate warmed, not all the plants that had taken refuge at low elevations migrated back to higher elevations. Some remained in the Gorge, having found a suitable home, especially in the shade of the cool, moist basaltic cliffs on the south side of the Gorge. At least twenty-five wildflower species normally found at elevations of 4,000 feet or greater are thriving at scarcely 100 feet above sea level in the Columbia Gorge. Among them are the shocking pink cliff penstemon (*Penstemon rupicola*), yellow desert-parsley (*Lomatium martindalei*), spreading phlox (*Phlox diffusa*), and white shooting star (*Dodecatheon dentatum*).

Of the thirteen regional endemics, that is, species whose range is restricted to the Columbia Gorge and vicinity, six are commonly found on vertical basaltic cliffs near the floor of the Gorge. Some of the endemics are so little known that they have no common names. The six cliff-dwelling endemics are *Bolandra oregana*, *Sullivantia oregana*, *Erigeron oreganus*, *Douglasia laevigata* var. *laevigata*, long-bearded hawkweed (*Hieracium longiberbe*), and *Penstemon barrettiae*, named after its discoverer, Mrs. P. G. Barrett, who lived in the Hood River Valley in the late nineteenth century. Two other endemics, Howell's daisy (*Erigeron howellii*) and kittentails (*Synthyris stellata*) with spikes of blue-purple flowers, are typically found growing on steep north-facing slopes but often on cliffs, as well. Many of these endemics grow along the trail to upper McCord Creek Falls in John Yeon State Park.

Detling speculated that the cliff-dwelling endemics may be relicts, that is, species more widely distributed at one time but now reduced to their present limited range. One of the plants, *Sullivantia oregana*, is found only at waterfalls, where it grows within reach of the spray. *Bolandra oregana* is a little less fastidious, sometimes settling for a merely damp cliff. The round, sharply toothed leaves of these two species, both members of the saxifrage family, are not always easy to distinguish, but the rather inconspicuous white flowers of *Sullivantia* bear no resemblance to the peculiar maroon crowns of *Bolandra*. Also growing on wet cliffs, often in association with *Bolandra* and *Sullivantia*, are several widespread species, such as Mertens' saxifrage (*Saxifraga mertensiana*), mist maiden (*Romanzoffia sitchensis*), and white shooting star (*Dodecathon dentatum*). A third cliff-dwelling endemic, *Erigeron oreganus*, is an attractive pink-rayed daisy invariably found under overhanging basalt cliffs, precisely as described in 1880 by Thomas Howell, an early Oregon botanist. Sometimes it is found behind waterfalls, as at Latourell Falls, but often on apparently dry cliffs, where the gnarled roots probe crevices for water. *Douglasia laevigata,* also an endemic, is perhaps more at home on vertical cliffs than any other plant of the Gorge. In April, it blooms on the vertical walls of Crown Point, at Mitchell Point thirty-three miles to the east, and at many places in between. Pink clumps of *Douglasia* literally hang over the heads of hikers on the McCord Creek Trail.

In mid- to late May, the succulent broadleaf stonecrop (*Sedum spathulifolium*) blooms on dry cliffs, rock outcrops, and talus slopes throughout the western Gorge. Many rocky places along the highways are brightened by these yellow flowers. Later on, in midsummer, bluebells (*Campanula rotundifolia*) adorn many of the same cliffs where stonecrop bloomed earlier. Around the first of August, bluebells are seen on the cliffs in Washington along Highway 14 at Cape Horn and along the Beacon Rock Trail.

Cut-leaf penstemon (*Penstemon richardsonii*) is a plant of dry vertical cliffs and rocky banks, generally at low elevations. It is the only species of penstemon that is found throughout the length of the Gorge. A species normally found east of the Cascade Range, it has migrated westward through the Gorge to suitable cliff sites as far west as Crown Point and Cape Horn. At Hole in the Wall Falls on Warren Creek, it blooms around the first of August.

Oregon bolandra (Bolandra oregana)

Sulfur buckwheat (Eriogonum umbellatum)

SUMMITS

Some of the high ridges above the Gorge attain elevations of 4,000 feet or more above sea level, high enough to reach into the subalpine (Hudsonian) zone. Subalpine flowers are seen on open rocky summits such as the top of Larch Mountain (4,056 feet), Indian Mountain (4,880 feet), and Big Huckleberry Mountain (4,202 feet). Characteristic plants include avalanche lilies (*Erythronium montanum*); Oregon campion (*Silene oregana*), a flower with incredibly fringed petals; cat's-ear lily (*Calochortus subalpinus*), the hairy inner face of the petals being responsible for the common name; the spectacular blue and green flowers of rockslide gentian (*Gentiana calycosa*); rock pennycress (*Thlaspi fendleri*); rusty saxifrage (*Saxifraga ferruginea*); sulfur buckwheat (*Eriogonum umbellatum*); and several species of penstemon.

MARSHES

Nestled in the coniferous forest of the western Gorge, at elevations between 2,800 and 4,000 feet, are perennially wet meadows or marshes. There may be as many as forty of these marshes in the Gorge, but only a few are accessible by road or trail. A large marsh can be seen below the viewpoint on Larch Mountain. Another place to find marsh plants is along the north and west shores of Rainy Lake.

Certain plants grow in practically every marsh in the Gorge: Jeffrey's shooting star (*Dodecathon jeffreyi*), marsh marigold (*Caltha biflora*), marsh violet (*Viola palustris*), northern starflower (*Trientalis arctica*), sticky tofieldia (*Tofieldia glutinosa*), green bog orchid (*Habenaria saccata*), and white bog orchid (*Habenaria dilatata*).

Other plants grow in many marshes of the Gorge. Fringed grass-of-Parnassus (*Parnassia fimbriata*) blooms by the thousands in some of the more western marshes in late August. Elephant-head lousewort (*Pedicularis groenlandica*) has tall spikes with little purple flowers, each a miniature elephant's head with an up-curled trunk. The blue flowers of staff gentian (*Gentiana sceptrum*) are rarely open, but the bumblebees have no trouble forcing their way inside, and out again. In the boggy areas of these marshes, one can find the insect-eating sundew (*Drosera rotundifolia*), whose ruby-jeweled leaves attract small insects to their doom.

Then there are species that are found in only a few marshes, plants like Oregon saxifrage (*Saxifraga oregana*), swamp laurel (*Kalmia occidentalis*), and buckbean (*Menyanthes trifoliata*), a plant with a lowly common name but a beautiful cluster of pink or white fringed flowers, usually at the edges of ponds.

In most of the marshes of the Gorge, the show begins in late May with marsh marigolds, shooting stars, and marsh violets, and it ends in September with great northern asters (*Aster modestus*), grass-of-Parnassus, and ladies' tresses (*Spiranthes romanzoffiana*), an orchid with greenish-white flowers arranged in a spiral around the stem.

PINE AND OAK WOODLANDS

An unusual feature of the Columbia Gorge is the presence of a sizeable group of plant migrants from the Rogue River Valley. The most recent Ice Age—about 12,000 years ago—was followed by a warm and dry (xerothermic) period that peaked about 6,500 years ago and was succeeded by a cooler and moister phase that has persisted until the present. Detling's hypothesis is that, during the xerothermic phase, the Rogue flora migrated northward through the Willamette Valley and the Columbia Gorge. Then, as the climate slowly cooled, many of the Rogue plants remained in the Gorge, especially in the warmer and drier eastern end, but became much less abundant in the area between the Gorge and the Rogue Valley.

The most prominent of these Rogue migrants is the Oregon white oak, which occurs in extensive stands in the eastern Gorge and in xeric "islands" in the western Gorge and the Willamette Valley. Many colorful wildflowers of the pine and oak woodlands are of Rogue Valley origin, such as small-flowered blue-eyed Mary (*Collinsia parviflora*), a small plant with quarter-inch-long flowers, each with a white upper lip and a deep blue lower lip; four-spotted clarkia (*Clarkia quadrivulnera*), with a dark red spot on each of its four pink petals; and balsamroot (*Balsamorhiza deltoidea*), its incredibly brilliant sunflowers borne above robust clusters of arrow-shaped leaves.

Four species of cluster-lily (*Brodiaea*) are found in the Gorge, mostly on grassy slopes in the east half of the Gorge and usually at low elevations. In a small open area at the south base of Wind Mountain, next to the highway, the bicolored cluster-lily (*Brodiaea howellii*) blooms in early May; dark blue ookow (*Brodiaea congesta*), on stems often two or three feet high, in late May; white cluster-lily (*Brodiaea hyacinthina*) in early June; and the harvest cluster-lily (*Brodiaea coronaria*), usually close to the ground, in mid-June.

Pine and oak woodlands provide habitat for the five Columbia Gorge endemics that are not cliff dwellers, including Suksdorf's desert-parsley (*Lomatium suksdorfii*); Columbia desert-parsley (*Lomatium columbianum*); Narcissus shooting star (*Dodecatheon poeticum*); Thompson's lupine (*Lupinus latifolius* var. *thompsonianus*); and Hood River milk-vetch (*Astragalus hoodianus*). These five species grow on gentle slopes and flats, in grassy openings in the pine and oak woodlands or in the open grassland near The Dalles. A sixth Gorge endemic found in the pine and oak woodlands, *Penstemon barrettiae*, is more likely to be found on cliffs and talus slopes. In early May, bright purple masses of Barrett's penstemon adorn cliffs on both sides of the Columbia near Mosier.

Around the first of July, when most of the flowers of low elevations in the eastern Gorge are gone for the year, there are still things worth looking for. Wandering among the oaks at Memaloose State Park, carefully skirting the patches of poison oak, you might see the tall buckwheat (*Eriogonum elatum*) or goldaster (*Chrysopsis villosa*), both of which seem almost immune to drought. Then it always comes as a surprise to find a beautiful green-banded mariposa lily (*Calochortus macrocarpus*) all by itself in a grassy glade. On a slender two-foot stem, it seems to float in the gentle summer air like a lavender butterfly, the Spanish word for which is mariposa. A flower like this—up to four inches across—would be torn apart by the gales of spring.

East of Bingen, the "old highway" turns off Highway 14 and travels around the north side of Rowland Lake, crossing Catherine Creek and then Major Creek at about two and a fifth miles. Here the Major Creek Road turns north and dead-ends in a couple of miles. You can park at the junction and walk the Major Creek Road, since traffic is extremely light. The narrow dirt road climbs about 200 feet at first, then stays level the rest of the way, winding through pine and oak woodlands with occasional meadows and rock outcrops in a lovely quiet valley.

Just about every wildflower species of Major Creek is right beside the road somewhere along the way. Between March 1 and June 1, at least eighty-five native wildflowers bloom here, including purple grass-widows (*Sisyrinchium douglasii*), yellow bells (*Fritillaria pudica*), glacier lilies (*Erythronium grandiflorum*), bigheaded clover (*Trifolium macrocephalum*), Shelton's violet (*Viola sheltonii*), dark blue larkspur (*Delphinium nuttallianum*), and light blue Columbia frasera (*Frasera albicaulis*), a member of the gentian family. In March and April, western buttercups (*Ranunculus occidentalis*) are everywhere.

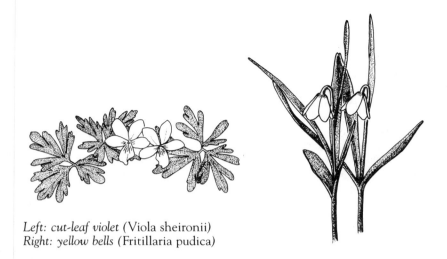

Left: cut-leaf violet (Viola sheironii)
Right: yellow bells (Fritillaria pudica)

GRASSLANDS

East of the Lyle area, trees are left behind as you enter the grassland of the Columbia Basin, more properly called the shrub grassland, since shrubs such as bitterbrush, mock orange, rabbit-brush, sumac (*Rhus glabra*), and big sagebrush (*Artemisia tridentata*) are also found at this end of the Gorge. Against the background of treeless hills, the season brings splashes of color. North of The Dalles Bridge over the Columbia, near the junction of US 197 with Highway 14, late April brings a fine roadside show: a Rogue Valley migrant, yellow balsamroot (*Balsamorhiza deltoidea*), blooming alongside two Columbia Gorge endemics, blue *Lupinus latifolius* var. *thompsonianus* and white *Astragalus hoodianus.*

The Dalles Mountain Road climbs the Columbia Hills on the Washington side of the river opposite The Dalles, starting at Highway 14 milepost 84.5 and eventually reaching an elevation of 2,200 feet. Along this eight-mile stretch of road, the wildflower show is a long one, with a brief prologue of purple grass-widows (*Sisyrinchium douglasii*), salt-and-pepper (*Lomatium piperi*), and a few other plants in February; main acts from March to July; and epilogues in September of yampah (*Perideridia gairdneri*) and in October of rabbit-brush (*Chrysothamnus nauseosus*). The progress of the seasons here brings as well the white blossoms of *Phlox hoodii*, white or pink daggerpod (*Phoenicaulis cheiranthoides*), yellow blanketflower (*Gaillardia aristata*), pink *Phlox speciosa,* and wavy-leaf thistle (*Cirsium undulatum*), and dozens of other colorful wildflowers, including six species of desert-parsley (*Lomatium*).

The genus *Lomatium*, in the parsley family, includes about seventy-five species and is exclusive to western North America. Fourteen lomatiums are represented in the Columbia Gorge, most in great abundance. Two are regional endemics whose range is largely within the boundaries of the Gorge. *Lomatium suksdorfii*, named in honor of Wilhelm Suksdorf, the most important botanist of the Gorge, occurs in pine and oak woodlands on both sides of the Columbia River, mostly at higher elevations. In mid-May, it blooms along the roads near Wasco Butte, southeast of Mosier. *Lomatium columbianum* is a handsome purple-flowered species most abundant near the floor of the Gorge. Its range, like that of *Lomatium suksdorfii*, lies mainly in the pine and oak woodlands. Around the middle of March, it can be seen blooming along Interstate 84 east of Memaloose State Park and along Highway 14 east of Lyle.

Lomatium laevigatum is yellow-flowered, with extraordinarily delicate and graceful foliage. It is a cliff dweller, its habitat the vertical basalt cliffs that line the Columbia River east of The Dalles. It can be seen on the cliffs just east of the little town of Wishram, blooming in mid-March. The very widespread *Lomatium grayi* grows on suitably rocky and dry sites throughout the Gorge, but especially in the eastern Gorge. Its yellow flowers are like those of *Lomatium laevigatum*, but its leaves are even more finely dissected and give off a characteristic pungent aroma when crushed or even brushed against. Around the first of April, *Lomatium grayi* blooms on hillsides and road cuts east of Bingen and on the sides of the Klickitat Valley just north of Lyle. *Lomatium triternatum* is perhaps even more common, growing throughout the Gorge and at all elevations. This rather sparse little plant is not showy, but it is found everywhere on open slopes and rocky banks, especially in the western half of the Gorge. In May, it blooms in abundance on the slopes next to Highway 14 at Cape Horn and at Dog Creek Falls.

Fragrant mock orange (*Philadelphus lewisii*) is a white-flowered shrub seen throughout the Gorge, but in open grassland it is more noticeable than in the forested areas to the west. In early June, it blooms on dry rocky areas along Highway 14 east of Lyle. Three other shrubs of the open grassland rival mock orange for showiness. The golden currant (*Ribes aureum*) is loaded with yellow flowers around April 1. Chokecherry (*Prunus virginiana*), a large shrub with long white drooping racemes, blooms along The Dalles Mountain Road in late April and May. Around the first of June, the wild cluster-rose (*Rosa woodsii*) puts on its show. All three of these shrubs inhabit moist spots in otherwise arid land, places such as stream banks and ditches.

Finally, about the first of October, both gray rabbit-brush (*Chrysothamnus nauseosus*) and green rabbit-brush (*Chrysothamnus viscidiflorus*) come into bloom, spreading golden yellow over the flats and lower hillsides along the highways near The Dalles and eastward. One can only wonder how these plants can summon the energy for such an effort after so many months of drought.

DUNES

Interesting plant communities are found on the sand dunes that occur here and there along the river from Mosier eastward. The sand sparkles with mica, a mineral not found in this region of the Cascade. In fact, the sand originated in the Rocky Mountains and arrived with the great flood that created the scablands. It was deposited in the area of The Dalles when the mighty torrent was momentarily backed up and ponded by the bottle-neck of the Gorge at Crates Point northwest of The Dalles. Sadly, the finest dune of the Gorge was lost in 1983 when the Oregon Highway Divi-sion covered it with gravel so as to avoid having to periodically remove sand encroaching on Interstate 84 east of The Dalles. However, smaller dunes remain along Interstate 84, on islands in the Columbia, in the Dal-lesport area (just across the river from The Dalles), and eastward along Highway 14.

Characteristic dune species include wiry knotweed (*Polygonum majus*), a spare little plant with tiny pink bell-shaped flowers; Suksdorf's broomrape (*Orobanche ludoviciana*), a root parasite usually blooming in mid-June, but most often found in the form of a four-inch blackened skele-ton protruding conspicuously from the sand, long after its brief flowering season has ended; bright yellow western wallflower (*Erysimum occidentale*); white evening primrose (*Oenothera pallida*); and sand-verbena (*Abronia mellifera*). The white flowers of the sand-verbena are only half open on bright sunny days, opening fully in the late afternoon and evening. The dunes east of The Dalles also feature the sky-blue flowers of the sand dune penstemon (*Penstemon acuminatus*), blooming in early May.

COLUMBIA RIVER SHORE

A wanderer on the shore of the river will find flowering plants rarely seen elsewhere in the Gorge, plants like the tall Columbia coreopsis (*Coreopsis atkinsoniana*), sneezeweed (*Helenium autumnale*), aromatic field mint (*Mentha arvensis*) with pale bluish flowers in tight clusters along the stem, wild licorice (*Glycyrrhiza lepidota*), and beggar-ticks (*Bidens cernua*), the seeds of which are perfectly designed to collect on pantlegs and socks. Also occasionally on the shore, in springy areas, is the deadly poisonous water-hemlock (*Cicuta douglasii*). Beware! Every so often someone mis-takes this for "wild celery," with generally fatal results.

Along the river, the season is not closely tied to the week or month, but rather to the level of the river. As a rule plant growth and flowering do not take place until the shore is exposed by the receding water. This, in turn, depends principally on the depth of the mountain snowpack in the Columbia River watershed. A wet, cold winter means high water and a late season, possibly not well underway until September. A low snowpack means that shoreline plants may start blooming in late July. Once the shoreline has been exposed, it becomes essentially a one-act show lasting about two months. Many shore plants, such as yellow monkey flowers (*Mimulus*), blue speedwells (*Veronica*), and hedge-hyssop (*Gratiola neglecta*), continue to bloom as long as the river keeps them wet.

From the Dalton Point boat-launching ramp on westbound Interstate 84 near milepost 29, one can walk miles of the shore east to Wahkeena Creek or west to the mouth of Bridal Veil Creek and beyond. The busy freeway above is only fifty yards away, but it is generally hidden by cottonwoods and tall reed canarygrass. It is still pretty much a lonely shore, with few visitors and a lot of variety, ranging from springs to muddy, sandy, or rocky shores like those at the mouth of Wahkeena Creek, where the great swamp groundsel (*Senecio hydrophilus*) grows. Across the river, at the Beacon Rock State Park moorage, the aromatic riverbank sage (*Artemisia lindleyana*) is abundant, its little yellowish flowers appearing in August or September.

FURTHER READING

Jolley, Russ. *Wildflowers of the Columbia Gorge.* Oregon Historical Society Press, 1988.

Clasping-leaved twisted stalk (Streptopus amplexifolius)

View from Hamilton Mountain Trail

PART II

HIKING

BY JOE WALICKI

Northwest residents are blessed with a wide variety of landscapes to enjoy: the rugged coastline, the high desert with its sweet-smelling sage, and the mountains, from snowcapped Mount Adams and Mount Hood to the steep walls and deep ravines of the Columbia River Gorge. For those who venture into the Gorge, just 45 minutes east from Portland, an area of exquisite waterfalls, pine-scented forests, and lush wildflower gardens await. The trails of the Gorge are as varied as each sunset, each one having its own distinctive and subtle beauty.

Although the western and central Gorge, the area with the most waterfalls, is the most popular destination for hikers, the drier eastern portion of the Gorge also attracts hikers, particularly when wet weather inhibits hiking in the wet western end. Throughout the Gorge, those hikers who have the energy to climb some of the longer, steeper trails are rewarded with sweeping vistas of a dramatic landscape.

The best way to appreciate this beauty is up close and slowly—by walking along the many miles of maintained trails that weave in and out of forest-covered valleys and crisscross the rushing streams. This chapter describes most of the one-day hikes available in the Gorge, from the short strolls to popular waterfalls, to steep climbs to grand vistas, to dry eastern hikes. Longer backpack trips are possible by combining some of these day hikes, or continuing onward when the day hikes described here return to the car.

Two combinations deserve special mention. The first is Gorge Trail 400, which generally parallels Interstate 84 from Bridal Veil to Wyeth. The purpose of the trail is to give hikers an opportunity to take an extended 35-mile trip through the Gorge during all seasons of the year, even when other trails in the Gorge are covered with snow. The trail can be walked a section at a time, or several sections can be combined for an extended outing. The trail can also be used to return to your car after doing a hike that returns you to the highway some distance from your starting place.

Another long trail is the Chinook Trail, proposed in 1988 by a group that formed under the name of the Chinook Trail Association. Their goal is to develop a 200-mile trail running the entire length of the Gorge, from Vancouver to Maryhill on the Washington side and from Biggs to Portland

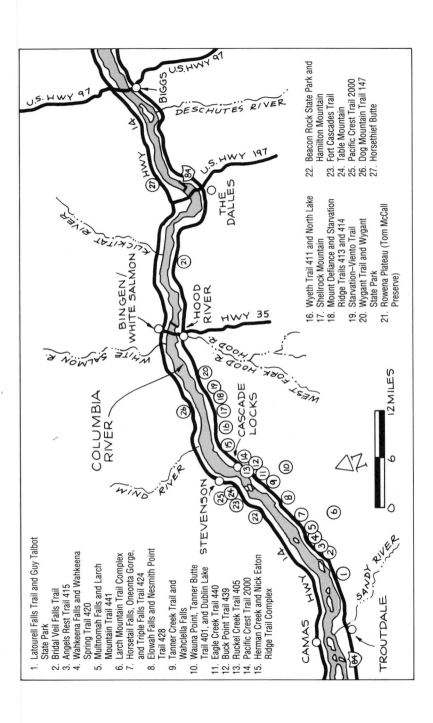

1. Latourell Falls Trail and Guy Talbot State Park
2. Bridal Veil Falls Trail
3. Angels Rest Trail 415
4. Wahkeena Falls and Wahkeena Spring Trail 420
5. Multnomah Falls and Larch Mountain Trail 441
6. Larch Mountain Trail Complex
7. Horsetail Falls, Oneonta Gorge, and Triple Falls Trail 424
8. Elowah Falls and Nesmith Point Trail 428
9. Tanner Creek Trail and Wahclella Falls
10. Wauna Point, Tanner Butte Trail 401, and Dublin Lake
11. Eagle Creek Trail 440
12. Buck Point Trail 439
13. Ruckel Creek Trail 405
14. Pacific Crest Trail 2000
15. Herman Creek and Nick Eaton Ridge Trail Complex
16. Wyeth Trail 411 and North Lake
17. Shellrock Mountain
18. Mount Defiance and Starvation Ridge Trails 413 and 414
19. Starvation–Viento Trail
20. Wygant Trail and Wygant State Park
21. Rowena Plateau (Tom McCall Preserve)
22. Beacon Rock State Park and Hamilton Mountain
23. Fort Cascades Trail
24. Table Mountain
25. Pacific Crest Trail 2000
26. Dog Mountain Trail 147
27. Horsethief Butte

on the Oregon side. The Oregon section of the trail would link together several existing trails, along with the Forty Mile Loop being assembled in the Portland metropolitan area. The Washington section, however, would consist mainly of new trail construction. For more information, write the Chinook Trail Association, P.O. Box 997, Vancouver, WA 98666-0997.

Preparation

Once you decide that seeing the Gorge by foot is an experience you don't want to miss, proper preparation and equipment and some knowledge of trail safety and etiquette will help create a more enjoyable experience and will make you want to return again and again to the Gorge for day hikes.

The most important part of preparation is selecting a trip to match your physical ability. If you have never hiked before, don't choose an 8-mile, 3,000-foot elevation gain hike—unless you don't mind being very sore the next day! Start with an "easy" hike with little or no elevation gain, such as Eagle Creek or Latourell Falls.

If you keep in good physical shape by daily exercise, one of the moderate or strenuous hikes might be more challenging. If these trips entice you and you haven't been exercising daily, try some vigorous walking around the neighborhood for about 30 minutes a day a couple of weeks before the trip. (This would be a good time to break in a new pair of boots.) A person who has never hiked before *could* walk 16 miles in one day, but the next morning he wouldn't want to get out of bed! Be especially sensitive to the needs of your hiking partner, especially if he or she has never hiked before. If children come along, choose a hike that is an appropriate length for young ones.

Many of the hikes in the Gorge traverse steep cliffs and visit the very brink of scenic viewpoints and waterfalls. Such locations are extremely dangerous for children. The trails described here are rated for child safety, but never let children run ahead or hike alone, even on the safest of trails.

Allow yourself plenty of time to complete the trip. The "time allowance" listed in this book is generous. You shouldn't have any trouble completing the hike in the time stated, including a nice long lunch break.

If the weather is stormy, avoid trips that take you to exposed areas such as Angels Rest, Mount Defiance, or Dog Mountain. The higher up you go, the more severe the weather will be. Be prudent. Take a low-elevation trail sheltered from the wind such as Latourell Falls, Triple Falls, or Eagle Creek. (The exposed areas are mentioned in the trail descriptions.)

Before you set out on your trip, make sure that you will be able to find the trailhead. Directions to trailheads are given in detail in each of the following trail descriptions. Read them carefully. Be aware, though, that roads and trailheads change, and if you can't find a trailhead, ask at a store, a gas station, or a ranger station.

EQUIPMENT

Proper equipment helps ensure an enjoyable hike. Good hiking boots are the most important piece of equipment a hiker can own. Shop around before choosing your first pair. Try several styles and sizes; size 9 in one manufacturer's boot may not be the same as another brand. Try on your boots with the thickness of socks you'll wear while hiking—for example, two thick woolen socks or one thick and one thin.

Before starting out on a hiking trip, be sure the boots are broken in. Try wearing them around the house for a week or two to stretch the leather and to get your feet used to them. Some boots, such as the lightweight nylon/leather combinations, take little breaking in. If there is any sign of soreness on your feet, put moleskin over the area immediately. This cloth-backed adhesive sticks to the skin and prevents blisters.

If you don't have a pair of boots, running shoes will do fine for short hikes on maintained trails. Don't let the lack of boots stop you from enjoying the Gorge.

Your other important piece of equipment is your day pack. There are many comfortable and practical day packs on the market. When shopping for one, look for the following features: padded shoulder straps; foam padding in the back of the pack (this protects you from sharp objects in the pack); a strap to secure the pack around the waist; a heavy nylon material, waterproofed and double-stitched throughout; and enough room to hold an average-size watermelon.

What you wear on a day hike in the Gorge depends on the season, the weather, and your preference. Jeans and a long-sleeve shirt will do most of the time. If the weather is unseasonably hot, shorts are a good idea, but you will want to be careful where you sit if you're allergic to poison oak. Poison oak is ubiquitous in the Gorge. Learn to recognize it. If a shrub or vine has leaves that appear in sets of three, stay away.

Since rain is possible any month of the year, carry a waterproof parka and pants, along with an extra sweater. This equipment can also be used to keep you warm in the event of a sudden drop in temperature. And don't forget a hat; you can lose half of your body heat through your head.

A wool shirt or sweater or a down vest is a good thing to carry, especially if the Gorge winds are really blowing.

WHAT TO TAKE ALONG

Food and water are essential items to carry even if you're only hiking for an hour or two. It's surprising how hungry and thirsty one can get just a short distance from the car. If the hike might take from 2 to 8 hours, pack a lunch. Granola bars, nuts and raisins, and cheese and crackers provide the calories and high energy a body needs while hiking. In case you are delayed, always carry a bit more food than you plan to consume. Try to avoid walking more than 2 hours without snacking; the body is using a lot of energy and needs a continuous supply of food to function efficiently.

Carry at least one full quart of water per person. Not having enough water is worse than carrying a little extra, especially in hot weather.

The Ten Essentials. Several items are considered essential equipment and should always be carried:

1. Extra clothing
2. Extra food
3. Sunglasses
4. Small flashlight with extra batteries and bulb
5. Pocket knife
6. Matches
7. Firestarter
8. First aid kit
9. Map
10. Compass

Plus one special addition: an emergency "space blanket."

Rodney Falls, Hamilton Mountain Trail

NAVIGATION

Know where you are at all times while hiking in the Gorge. Not reading trail signs at trail intersections or not knowing which trail to take could mean an extra-long walk or even a night out in the woods. Since the trail system in the Gorge can be complex, trail intersections are particularly important: remember each and every intersection you pass through, and remember which direction you turned. If need be, take notes or mark your map as you pass through each intersection. Read trail descriptions and maps before setting off, and carry a detailed map with you at all times. Purchase the U.S. Forest Service map "Trails of the Columbia Gorge" to learn about trails not shown on maps included here, and always carry a USGS topographic map of the area in which you plan to hike. In addition, carry a compass with you and check it every now and then to know the general direction of travel.

Trail Signs. Trail signs sometimes disappear, especially at trailheads. Once on the trail, the signs are usually in place. If you feel sure you are at the correct trailhead but there is no sign, follow your map and, when you reach the first trail crossing, compare the signs on the trail with the numbers on the map to verify your position. Report the loss of signs to the Forest Service or other appropriate agency.

SAFETY AND ETIQUETTE

Following a few general pointers about safety and etiquette will enhance the enjoyment of your trip. Hike at a steady pace, but stop frequently for rests. Be extra cautious at unfenced viewpoints. If an injury does occur, one person should stay with the injured party and another should hike out and contact the county sheriff. If you are hiking alone, tell someone where you are going before you leave home, and if you are injured, stay on the trail. An 8-hour first aid course from the American Red Cross could be helpful in any emergency.

If there were any hazardous conditions on the trail, such as loss of trail due to landslides, notify the appropriate state or federal agency.

Don't leave any valuables in your car.

Watch the time from the parking lot to your destination, and realize that generally a 3-hour uphill climb will take 2 hours downhill.

Be considerate of others; don't shout or scream unless in an emergency. Don't leave any litter, but do pick up what someone else has left. Don't pick flowers or other plants; several threatened or endangered species live in the Gorge.

Don't drink the water directly from any stream unless it has been purified first. The danger of ingesting *Giardia* and other parasites is increasingly likely, so purify all drinking water by using purification tablets or a special filter. Better yet, bring water from home.

A PERSONAL NOTE

Whether you're a beginning hiker or an experienced backpacker, once you've hiked in the Gorge, you will return time after time. There's something special about these lovely trails and the land it takes you through that stays with you long after the trip. Possibly it's a sense of peace or that good tired feeling, or just a sense of accomplishment in reaching your planned destination.

Whatever your feelings are, they'll be good feelings. Good luck and great hiking!

HOW TO SELECT A HIKE

Preliminary information for each hike is given in the information block preceding the hike. Before selecting a hike, skim the information block. A description of the hike and how to get to it follows each informa-tion block. Most directions for Oregon are given from Interstate 84 (or the Columbia River Highway) eastbound. On the Washington side, directions for most hikes are given from Highway 14. For trailheads located on other roads, call a Forest Service ranger station to check snow level if use is in early spring. An explanation of the information blocks follows.

Difficulty. **Easy:** Up to 5 miles and a maximum 1,000-foot elevation gain. **Moderate:** 5 to 10 miles and between 1,000 and 3,000 feet of eleva-tion gain. **Strenuous:** More than 10 miles or more than 3,000-foot eleva-tion gain.

Child Safety. **Good:** There is little danger to children along the entire length of the trail. (For very small children, try some of the very short na-ture trails or interpretive trails. Three such trails described in this chapter are the two trails at Bridal Veil State Park and the Fort Cascades Trail east of North Bonneville.) **Moderate:** There is some danger to children, usu-ally in certain locations along the trail; discretion is advised, particularly with small children. **Dangerous:** Most sections of the trail are dangerous for small children; avoid if hiking with children.

Time. An estimated time is given to do the complete trip, allowing plenty of time for rests, photo breaks, and just plain enjoying the trip.

Distance. Total distance is given in miles from trailhead to destination and back to trailhead.

Elevation Gain. The amount of elevation gained is given in feet from the starting point to the destination. Usually, the higher the elevation gain, the harder the trip. Gains of more than 1,500 feet should be avoided by beginners.

USGS Map. The relevant U.S. Geological Survey map is given for each hike.

Viewpoints/Attractions. Scenic features or other features that make this area special are given.

The hiking trips in this chapter are listed from west to east along Interstate 84 and Highway 30 (the Columbia River Highway, also known as the scenic highway) in Oregon and from west to east along Highway 14 in Washington.

Note: Just as this book was going to press, two major forest fires occurred in the Gorge. Both were extinguished within a few days, but not before they had done considerable damage. The largest of the fires began near Multnomah Falls and spread west to Bridal Veil Creek. Because the fire was confined to the ground cover, most larger trees were not destroyed, but trails in the area were closed due to danger of rockslides and because some footbridges were destroyed. The trails closed at the time of publication included Angels Rest 415, Wahkeena Falls 420, Multnomah Falls 441, Return 442, and Perdition 421. A smaller fire occurred in the Wauna Point area. Although trail restoration work was underway at the time of publication, check with the Forest Service for current status of trails in either area.

Hikes

OREGON SIDE

◆ LATOURELL FALLS TRAIL AND GUY TALBOT STATE PARK

Difficulty: Easy
Child safety: Moderate
Time: 2 hours
Distance: 2 miles, round trip
Elevation gain: 300 feet
USGS map: Bridal Veil
Viewpoints/attractions: Lower falls, close to parking lot; upper
    falls, at south end of picturesque valley

Latourell Falls, an easy but pretty hike, is especially popular because it is the closest major falls to Portland. Within 40 minutes after leaving the city, you can be in a remote little valley, seemingly hundreds of miles

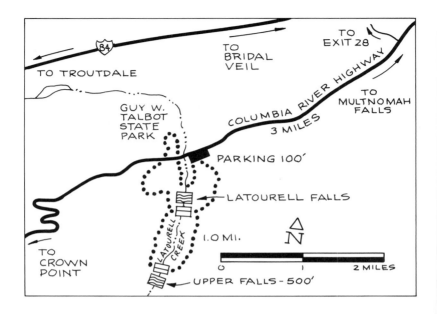

from civilization. Its easy access and low elevation gain make it a good first hike or a good trip for breaking in a new pair of boots.

From I-84, take Bridal Veil exit 28. Travel 3 miles west along the Columbia River Hwy to the trail parking lot. The trail, starting from the parking lot, leads you to the top of the lower falls and then continues up the valley to the upper falls, returning to the parking lot via the opposite side of the valley. Two viewpoints overlooking the Columbia River add to the special quality of this trail.

◆ BRIDAL VEIL FALLS TRAIL

Difficulty: Easy
Child safety: Moderate
Time: 30 to 45 minutes
Distance: 1 mile, round trip
Elevation gain: 100 feet
USGS map: Bridal Veil
Viewpoints/attractions: Uniquely shaped falls

The hike down to Bridal Veil Falls is so easy that a person who has never hiked before will find the experience very comfortable.

From I-84, take Bridal Veil exit 28. Travel west 1 mile along the

View from Overlook Loop Trail, Bridal Veil Falls State Park

Columbia River Hwy to Bridal Veil State Park. From the east end of the parking lot, the trail leads downhill to the creek and then uphill a short distance to a viewing platform directly in front of the falls. The water cascades over the lip of the falls as evenly as a large water fountain.

To the north of Bridal Veil Falls is the site of Bridal Veil Lumber Company, which is planned for conversion to a park. The trail from the

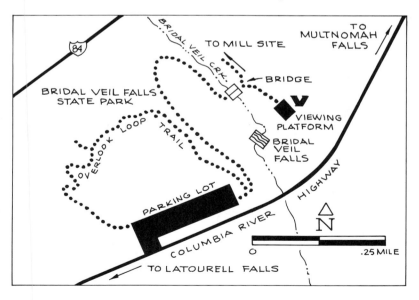

falls to the mill site is presently gated and locked, but will presumably be restored to public use.

The climb back up to the parking lot is moderately steep but of short duration.

Also available at Bridal Veil Falls State Park is a short paved nature trail known as the Overlook Loop Trail. It leaves one end of the parking lot and returns to the other. Along the way it passes through camas meadows and offers several views of the Columbia. It also offers a view of the Pillars of Hercules, a 120-foot basalt tower to the west.

◆ ANGELS REST TRAIL 415

Difficulty: Moderate
Child safety: Moderate
Time: 5 hours
Distance: 4.5 miles, round trip
Elevation gain: 1,400 feet
USGS map: Bridal Veil
Viewpoints/attractions: Panoramic view of Gorge

If you don't want to travel too far from Portland and want to experience a *real* Gorge hike, take the trail to the top of Angels Rest, a spectacular viewpoint.

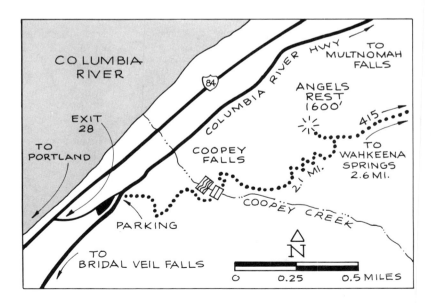

From I-84, take Bridal Veil exit 28. At the junction of this exit and the Columbia River Hwy, there is a gravel parking lot. The trail is just across the road to the northeast.

This picturesque trail traverses through deciduous and evergreen forests, crosses a number of pretty streams, and passes the top of Coopey Falls. Although the trail is moderately steep, there are many places along the way that invite resting. When the trail reaches the ridge, it offers panoramic views of the Columbia Gorge. To the east, Trail 415 leads to Wahkeena Spring.

Once on top, use extreme caution. The edges of the cliffs are rounded and footing near the edge is insecure.

◆ WAHKEENA FALLS AND WAHKEENA SPRING TRAIL 420

Difficulty: Easy to moderate
Child safety: Moderate
Time: 4 hours
Distance: 3 miles, round trip
Elevation gain: 1,200 feet
USGS maps: Bridal Veil and Multnomah Falls
Viewpoints/attractions: Falls, miniature canyon, springs

If you enjoy finding your way through a maze of trails, the Wahkeena/Multnomah Falls area should satisfy you perfectly. This area has more trail intersections per square mile than any other section in the Gorge. Take your time and read the signs and maps carefully, and note every intersection you pass through. If you get lost, just head downhill on almost any trail, and you'll eventually reach the Columbia River Highway.

From I-84, take Bridal Veil exit 28. Travel east 3 miles on the Columbia River Hwy, to a parking lot and the trailhead. The trail to Wahkeena Spring travels uphill through many switchbacks and is steep at times. About 1 hour from the parking lot, the trail enters a miniature canyon with tall Douglas firs, steep rock walls, and a bubbling stream.

As you approach the headwaters of Wahkeena Creek, you'll reach the intersection of Trail 420 and Angels Rest Trail 415. Turn right and in a couple hundred feet you'll find Wahkeena Spring gushing from the ground. It is considered one of the few sources of water in the Gorge that's safe to drink. This is a fine place to rest and have a picnic.

Trail 415 continues west to Angels Rest, and Trail 420 continues east to Devils Rest Trail 420C and Larch Mountain Trail 441. Devils Rest Trail is a little-used trail that climbs steeply at first, then levels out before coming to a viewpoint about 1.5 miles from Trail 420.

Wahkeena Falls

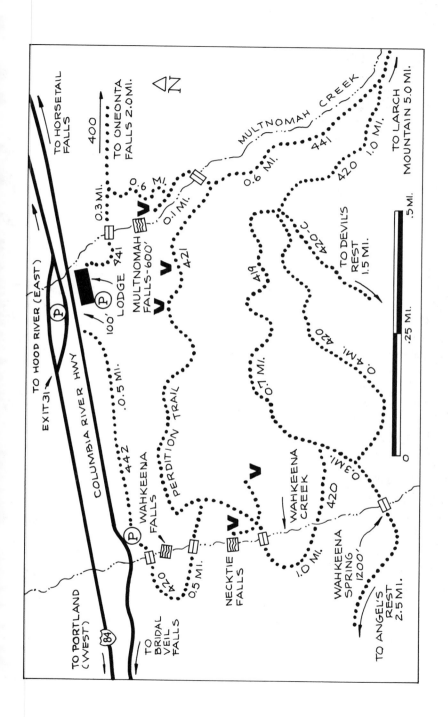

◆ MULTNOMAH FALLS AND LARCH MOUNTAIN TRAIL 441

Difficulty: Easy to Moderate
Child safety: Moderate
Time: Top of falls, 2 hours; metal bridge, 5 hours
Distance: Falls, 2.5 miles, round trip; metal bridge, 4 miles, round
trip
Elevation gain: Falls, 500 feet; metal bridge, 1,500 feet
USGS maps: Bridal Veil and Multnomah Falls
Viewpoints/attractions: Highest falls, views of river, picturesque
stream

The most popular spot in the Columbia Gorge is undoubtedly Multnomah Falls. On any sunny Saturday or Sunday year-round hundreds of
people will be there, taking pictures of Oregon's tallest waterfall, eating a
meal in the historic lodge, and buying souvenirs by the bagful. In the summer months, the Forest Service operates a small visitor center behind the

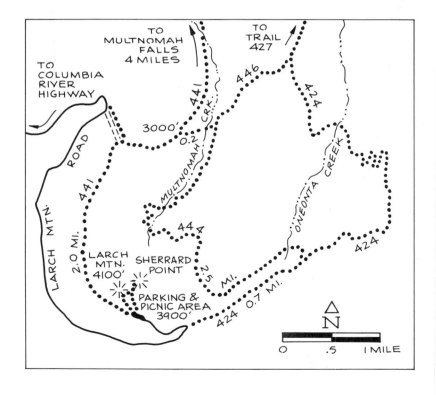

lodge where friendly rangers answer questions about Gorge trails and the natural history of the Gorge.

From I-84, take Multnomah Falls exit 31, to Multnomah Falls Lodge. The trail starts immediately east of the lodge and is paved all the way to the top of the falls. The grade is moderately steep but rewards the walker with an unsurpassed view of the Columbia River once the viewing platform is reached. Anyone in reasonably good condition can make it to the top, including small children, although parents should keep a watchful eye on them.

Larch Mountain Trail 441 continues upstream from the top of the falls and passes a number of beautiful smaller waterfalls. The deciduous forest changes to an evergreen forest, and the creek fills with huge boulders. Many hikers feel that this stretch of trail is the prettiest in the Gorge, but don't look for any larches: not a single larch grows on Larch Mountain.

About 2 miles from the parking area is a large metal bridge across Multnomah Creek. Two or three hundred yards beyond the bridge, a small path leads down to the right to a clearing next to the creek. This is a good spot to have lunch. The trail continues uphill 4.8 miles, crossing Multnomah Creek one more time before terminating at the picnic area near the summit of Larch Mountain. From the parking lot nearby, a short trail leads to spectacular views from Sherrard Point.

◆ LARCH MOUNTAIN TRAIL COMPLEX

Difficulty: Easy
Child safety: Good
Time: 4 hours
Distance: 5.5 miles, round trip
Elevation gain: 1,100 feet
USGS map: Multnomah Falls
Viewpoints/attractions: Mountains of Columbia Gorge—Mount Hood, Mount Adams, Mount St. Helens, and Mount Rainier

Do this trip on a sunny day. You will long remember the panoramic vista from the viewpoint on Sherrard Point, a short walk north from the parking lot. There are numerous picnic tables in the area, and it's a great place to escape the high temperatures of Portland in the summer. Bring your own water.

From I-84, take Corbett exit 22. Proceed uphill to the Columbia River Hwy, then turn left and follow signs to Larch Mountain (about 17 miles). The trail begins at the west end of the parking lot at the top of Larch Mountain.

To begin a picturesque loop trip, start on Trail 441, the Larch Mountain Trail, and head downhill through a thick young forest. After about 45 minutes, watch for a trail on the right. This "cut-off" trail eventually crosses Multnomah Creek and intersects Trail 444. Head uphill on 444 past a small swamp and through a grove of old-growth Douglas fir. After intersecting Trail 424, begin a moderately steep climb back to the road and parking lot.

The only views on this trip are from the parking lot and Sherrard Point.

Triple Falls on Oneonta Creek

◆ HORSETAIL FALLS, ONEONTA GORGE, AND TRIPLE FALLS TRAIL 424

Difficulty: Easy
Child safety: Moderate
Time: Ponytail Falls, 1 hour; Oneonta Creek/Gorge viewpoint,
  2 hours; Triple Falls, 3 hours
Distance: Ponytail Falls, 1.5 miles, round trip; Oneonta
  Creek/Gorge viewpoint, 3.0 miles, round trip; Triple Falls,
  5.0 miles, round trip
Elevation gain: 700 feet to Triple Falls
USGS map: Multnomah Falls
Viewpoints/attractions: Walk behind a falls, three falls in one,
  scenic canyon

The special attractions on this trail system are a walk behind Ponytail Falls, a view of Oneonta Gorge from above, and a view of unique Triple

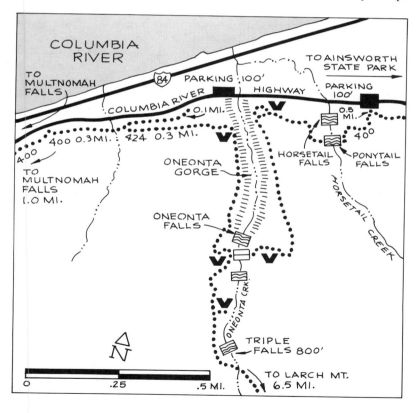

Elowah Falls, John Yeon State Park

Falls. If time is limited, just go as far as Ponytail Falls, but if you want to take a pleasant hike for a day, pack a lunch and walk to Triple Falls along a scenic trail in the Oneonta canyon. There's an ideal spot to eat and view the falls as the trail descends to the creek.

Beware: the profuse waterfalls in this area are occasionally mislabeled on some maps.

From I-84, take Dodson/Ainsworth State Park exit 35. Travel 1.4 miles west on the Columbia River Hwy, to the parking lot at Horsetail Creek and the trailhead. After crossing Oneonta Creek above Triple Falls on a footbridge, Trail 424 continues south, climbing for 6 miles and eventually reaching Larch Mountain Road, 0.25 mile east of the parking lot.

In the hot summer months, try wading up Oneonta Creek from the Columbia River Highway. For 45 minutes you'll pick your way around boulders and through deliciously cold water up a narrow gorge, at the end of which is a close-up view of seldom-seen Oneonta Falls and a tiny beach to relax on.

◆ ELOWAH FALLS AND NESMITH POINT TRAIL 428

Difficulty: Easy to Elowah Falls; strenuous to Nesmith Point
Child safety: Moderate
Time: Falls, 1.5 hours; Nesmith Point, 10 hours
Distance: Falls, 2 miles, round trip; Nesmith Point, 10 miles round trip
USGS maps: Multnomah Falls and Tanner Butte
Viewpoints/attractions: Classic "bowl" falls, view of Columbia River and Hamilton Mountain

For a short scenic hike, follow the trail signs to either a bridge below Elowah Falls or viewpoints above the falls. McCord Creek, which feeds the falls, drops into one of the classic "bowls" of the Gorge. To really feel the size of this area take the upper trail, which goes almost all the way around the upper part of the bowl and then visits Upper McCord Creek Falls. Use caution on the portion of trail that is high above the valley floor.

From I-84, take Dodson/Ainsworth State Park exit 35. Travel 2.5 miles east on Columbia River Hwy to a parking lot. Nesmith Point Trail, which branches off the main trail after a short distance from the parking lot, climbs steeply through groves of bigleaf maple and mixed hardwood forest. Many hikers use this trail as a conditioning hike prior to climbing Mount Hood. About 3.5 miles from the highway, the trail levels out and in 1.5 miles reaches Nesmith Point overlooking the Columbia River. This is one of the highest points on the rim of the Gorge.

Close to Nesmith Point, Horsetail Creek Trail 425 takes off from an old jeep trail and heads west 5 miles along the rim to Oneonta Trail 424. The lower trail drops into the valley, and a bridge crosses the creek below the base of the falls. The trail continues 3 miles to Tanner Creek and Bonneville Dam as Trail 400.

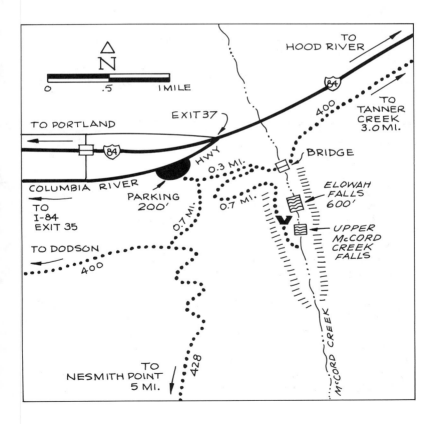

104 ♦ COLUMBIA RIVER GORGE

♦ TANNER CREEK TRAIL AND WAHCLELLA FALLS

Difficulty: Easy
Child safety: Moderate
Time: 2 hours
Distance: 2 miles, round trip
Elevation gain: 300 feet
USGS maps: Bonneville Dam and Tanner Butte
Viewpoints/attractions: Falls, huge "bowl"

For a cool and easy trip in the summer, hike to Wahclella Falls (also known as Tanner Falls) and enjoy a shady spot under the limbs of huge Douglas firs.

From I-84, take Bonneville Dam exit 40. Find a paved parking area south of the exit. The trail starts as a gravel road and in a few hundred yards becomes a small trail hugging the east side of the canyon. Eventually the trail forks into a loop: choose one fork, then return on the other. On the east side of the canyon, the trail crosses some landslides. Although the trail has been rebuilt in recent years, exercise caution. On the west side, notice the huge bowl created by a very large landslide, also evidenced by the gigantic boulders below.

At the end of the trail near Tanner Falls, there are a couple of nice spots to sit and watch the falls as they descend into one of the larger "bowls" in the Gorge.

♦ WAUNA POINT, TANNER BUTTE TRAIL 401, AND DUBLIN LAKE

Difficulty: Moderate to strenuous
Child safety: Moderate
Time: Wauna Point, 4 hours; Dublin Lake Loop, 8 hours
Distance: Wauna Point, 5.5 miles, round trip; Dublin Lake via
    Tanner Butte trail, Tanner cut-off 448, Road 777, 9.5 miles,
    round trip
Elevation gain: Wauna Point, 1,600 feet; Dublin Lake, 2,200 feet
USGS maps: Bonneville Dam and Tanner Butte
Viewpoints/attractions: View of dam and lake

Wauna Point and Tanner Butte are located in some of the wildest parts of the Columbia Gorge, which will be apparent as you bounce along the gravel road to the trailhead and wonder where the other cars are.

From I-84, take Bonneville Dam exit 40. Proceed south on Forest Service Road 777 for 2.5 miles. From the parking area, the Tanner Butte trail climbs steeply at times through stands of Douglas and noble fir. About 2 miles out, Trail 402 leads left for a 0.4-mile hike to Wauna Point where,

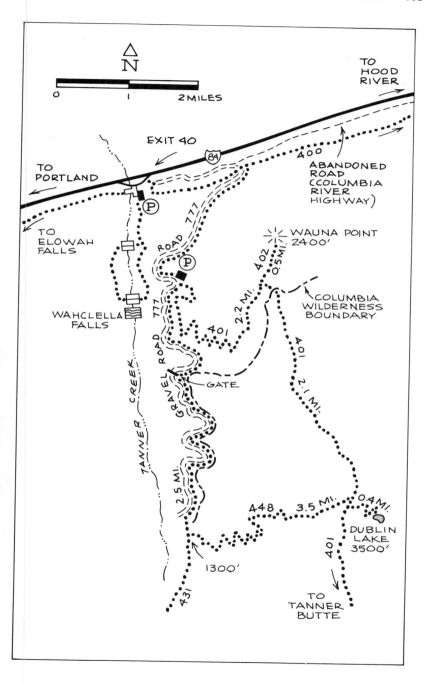

Wahclella Falls on Tanner Creek

during most weekends, you'll have the view to yourself. The official trail leads to a point covered by trees. For the real view below the point, turn left a few hundred feet before the point and bear downhill on an unofficial trail.

To change this moderate hike to a strenuous one, continue south on Trail 401 for another 2 miles and drop down to Dublin Lake for a swim.

Tanner Butte is about 4.5 miles farther south. Backtrack to Tanner Butte cut-off Trail 448 and descend for about 3.5 miles. When you reach Forest Service Road 777, follow it north for 2.5 miles downhill to your car.

◆ EAGLE CREEK TRAIL 440

Difficulty: Easy
Child safety: Dangerous
Time: 5 hours
Distance: 7 miles, round trip
Elevation gain: 600 feet
USGS maps: Bonneville Dam and Tanner Butte
Viewpoints/attractions: Scenic canyons, waterfalls

Eagle Creek Trail is one of the most popular trails in the Gorge because it is relatively flat over most of its route and it passes through one of the most scenic canyons in the Northwest. Punch Bowl Falls, Loowit Falls, Tunnel Falls—all contribute to a very exciting hiking experience. They also contribute to making Eagle Creek perhaps the single most popular trail in the Gorge. If possible, save this hike for a midweek trip to avoid the throngs.

In places, the trail is very exposed. This is not a hike for children.

From I-84, take Eagle Creek exit 41. Proceed 0.75 mile south on Eagle Creek Road, to the road-end parking lot. A good destination is the metal bridge that crosses the canyon, some 150 feet above the creek, about 3.5 miles from the parking lot. There are a number of established campsites near the trail once you cross the bridge and head south. Have lunch either at the bridge or go another 5 or 10 minutes to the primitive campground and sit next to the creek.

◆ BUCK POINT TRAIL 439

Difficulty: Easy
Child safety: Good
Time: 1 hour
Distance: 1.5 miles, round trip
Elevation gain: 500 feet
USGS map: Bonneville Dam
Viewpoints/attractions: Indian pits, view of Bonneville Dam and Eagle Creek

The Buck Point Trail was previously known as the Ruckel Ridge Trail, and the Forest Service used to maintain the trail 3 miles farther, to the Benson Plateau. Today, however, the trail is not maintained past a power line less than a mile from the road. Beyond that point, much of the trail across a large rockslide has been destroyed by recent slides. As a result, the edge of the rockslide is the safe place to turn around. All is not lost, however, since the views from the power line and the rockslide are worth the short trip, and the edge of the rockslide is marked by several pits

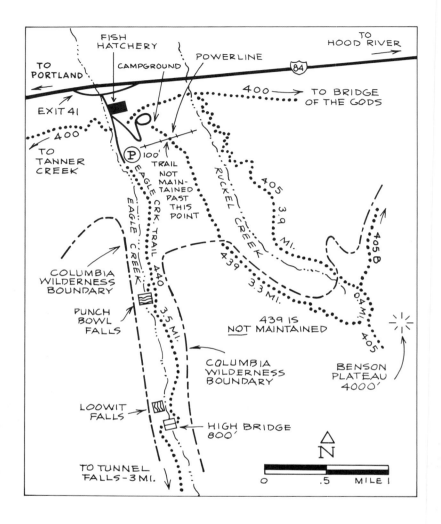

thought to have been excavated by Indians.

From I-84, take Eagle Creek exit 41. Proceed to the Eagle Creek Fish Hatchery and the parking lot next to it. To reach the Buck Point Trail, walk up the road toward Eagle Creek Campground, and turn left on Gorge Trail 400. Follow this trail past a sign for Buck Point Trail 439, then turn right. The trail enters Eagle Creek Campground, then resumes on the south side of the campground next to campsite 6.

This short trail gradually steepens as it climbs 500 feet to a viewpoint under the power line. The trail then reenters the woods, and emerges a few hundred feet later at the rockslide.

Loowit Falls on Eagle Creek

◆ RUCKEL CREEK TRAIL 405

Difficulty: Strenuous
Child safety: Moderate
Time: 8 hours
Distance: 8.6 miles, round trip
Elevation gain: 3,600 feet
USGS maps: Bonneville Dam and Tanner Butte
Viewpoints/attractions: View of river and Benson Plateau

Gorge Trail 400 near Ruckel Creek

This trail stays on the east side of the Ruckel Creek canyon, passing many steep cliffs lined with wildflowers in the spring. The first half of the trail offers a few viewpoints, but the second half is in predominately deep forest before reaching Benson Plateau.

From I-84, take Eagle Creek exit 41. Proceed to the Eagle Creek Fish Hatchery and the parking lot next to it. To reach the Ruckel Creek Trail, walk up the road toward Eagle Creek Campground, and turn left on Gorge Trail 400. Follow this trail past a sign for Buck Point Trail 439 and farther on, just past Ruckel Creek itself, to Ruckel Creek Trail 405. Turn right on Trail 405, leaving Trail 400, which continues east to Bridge of the Gods. Four miles later, the trail reaches 4,000-foot Benson Plateau. Carry plenty of water on this trip.

◆ PACIFIC CREST TRAIL 2000

Difficulty: Easy
Child safety: Good
Time: 3 hours
Distance: 4.5 miles, round trip
Elevation gain: 600 feet
USGS maps: Bonneville Dam and Carson
Viewpoints/attractions: Famous trail, Dry Creek

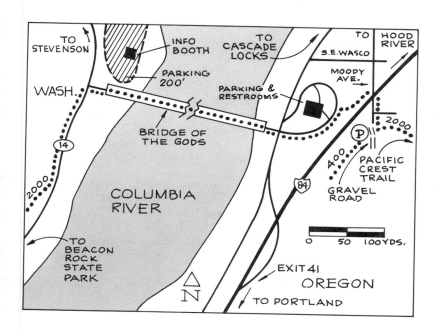

The Pacific Crest Trail (PCT) 2000 follows the Cascade Range south from the Canadian border in Washington, through Oregon, and then the length of the Sierras through California to the Mexican border, 2,080 miles to the south. The trail is always well maintained and built at a comfortable grade for horse and hiker use.

From I-84, take Cascade Locks exit 44. Proceed to the south end of the Bridge of the Gods. The trail starts across the road from the parking lot and rest rooms.

The stretch of trail immediately south of the Columbia River, passing through beautiful deciduous and evergreen forests, is good for beginners and children. It includes a nice lunch stop at the turnaround point, Dry Creek.

The trail then continues uphill to Benson Plateau and Wahtum Lake, intersecting many trails along the way.

◆ HERMAN CREEK AND NICK EATON RIDGE TRAIL COMPLEX

Difficulty: Easy to strenuous
Child safety: Good
Time: Herman Creek Camp, 3 hours; trails 406, 408, 437, 447, 7 hours
Distance: Herman Creek Camp, 3 miles, round trip; trails 406, 408, 437, 447, 7 miles, round trip
Elevation gain: Herman Creek Camp, 800 feet; intersection of trails 408 and 437, 2,600 feet
USGS map: Carson
Viewpoints/attractions: Herman Creek Camp, Indian Point, view of Columbia River

Two worthwhile trips take off from the old Forest Service Work Center or Herman Creek Campground (the campground is closed in winter): an easy hike to the Herman Creek camp area, which includes a picnic area; and a more vigorous hike uphill to an interesting geologic formation, Indian Point.

From I-84, exit at the weigh station, or from downtown Cascade Locks follow Forest Lane east. In either case, drive east past the fish hatchery to Herman Creek Work Center and Herman Creek Campground.

Follow Herman Creek Trail 406 uphill under a power line, along an old logging road, and eventually to the intersection of Gorton Creek Trail 408. Herman Creek Campground is located at this point, along with a spring flowing downhill toward the creek. This is a good place for lunch.

To make this trip into a vigorous outing, follow Trail 408 uphill 2.5 miles, through a grove of old-growth Douglas fir to Trail 408C, which leads to the unique Indian Point landmark and viewpoint. Return via trails 437 and 447, enjoying a spectacular view of the Gorge and Columbia River as you descend to Herman Creek Trail.

Trail 408 continues 6 miles south to Green Point Mountain and Rainy Lake. Trail 406 continues south to PCT, which goes on 11.5 miles to Wahtum Lake.

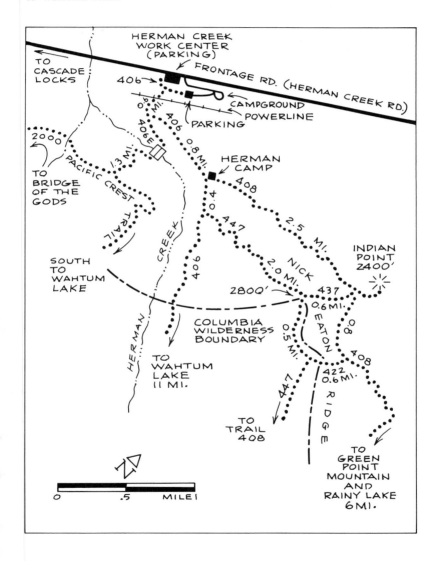

◆ WYETH TRAIL 411 AND NORTH LAKE

Difficulty: Moderate to strenuous
Child safety: Moderate
Time: 10 hours
Distance: 11.2 miles, round trip
Elevation gain: 3,800 feet
USGS map: Carson
Viewpoints/attractions: North Lake, views of Columbia River and
    Carson, Washington

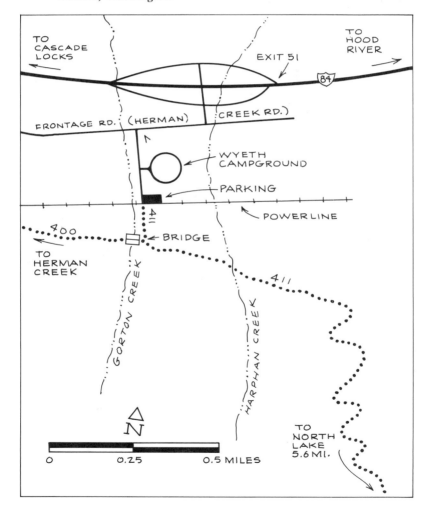

From I-84, take Wyeth exit 51. Turn south onto Herman Creek Road (Frontage Road), then turn west to Wyeth Campground, on the left after 0.25 mile. The trail starts at the south end of the campground.

From the campground, hike up Gorton Creek for a short distance, then make a sharp left at the intersection of Gorge Trail 400 and a bridge. The trail to the right (400) over the bridge travels west toward Herman Creek.

An 1872 wagon road on Shellrock Mountain

In a short time, cross Harphan Creek (no bridge), and begin a steep ascent; in about 2.5 miles you have a fine view looking north to the Columbia River. On the far side lie the town of Carson and the Wind River Valley.

To turn this trip into a strenuous exercise, follow the trail south to North Lake, 5.6 miles from the trailhead. The Forest Service describes this lake as "flanked by sun-washed cliffs and dense conifer-shaded forest." An easier way to North Lake, of course, would be to hike in from Forest Service Road 2820, only 0.8 mile, but then you wouldn't get the exercise.

◆ SHELLROCK MOUNTAIN

Difficulty: Easy
Child safety: Dangerous
Time: 2 hours
Distance: 2.5 miles, round trip
Elevation gain: 1,000 feet
USGS map: Mount Defiance
Viewpoints/attractions: 1872 wagon road, views of Wind Mountain

The loose rock slopes of Shellrock Mountain have always presented a major obstacle to attempts to build a road through the Gorge. This short

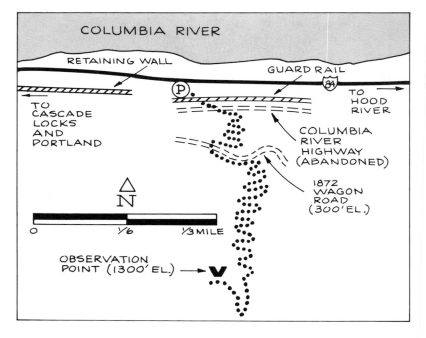

hike visits portions of the first two roads that overcame that obstacle.

The hike begins on the shoulder of I-84 eastbound. Watch for a lengthy steel retaining wall near milepost 52; at the east end of the retaining wall, pull well off the freeway and park at the west end of a guard rail. Step over the guard rail and walk east on the old roadbed of the Columbia River Hwy. Follow the old roadbed east a short distance. At a point where several piles of rock block the roadway, look for a trail on the right that switchbacks up through the rockslide, eventually reaching a stone roadbed a few hundred feet higher. This higher roadbed is one of the few remains of a wagon road constructed through the Gorge in 1872. Follow the old roadbed east, looking for the resumption of the trail up the mountain.

The trail ends at a small observation point built to observe landslides on Wind Mountain, on the Washington side of the Gorge.

◆ MOUNT DEFIANCE AND STARVATION RIDGE TRAILS 413 AND 414

Difficulty: Easy to strenuous
Child safety: Good
Time: Short loop, 2 hours; Mount Defiance, 10 hours
Distance: Short loop, 2 miles, round trip; Mount Defiance, 12 miles, round trip
Elevation gain: Short loop, 700 feet; Mount Defiance, 4,800 feet
USGS map: Mount Defiance
Viewpoints/attractions: Views of the Columbia River and Dog Mountain

For a nice, short trip with a variety of terrain and views, make a brief loop on Trails 413 and 414. You'll make three pleasant creek crossings, gain some elevation, and make a quick descent back to the parking lot. In the first mile, you'll see Cabin Creek Falls, Hole in the Wall Falls, and Lancaster Falls. During spring runoff, some of the creek crossings may be somewhat difficult; use caution.

From I-84, take Starvation Creek State Park exit 55. Proceed to the west end of the parking lot. For the short loop, follow Trail 413 for about 1 mile, then turn left on Trail 414 and follow it south, then east back to your car. A good spot to eat lunch, with a great view, is about 5 minutes downhill from the high point on Trail 414.

For a very strenuous loop trip, continue west, then south on Trail 413 to Mount Defiance (elevation 4,960 feet) to find sweeping panoramic views in all directions (along with a microwave tower). Then hike downhill toward Warren Lake via trail or gravel road, eventually connecting with Trail 417 and then with Starvation Ridge Trail 414. This heads north and returns to the parking lot, while passing through some fine views north and to Starvation Creek valley.

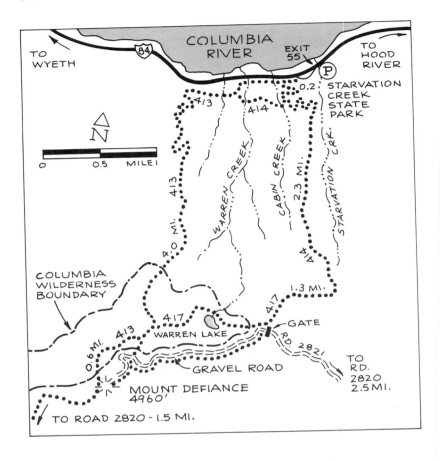

For an easier way to Mount Defiance, start at the southern terminus of Mount Defiance Trail 413 on Forest Service Road 2820, accessible via Hood River.

◆ STARVATION–VIENTO TRAIL

Difficulty: Easy
Child safety: Good
Time: Less than 1 hour
Distance: 2.2 miles, round trip
Elevation gain: Negligible
USGS map: Mount Defiance
Viewpoints/attractions: Columbia River Highway

An original 1915 milepost on the Columbia River Highway near Viento State Park

This short trail follows an abandoned section of the roadbed of the Columbia River Highway from Starvation Creek State Park to Viento State Park. Along the way, watch for an original cement milepost, one of only three still standing, not to be confused with a wooden post nearby. This milepost marker was installed in 1915; the cement mileposts now lining the Columbia River Highway are replicas, installed in 1991.

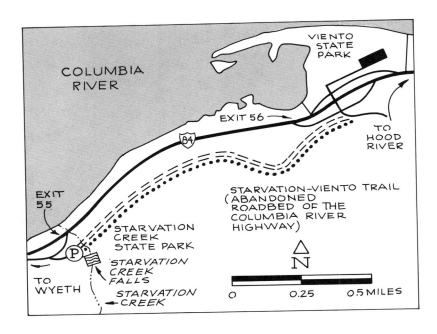

For the west trailhead, from I-84 take Starvation Creek State Park exit 55, and walk east through the park. For the east trailhead, from I-84 take Viento State Park exit 56, and find the trailhead immediately south of the exit. Regardless of which trailhead you start from, simply follow the old roadbed.

◆ WYGANT TRAIL AND WYGANT STATE PARK

Difficulty: **Easy to moderate**
Child safety: **Moderate**
Time: **3 to 6 hours**
Distance: **4 to 8 miles, round trip**
Elevation gain: **1,200 to 2,200 feet**
USGS maps: **Hood River and Mount Defiance**
Viewpoints/attractions: **Columbia River Highway, views of Dog Mountain and Columbia River**

This hike leads to a wooded former site of a Forest Service fire lookout tower. Because this area is so far east in the Gorge, one can expect a little drier weather and a change in vegetation, including gnarled oak trees.

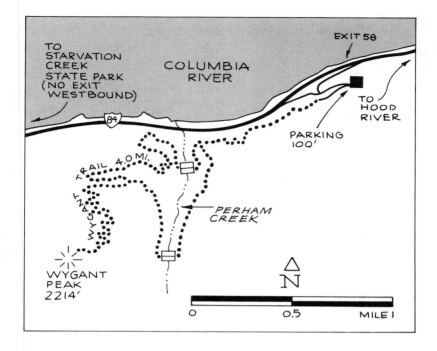

From I-84, take exit 58 and park at the east end of the wayside, then walk up a road to the west to find the trail. Begin heading west on the trail and shortly you will be on the abandoned roadbed of the Columbia River Highway. After 0.25 mile, watch for an unsigned trail on the left.

There are a couple of views along the trail before and after crossing Perham Creek. Continuing to the end of the trail will turn this trip into a moderate one. Have a snack at one of the viewpoints beyond the creek. If you're looking for some variation on the return trip, the volunteer-built Chetwoot Trail can be used to return on the east side of Perham Creek.

◆ ROWENA PLATEAU (TOM MCCALL PRESERVE)

Difficulty: Easy
Child safety: Moderate
Time: 2 hours
Distance: 1.5 miles, round trip
Elevation gain: 200 feet
USGS map: Lyle
Viewpoints/attractions: Panoramic view, unique wildflowers and
    other plants

Tom McCall Preserve, Rowena Plateau (photo by Joe Walicki)

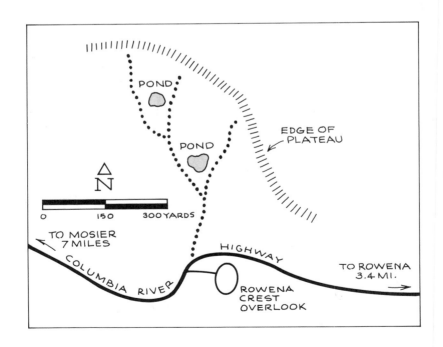

POND

POND

EDGE OF
PLATEAU

△
N

0   150   300 YARDS

TO MOSIER
7 MILES

COLUMBIA RIVER

HIGHWAY

TO ROWENA
3.4 MI.

ROWENA
CREST
OVERLOOK

This Nature Conservancy preserve is located near the Rowena Loops. In the spring the plateau is alive with multicolored flowers. Be extremely careful at the edges of the cliffs—they are rounded and the soil could easily give way. Carry a wind parka with you as the high plateaus are windy most of the year.

From I-84, take Rowena exit 76. Turn south onto the Columbia River Hwy, and drive 3.4 miles west, following signs for "Rowena Crest Viewpoint." Watch for a turnout on the right, next to a set of wooden steps over a barbed wire fence. The trail is marked by a sign just inside the wire fence that reads "Governor Tom McCall Preserve at Rowena Plateau." From this point the trail heads gently downhill, past two small ponds, and eventually to the edge of the cliffs overlooking the Columbia River.

WASHINGTON SIDE

◆ BEACON ROCK STATE PARK AND HAMILTON MOUNTAIN

Difficulty: Easy to moderate
Child safety: Moderate
Time: 5 hours
Distance: 7 miles, round trip
Elevation gain: 2,100 feet
USGS map: Beacon Rock
Viewpoints/attractions: Rodney and Hardy Falls, view of Bonneville Dam and Mount Adams

The trails in Beacon Rock State Park include a short, easy nature walk, a steep but short hike up Beacon Rock, and a muscle-stretching trip to the top of Hamilton Mountain. The nature trail is just west of Beacon Rock, on the south side of the highway, and leads to tiny Ridell Lake. The trail up Beacon Rock itself is marvelously engineered and takes only about 45 minutes; although most of the trail has railings, exercise caution with children.

On Hwy 14, drive 7 miles west of the Bridge of the Gods to Beacon Rock State Park. The trail to the top of Hamilton Mountain starts at the parking lot for the picnic area, located 0.5 mile north from Hwy 14. Follow the trail uphill from the picnic area, cross under a pair of power lines, and take a break at Hardy and Rodney falls, one of the more beautiful areas in the Gorge. After your break, continue steeply uphill to a fork, bearing right, and continue uphill to your first major viewpoint overlooking the Columbia River. If the weather is deteriorating, go no farther, as the winds only increase the higher you go.

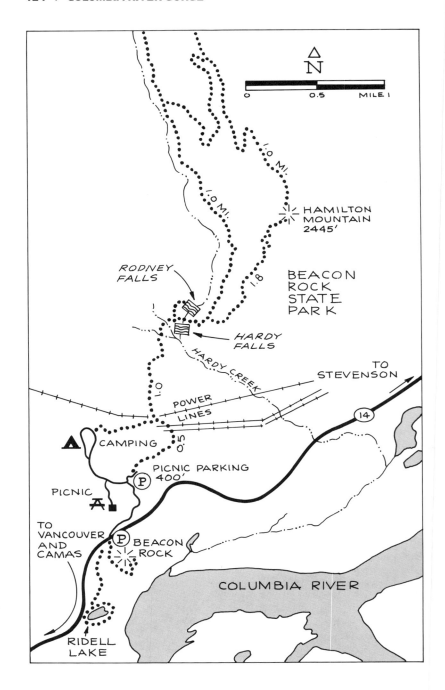

△
N

0   0.5   MILE 1

HAMILTON
MOUNTAIN
2445'

1.0 MI.

1.0 MI.

RODNEY
FALLS

BEACON
ROCK
STATE
PARK

1.8

HARDY
FALLS

HARDY CREEK

TO
STEVENSON

1.0

POWER
LINES

14

CAMPING

0.5

PICNIC PARKING
400'

P

PICNIC

TO
VANCOUVER
AND
CAMAS

P   BEACON
ROCK

COLUMBIA RIVER

RIDELL
LAKE

Beacon Rock Trail

After another rest, continue uphill on a mostly exposed trail and eventually to the top of Hamilton Mountain with views of Bonneville Dam and Mount Hood peeking over the Gorge mountains.

Return the way you came or, if you have a compass and a topographic map, try the longer route by continuing north from the summit, then dropping back down to Hardy Creek and rejoining the route near Hardy Falls.

◆ FORT CASCADES TRAIL

Difficulty: Easy
Child safety: Good
Time: 1 hour
Distance: 1.5 miles, round trip
Elevation gain: Negligible
USGS map: Bonneville Dam
Viewpoints/attractions: Views of the Columbia below Bonneville
    Dam; site of historic Fort Cascades

The U.S. Army built Fort Cascades at this site in 1850. After the Army vacated the fort at the beginning of the Civil War, the buildings became the community of Cascades, which survived until the flood of 1893 destroyed the entire town. The site of the town is now listed on the National Register of Historic Places, and the Army Corps of Engineers has built a 1.5-mile interpretive trail. Numbered markers are described in a brochure available at the site.

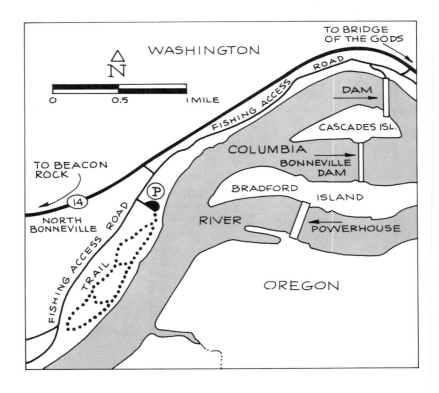

From Hwy 14, turn south at milepost 38.5, between North Bonneville and the Second (North) Powerhouse of Bonneville Dam. Proceed to Fort Cascades Historic Site parking area, off of Fishing Access Road.

◆ TABLE MOUNTAIN

Difficulty: Moderate
Child safety: Dangerous
Time: Up to 7 hours
Distance: Up to 14 miles, round trip
Elevation gain: 3,300 feet (summit of Table Mountain)
USGS map: Bonneville Dam
Viewpoints/attractions: Views of Columbia Gorge

The trail to the summit of Table Mountain starts out on Tamanous Trail 27, then joins the Pacific Crest Trail 2000, and finally strikes off on

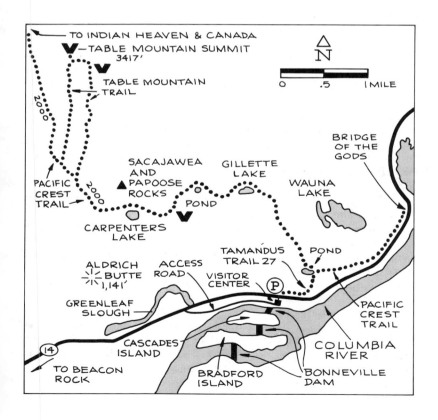

its own. The summit area of Table Mountain is not safe for children.

On the north side of Hwy 14 at milepost 39.8, find the trailhead at the east end of the parking lot across from the visitor center at the North Powerhouse of Bonneville Dam. Follow Trail 27 to the Pacific Crest Trail, which passes through an area of small lakes and, in 3.5 miles from the highway, reaches a viewpoint where Bonneville Dam and the Greenleaf Slough area can be seen. The trail then passes south of Sacajawea and Papoose rocks, known to local climbers as Rabbit Ears. After turning north, the Pacific Crest Trail 2000 turns west and north, while the Table Mountain Trail continues north to the summit of Table Mountain, 7 miles from Fort Rains.

◆ PACIFIC CREST TRAIL 2000

Difficulty: Easy
Time: 4 hours
Distance: 6 miles, round trip
Elevation gain: 200 feet
USGS map: Bonneville Dam
Viewpoints/attractions: Famous trail, Gillette Lake

The Washington section of the Pacific Crest Trail begins near the Bridge of the Gods, in order to accommodate hikers who use the bridge to connect the Oregon and Washington sections of the trail. The trail works its way north, eventually to the Canadian border, 520 miles away.

On Hwy 14, find the trailhead 400 yards west of the north end of the Bridge of the Gods (see map for the Pacific Crest Trail on the Oregon side). Parking is available at the visitor information area just east of the bridge.

The first mile of the Pacific Crest Trail is almost level as it heads west through a young forest, paralleling Hwy 14, and in 1 mile passing alongside a few dwellings and the main road at a community known as Fort Rains. At mile 1.5, Tamanous Trail 27 joins from the west. Trail 2000 then turns north and climbs uphill, passing a few small ponds. In 3 miles the trail intersects a road and a pair of power lines before dropping down to Gillette Lake, a good stopping point. The trail passes Greenleaf Overlook, a pleasant viewpoint, 1.5 miles farther west.

The trail continues west, then north past Table Mountain (9 miles from the Bridge of the Gods; see Table Mountain Trail), Three Corner Rock (15 miles from the bridge; excellent views), and then to the Indian Heaven Wilderness Area, the William O. Douglas Wilderness Area, and Mount Rainier National Park. Numerous guidebooks provide mile-by-mile descriptions of the entire trail.

The Pacific Crest Trail 2000 near Bridge of the Gods (photo by Joe Walicki)

◆ DOG MOUNTAIN TRAIL 147

Difficulty: Moderate
Child safety: Moderate
Time: 6 hours
Distance: 7 miles, round trip
Elevation gain: 2,800 feet
USGS map: Bonneville Dam
Viewpoints/attractions: Flowers in May, views of Mount Adams, Mount St. Helens, and Mount Hood

This trail has seen considerable changes over the years. The western portion was once part of the Pacific Crest Trail until 1985 when the new route was opened just north of the Bridge of the Gods. In 1986, much of the Dog Mountain Trail was rebuilt east of its former location. Wildflowers are abundant in the spring, so bring your flower book and camera.

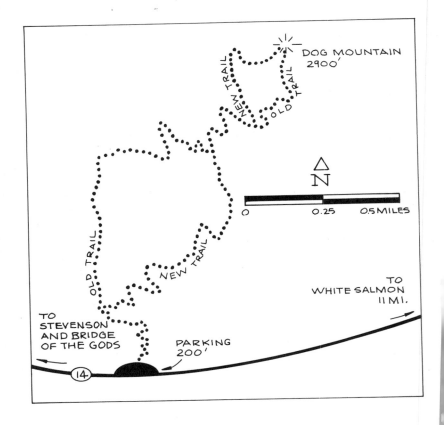

Carry plenty of water, as this can be a hot hike in the summer.

On the north side of Hwy 14, 12 miles east of the Bridge of the Gods, find a parking lot and the trailhead. To take the new route to the summit, take the right fork at mile 0.5.

◆ HORSETHIEF BUTTE

Difficulty: Easy
Child safety: Moderate
Time: 2 hours
Distance: 1 mile, round trip
Elevation gain: 100 feet
Viewpoints/attractions: Interesting rock formations and petro-
   glyphs, views of the Columbia

If you drive up the Gorge looking for a short hike, but are met only by rain, try driving as far as Horsethief Butte, a basalt mesa overlooking the eastern end of the Gorge, not far from The Dalles. Horsethief Butte may have once been popular with rustlers, who (one assumes) hid stolen horses within the mesa. Unfortunately, it was also popular with arrowhead hunters, who dug up much of the area in search of artifacts. Today, digging is

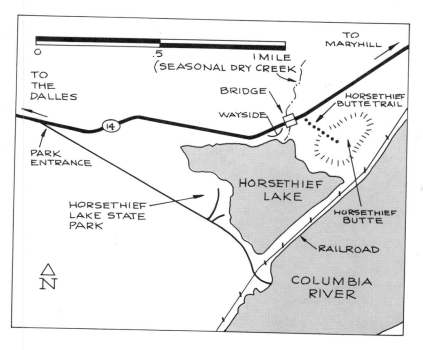

prohibited, and the most common visitors come to practice rock climbing on the short, steep walls.

The trail begins on Highway 14 at milepost 86.3, 1.2 miles east of the entrance to Horsethief Lake State Park. Limited parking can be found on the north side of the highway, or park at a wayside, across the bridge to the west.

The short trail seemingly leads to the blank north wall of the mesa, but closer examination reveals an entrance to interior corridors within the mesa. Once within the mesa, explore to your heart's content, but keep a close watch on children who might venture too close to the cliffs. Also watch out for rattlesnakes.

FURTHER READING

Lowe, Don, and Roberta Lowe. *50 Hiking Trails: Portland & Northwest Oregon.* Touchstone Press, 1986.

————. *35 Hiking Trails: Columbia River Gorge.* 2d ed. Touchstone Press, 1988.

Plumb, Gregory A. *A Waterfall Lover's Guide to the Pacific Northwest.* 2d ed. The Mountaineers Books, 1989.

Dagger pod (Phoenicaulis cheiranthoides)

CLIMBING

By Jeff Thomas

From the front porch of the Skamania community store, the basalt walls on the south side of the Columbia River dominate the view. The setting sun of a long summer's evening often alters their dreary black color to a surrealistic red. A tired climber just off a difficult route on Beacon Rock can easily fantasize what the climbing potential of the Gorge would be if only it were granite, or quartzite, or sandstone. Beacon would be a minor bump in a vast playground twenty times the size of Yosemite or the Verdon. The climbing would never stop.

The fantasy quickly fades with the alpenglow. Columbia River basalt is one of the worst mediums on which to climb in North America. Rooster Rock, Pillars of Hercules, Crown Point, St. Peters Dome, Rabbit Ears, and other formations in the Gorge were attractive to early climbers only because of their proximity to Portland and their lure as isolated summits. With the possible exception of the regular route on Rooster Rock, these formations are wisely admired from afar by most modern climbers. Today, rock climbers regularly frequent only three formations in the gorge: Broughton Bluff at the western end of the Gorge, Beacon Rock in the central portion of the Gorge, and Horsethief Butte near The Dalles in the eastern end.

Ice climbers face a similar paradox. The Gorge could be a great place to climb. In the clutches of a hard freeze, it becomes a great place to climb. Never mind that the interstate is closed, a tractor-trailer rig is jack-knifing in front of your car, and the 40-knot wind gusting to 80 knots just tore your door off. Ice is the ultimate way to explore the otherwise inaccessible walls of rotten basalt. Although the Columbia Gorge is blessed with numerous waterfalls and seeps, the maritime climate of the lower Gorge rarely allows freezing weather long enough to form climbable ice. But unlike the frustrated rock climber, the patient ice climber can occasionally find happiness. Once every 3 to 5 years the waterfalls of the Columbia River Gorge freeze. Since the time when modern ice climbing tools and technique became available, freezes have occurred in January 1974, January and February 1979, December and January 1979–80, December 1983, November and December 1985, February 1989, and December 1990. Often the conditions that bless the Gorge with ice curse Portland with freezing rain. Chaos ensues, the difference being the average citizen is highly

Placing protection on the Little Wing route, Beacon Rock (photo by Jeff Thomas)

inconvenienced while the ice climber is wild with joy, which is as it should be.

SAFETY CONSIDERATIONS

Listed below are brief descriptions of the most popular climbing spots, but first a word of caution. If you lack training *or* experience, stop reading now. This chapter is a road map to selected locations, not an instruction manual. Rock and ice climbing involves certain inherent dangers. Competent training cannot be gained from the pages of any book, much less a guidebook. If you want to learn how to climb contact the Mazamas of Portland, The Mountaineers of Seattle, or a commercial guide. *Do not attempt any of these climbs unless you are a competent, experienced climber.*

Rock Climbing

For more information on the three areas described very briefly below, particularly the many routes established on Beacon Rock, see *Oregon Rock,* listed at the end of this chapter.

BROUGHTON BLUFF

Broughton Bluff offers several advantages. It is close to Portland and its southwest exposure moderates the effects of the ferocious east wind. It offers many short climbs that can be led or top-roped. The disadvantages of Broughton Bluff are dirt and vegetation (including poison oak).

From I-84, take exit 18 and follow signs to Lewis and Clark State Park. After parking, walk south along the road to a steep hillside. A well-worn path begins at the foot of the hillside and leads to the main cliffs. A fork in the trail offers a choice between the cliffs facing north and those facing the Sandy River on the west. The north face is very steep, while the west-facing cliffs are more extensive. The descent route is between the north and west faces via a third-class trail that joins the main trail near the fork.

HORSETHIEF BUTTE

Horsethief Butte is often used as a practice area for bouldering and top-roping. Best of all, it is in the rain shadow of the Cascade Range and is often dry when the lower Gorge is wet.

From I-84, take exit 87, cross the Columbia River on The Dalles Bridge, and continue 3 miles to Washington state Highway 14. Turn right and drive 2.9 miles. Just after crossing a small bridge, park on the left. (Additional parking is available just to the west, at a historical marker.)

On the right, a path leads south toward a rock mesa. Inside the mesa, and around the periphery, are many boulder and top-rope problems on excellent rock.

BEACON ROCK

Beacon Rock is an 848-foot-high andesite volcanic plug in Beacon Rock State Park on the north bank of the Columbia River just west of Bonneville Dam. Climbing is allowed on the south (river) face only, but that face offers more than sixty routes of all degrees of difficulty on high-quality rock.

Follow Washington state Hwy 14 to the north side of the rock at milepost 34.8. Park in the rest room parking lot on the south side of the highway, then from the east end of the parking lot follow a developed trail toward the river to the southeast corner of the rock. Five of the most popular routes are described below. A word of warning: poison oak proliferates at the base of the climbs. You have to decide if your itch to grab rock is greater than the itch produced by the obnoxious little bushes.

Cruisemaster (I–5.7). Protection to 2 1/2 inches with an emphasis on small to medium wired nuts. After descending from the parking area, and before reaching the railroad tracks, follow a trail west 20 feet to the base of the rock and a weird-shaped oak tree. Fifteen feet left of the oak tree is a thin crack that breaks a bulge 5 feet off the ground and a beautiful slab above. Follow the thin crack 60 feet to an overhang. Move left 5 feet and climb an overhang above into a dihedral. Follow the dihedral until it is possible to move right to a large ledge and a bolt belay. To descend, follow fourth-class ledges left 50 feet to two bolts. One 150-foot rope will reach the ground.

Southeast Face (III–5.7). Protection to 2 inches. After descending from the parking lot, follow a trail along the base of the rock west for 100 feet. The climb starts in a small clearing with three large boulders just after the trail starts to climb slightly. *Pitch 1:* Climb either of two small low-angle corners up and right 15 to 20 feet. Proceed straight up broken but solid rock about 80 feet. Belay on a large ledge with a dead snag ("Snag Ledge"). *Pitch 2:* Follow a broken ledge system 100 feet right to a bolt belay. *Pitch 3:* Climb a shattered groove up and left 20 feet. Move right about 15 feet to a small stance on a slab. Alternatively climb straight up from the bolts to the belay. *Pitch 4:* Follow right-facing dihedrals (or the slabs just right of the dihedrals), which eventually force the route onto the east face. Climb up to a large ledge with a tree ("Tree Ledge"). At this point many parties rappel using two ropes. *Pitch 5:* Follow dihedrals up and left 150 feet to a large broken area with grass and brush. *Pitch 6:* Walk up indistinct trails through a brushy section to a 20-foot chimney. Climb the

Climbing on the Little Wing route, Beacon Rock (photo by Jeff Thomas)

chimney and follow a ramp up and right to an easy ridge. The ridge leads to the westside hiking trail, which can be followed down to the northside parking area.

Right Gull (III—5.10A or 5.8). Protection to 2 1/2 inches. The majority of the climbing on this route follows cracks in dihedrals. The crux is a tricky boulder problem off the second belay. It can be bypassed on the right by an easier variation. *Pitch 1:* Follow the first pitch of the Southeast Corner. *Pitch 2:* From the left side of Snag Ledge, step down and left 10 feet. Climb a right-facing dihedral 80 feet to the top of a pinnacle. Step up and left to a second, higher pinnacle and belay. *Pitch 3:* Climb a short, thin crack above, or step down to the sharp pinnacle on the right and climb straight up past a pin. Both variations end on a ledge. Gain another ledge 25 feet above via one of two jam cracks that start on the left. *Pitch 4:* Move left again and climb another jam crack to a ledge. Step right and climb a right-facing dihedral to vegetated ledges. *Pitch 5:* Walk up indistinct trails through a brushy section to a 20-foot chimney. Climb the chimney and follow a ramp up and right to an easy ridge. The ridge leads to the westside hiking trail, which can be followed down to the northside parking area.

Little Wing (I–5.8). Protection to 2 1/2 inches. Little Wing has more than one pitch, but the first pitch has become quite popular and is done either for its own sake or as an alternative start to Right Gull. The route starts near the Southeast Corner route. *Pitch 1:* Walk slightly uphill from the low-angle start for the Southeast Corner. Climb a left-facing corner 30 feet. Before intersecting the regular Southeast Face route on the right, move up a shallow crack that widens as you climb higher. Continue up the Right Gull or the Southeast Face, or rappel.

Dod's Jam (III–5.10c). Protection to 2 1/2 inches. This is a classic climb that never grows old. From the Southeast Corner, follow the trail along the base of the south face past two 2-foot-high, man-made tunnels. Rope up at the third tunnel. *Pitch 1:* Face-climb up and left to a crack system; follow it up and left 120 feet to a tiny belay stance. *Pitch 2:* Jam, stem, or layback the overhanging off-width above to the top of a pillar. Follow the crack above to Big Ledge. *Pitch 3:* Walk right, around the prominent buttress above Big Ledge. Climb a hand/fist crack to an alcove. Continue over an overhang and face-climb up and right to a belay stance. *Pitch 4:* Climb either of two overhangs on the right and left sides of the amphitheater above. Belay below a thin crack higher up. *Pitch 5:* Climb either the thin crack directly above the belay or the off-width on the left. Descend the westside hiking trail to the northside parking area.

Ice Climbing

The potential for ice climbing in the Columbia River Gorge has barely been tapped. The best plan of action is to spend several days in the following four areas. If you find yourself and the ice in good form, go exploring and run wild.

Many small falls and smears are located between Troutdale and Crown Point but the *real* climbing starts at Crown Point with Crown Jewel, a two-pitch smear reaching a maximum angle of eighty degrees. From I-84 eastbound, park next to a gate immediately across from Rooster Rock. Hike over to the railroad tracks and then walk a few minutes east to Crown Point. Crown Jewel is the only easy multipitch climb in the Gorge. However, if there is any wind at all (is the pope Catholic?), you will suffer. To descend, hike up to the top of Crown Point and bash down an ugly gully on the west side.

Shepperds Dell is a good place if you want some (very little) shelter from the wind and are looking for one-pitch climbs that can be led or top-roped. From I-84, take Bridal Veil exit 28. After leaving the freeway, turn

Ice climbing near Bridal Veil

right at the intersection with the Columbia River Hwy and drive 2 miles past Bridal Veil Falls State Park and Shepperds Dell. A series of six water-falls formed by seeps on a mossy green wall are visible just above the high-way. Park just after the first fall in an open area on the right. To descend from the top of the falls, either rappel (two ropes are needed for most of the climbs) or walk west to the end of the cliff.

Several longer climbs have been completed or attempted along the Columbia River Highway between Bridal Veil and Multnomah Falls, in-cluding a long gully just to the right of the Multnomah Falls amphitheater. From I-84, take Bridal Veil exit 28. Turn left onto the Columbia River Hwy. Choose a likely line.

On the Washington side of the Gorge, just east of the Cape Horn viewpoint and above Washington state Hwy 14 in the vicinity of milepost 25, are a series of small falls, some of which are visible from the road, and some of which require a short hike to see and climb.

FURTHER READING

Thomas, Jeff. *Oregon Rock*. The Mountaineers Books, 1983.

WINDSURFING

By Bowen Blair, Jr.

The unique climatic and geologic conditions of the Columbia Gorge have made windsurfing one of the most popular recreational activities—for both spectator and participant—in the National Scenic Area. Climatic oddities that make 30-mile-an-hour winds commonplace during the late spring and summer have catapulted the Gorge to a preeminent position among world windsurfing sites. Dozens of specialty stores that cater to windsurfers have opened throughout the Gorge, and world-class tournaments are now annual events in Hood River, Cascade Locks, The Dalles, and other Gorge cities. On a typical summer weekend, hundreds of sailors can be found at popular windsurfing sites such as Swell City, Doug's Beach, and the Hood River Sailpark/Marina, and as many as a thousand others will be zipping across the waves at another dozen sites.

In late spring and summer, prevailing winds are from the west, beginning as gentle zephyrs in the Gorge's western portal and building into a roaring crescendo in the east. The prevailing westerly winds are propelled by differences in the pressure gradients found on either side of the Cascade Range: low pressure and warm, rising air in the Columbia Plateau east of the Cascade Range, and high pressure and cool, heavy air west of the Cascades, caused by the cold Pacific Ocean. High-pressure areas flow into areas of low pressure, and the Columbia Gorge is the only sea-level passage through the Cascade Range. Consequently, the high pressure west of the mountains drives air through the Gorge, growing in intensity as it is squeezed between the Gorge rims—much like water is squeezed through a funnel—until it spills out into the Columbia Plateau in eastern Oregon.

About the only time the wind doesn't blow during the spring and summer months is when a low-pressure system covers both sides of the Cascade Range. Thankfully, this period is rare and usually of short duration.

From the windsurfer's perspective, an additional benefit derives from the east-to-west flow of the Columbia River, against the prevailing winds. Sailors, therefore, may sail all day on one reach of the river without the additional effort required if the current and wind flowed in the same direction. These countervailing forces also create large swells and chop—particularly on the long, straight sections of the river—that add to the excitement and challenge of sailing the Gorge.

From fall to early spring, the climatic conditions reverse, and frigid air from the Columbia Plateau flows through the Gorge to meet air west of the Cascade Range that has been warmed by the Pacific Ocean's Japanese current. Winter winds are less consistent but stronger than their summer counterparts. Seventy-mile-an-hour winds in the Gorge's western portion are not uncommon during this season. The Gorge—for obvious reasons— is not a particularly popular windsurfing area during the winter.

Preparation

EQUIPMENT

In many sports, having the correct equipment is a luxury that merely improves the participant's prowess. While this is true for certain windsurfing equipment, much of it—because of the Gorge's strong winds and cool temperatures—is a virtual necessity. Some equipment, moreover, is required by law.

Windsurfing at Mosier

Wet Suits and Dry Suits. Anyone who sails the Gorge on a regular basis should invest in a good wet suit or dry suit. The average water temperature of the Columbia River in May and June is in the mid-fifties to low sixties (Fahrenheit). The summer months of July and August are slightly warmer—sixty-seven and seventy degrees, respectively—but even seventy-degree water can chill a person who is constantly climbing in and out of the water and exposed to 30-mile-an-hour winds. Hypothermia is always possible. Sailors in September through April may want to wear warm clothes under their dry suits in addition to boots, gloves, and a hood.

Flotation Devices. Personal flotation devices (PFDs) are more than a good idea for sailing the Gorge—they are required by law. Sailing in high winds and a 5-foot chop can cause injuries. Cramps—especially in the Columbia's cold water—are not uncommon. A PFD can make the difference between whether an injured or cramped sailor makes shore safely or not. On a less life-threatening level, PFDs provide extra buoyancy that will make a beginning high-winds sailor feel more secure during his or her waterstarts (waterstarts are the preferred method of sailing in the Gorge, where high winds and waves make uphauling—the process of hauling the mast, sail, and boom out of the water with a line attached to the boom— impractical if not impossible).

Footwear. Footwear with nonslip soles helps you negotiate riprapped shores, as well as protecting your feet from broken glass or sharp rocks that may be invisible under the surface. The thicker the sole, obviously, the greater the protection.

Other Equipment. Make sure your sailing equipment is in good shape. A broken boom, or even a split line, can transform a mild inconvenience into a major disaster in the middle of a barge lane. If you rent equipment, rent from an experienced shop, many of which exist in the Gorge, especially in Hood River and The Dalles. Have the correct-sized sail. Take enough time—especially if you are renting equipment—to ensure you have all of your equipment before you drive to your site. Count your battens! Five minutes of review at this point may save you an hour later.

A "mast leash" that connects the board and the mast also should be mandatory equipment in the Gorge, where the high winds and steep chop can easily separate the two.

The Oregon State Marine Board highly recommends that Gorge sailors carry flares. Many PFDs have pockets to accommodate flares and other safety equipment, including folding knives, a screwdriver, and perhaps a pair of pliers.

SAFETY PRECAUTIONS

Many of the conditions that make windsurfing in the Columbia Gorge an enjoyable experience also can make it a dangerous one—especially for those not accustomed to high-wind conditions. Most precautions are commonsensical. Knowing the local hazards, using proper equipment and keeping it maintained, and not exceeding your skill level are prudent measures that will allow you to enjoy the Gorge season after season. Some of the most frequently encountered hazards are described below.

Parking. Not all of the hazards with which to contend are found in the river. Traffic problems—especially along Washington state Highway 14, which parallels the Columbia River—can also be dangerous. Parking spaces along several excellent windsurfing sites in Washington often consist of only a highway shoulder, and competition for spaces can be intense among windsurfers and sightseers. The problem is exacerbated by frequent logging trucks that barrel down Highway 14 at speeds exceeding 65 miles an hour.

When approaching a windsurfing site, use your turn signals. If you find yourself passing your destination, do not slam on your brakes but continue onward until a safe turnaround is found.

Trains may also be hazardous, especially on the Washington side where windsurfers often must cross—either by car or by foot, loaded down with gear—the Burlington Northern tracks to reach the river. Twenty-four trains a day run these tracks at speeds approaching 70 miles an hour. Look carefully before crossing!

Once you have parked, be especially cautious unfastening your board from the roof carrier. Keep the windward rail of the board turned slightly downward during high winds, and never leave an unsecured board on the roof carrier. Unfortunately, it is not too uncommon to see uncared-for boards blowing end over end through a parking lot to the detriment of people, cars, and, needless to say, the board.

Barges. Perhaps the greatest danger to windsurfers in the Gorge—certainly the most frightening—is presented by the barges that regularly ply the Columbia. As large as 30 feet high and 650 feet long, barges have extremely limited maneuverability.

Running at speeds of 6 to 10 miles an hour, these huge vessels seem to materialize out of nowhere—especially to the windsurfer who is concentrating on sailing. Warning horns often are lost in the wind.

It is difficult for captains to see windsurfers since barges often have blind spots up to ten lengths long in front of their bows. If the captain actually sees a windsurfer in his path—and one captain described an area crowded with windsurfers as looking like "fleas on a hot skillet"—he may be unable to avoid the sailor. A fully loaded barge heading downriver can require several miles to stop, and even under full reverse power requires at least half a mile. Lateral maneuverability is restricted by wind conditions, as well as by the limits of the barge channel.

Several other, generally lesser-known problems are associated with barges and other commercial vessels. First, because of their enormous size, barges block the wind. This "wind shadow" can rob a windsurfer of his or her ability to sail out of harm's way. The wind shadow is most dangerous when the wind is blowing from directly behind the barge, creating a situation where a windsurfer may be helpless in the path of an advancing barge.

Second, a tugboat's powerful propeller causes suction that may be strong enough to pull a nearby windsurfer under the boat and into the propeller.

Third, the direction a barge is heading can be deceptive. An empty barge acts like an enormous sail that the captain may have to angle into the wind in order to stay on course. A barge that looks as though it were heading in a direction that would bypass a windsurfer may actually be bearing down upon him or her.

Lastly, windsurfers should watch for tugboats towing log rafts. The cable between the boat and raft is frequently hidden, as is true also of the submerged rafts. Do not sail closely behind tugboats, no matter how tempting their wake may be!

How does one avoid being run over by a barge? Most importantly, before you sail a new area make certain you know where the barge channel is located or, if there is no channel, where the barges customarily run. Ask other windsurfers. If you cannot avoid the channel, exercise extreme caution when crossing it.

There is no substitute, however, for vigilance. Check frequently for barges, up- and downriver. Remember that their warning horns may go unheard in the wind. Do not become so focused on your sailing that you are unaware of what is happening around you. If you suddenly notice fewer sailors than before, be especially alert, since this may signify the approach of a barge.

When a barge is sighted, do two things. First, sail to shore. Do not merely leave what you believe to be the barge channel or, if no channel exists, where you believe the barge is heading. Bearings may be misleading, and captains may prefer different sections of the river, particularly in the deeper waters above Bonneville Dam.

Second, warn other sailors of the barge's approach. The sudden exodus of sailors should alert stragglers of the impending danger.

Climatic Hazards. Before sailing a new area, ask other sailors about any unusual wind or current conditions at the site. Remember that the wind is usually stronger in the middle of the river than at shore.

Make sure you are dressed properly. The Columbia River is cold, particularly during the spring snowmelt season, and a 30-mile-an-hour wind can chill a windsurfer—especially a tired one—even in the relatively moderate temperatures found in July and August.

Floating and Other Hazards. Logs that have escaped from rafts and are partially submerged—called "deadheads"—are occasionally found in the river and are especially difficult to see. Indian fishing nets, visible by their floats—sometimes no more than empty plastic gallon bottles—are more common.

Watch for these hazards, and give fishing nets a particularly wide berth so as not to scare fish away or, at worst, rip the nets. If you do find yourself among the nets, lay on your board with your sail on top of the water until you float clear.

Much of the Columbia River's shores are covered with riprap, large boulders used to prevent bank erosion. Riprap is difficult to negotiate under the best of conditions and is close to impassible when covered with spray, especially when you are carrying a board and sail in high winds. However, most popular sites have fairly well-defined paths. Be careful when stepping off your board near shore—you usually cannot see on what you are landing. Use protective footwear and be particularly wary of broken glass. Windsurfing is considerably more difficult with a broken ankle or a sliced foot.

SAILING TIPS

The Columbia Gorge is not a safe place for novice windsurfers unless they are closely supervised by a certified instructor. Many stores, especially in Hood River and The Dalles, have numerous instructors available during the popular spring and summer months. Advance reservations are recommended but not always necessary.

Accomplished windsurfers who are new to high-wind sailing should choose their sites carefully. The Gorge offers several enclosed lakes (Horsethief Lake and Drano Lake, for example) and other semiprotected areas (including The Hook near Hood River and The Dalles Boat Basin) where beginning high-wind sailors can become acclimated. Do not venture into the main channel unless you are proficient at waterstarting.

All Gorge sailors should heed the following advice.

Buddy System. Do not sail alone. Sail with a friend and periodically check on each other. Make sure you both have keys to the car if something goes wrong. High-wind conditions in the Gorge are too dangerous to risk by yourself, even if you are an accomplished sailor, since equipment can always break.

Local Hazards. Do not sail in an area unless you know the local hazards. Ask other sailors about quirky wind conditions, river obstacles, currents, and customary barge lanes. If other sailors are uncertain—or even if they are not—spend a half-hour or so observing the conditions.

Remember, as soon as a barge appears, sail to shore and warn others.

Rights-of-Way. Knowing the sailing rights-of-way is mandatory, especially for crowded areas like the Hood River Marina, the Spring Creek Fish Hatchery, Swell City, and Doug's Beach. Sailboarders on starboard tack have the right-of-way over boards on the port tack. A downwind board has the right-of-way over an upwind board on the same tack. An overtaking sailboarder must keep clear of the board being overtaken. And (as if it were necessary) commercial vessels have the right-of-way over windsurfers.

Watch for other sailors, particularly when you are jibing and tacking.

Personal Limits. Know your limits. Do not sail if the wind or river conditions will overpower your ability or equipment. Remember that conditions generally are stronger in the middle of the river than on shore. Conditions change. Do not hesitate to wait out—whether for an hour or an afternoon—severe weather.

Wear warm clothing, and use properly maintained and attuned equipment.

Warm up your muscles—and your equipment—gradually. Start with short reaches that do not take you into deep water, fast current, or the barge channel. If you pull a muscle, cramp, or break important equipment, it is far better to do so near shore.

Rest periodically and replenish your fluids. Do not take that last, long reach across the river that will completely exhaust you. As in many sports, it is this final run that often leads to disaster. Drink plenty of fluids. It is surprising how dehydrated one can become despite the cooling breeze and water. If you are going to drink alcohol (and remember that alcohol is prohibited at many windsurfing sites), do so when you are finished sailing and after you have driven home.

Self-rescue. If you sail the Gorge often enough, eventually you will need to perform a self-rescue. Whether through equipment failure (ripped sail, broken boom, or separated universal), unanticipated weather conditions, or injury, it probably will happen.

Do not panic. Know beforehand how to accomplish the self-rescue.

Leave the barge channel. You may be able to make progress by uphauling your sail (if you have an uphaul) partially out of the water and luffing your way to shore. It may, however, be necessary to untie the outhaul line, wrap the sail around the mast and position it and the boom on top of the board, and paddle to safety. Aim for the nearest shore and paddle with the current. Your friend (the buddy system?) will be able to pick you up, since few parts of the Columbia River are inaccessible by car.

You may be forced to ditch your rigging. Stay with your board, however, which will help you float. Equipment is expendable, life is not.

If you need help, climb on your board and wave both arms over your head in a crossing motion. Someone should see you.

Windsurfing Locations

The following are brief descriptions of the most popular windsurfing sites in the Columbia Gorge. They are ranked according to relative difficulty: beginner, intermediate, and expert. These rankings, however, are only relative. A beginner ranking does not apply to a novice windsurfer but to a novice high-winds windsurfer, one who already has mastered the fundamentals of windsurfing. Weather conditions will also affect the rankings: a 40-mile-per-hour wind, for instance, may turn a beginner's site into an expert site.

As mentioned earlier, windsurfing is a recent addition to the Columbia Gorge. Some sites have undergone considerable improvements in the past few years, and more are scheduled for the immediate future. Oregon, for example, published a windsurfing study in December 1986 that details and prioritizes for the state legislature necessary improvements for numerous sites. Therefore, some of the following information, particularly regarding facilities, parking, and beach access, may become outdated.

Sites are presented in geographic order, from west to east, with sites on the Oregon side listed first, followed by sites on the Washington side. Descriptions include parking, rigging area, beach access, facilities, and special hazards. The discussion of special hazards, however, is not meant to be exhaustive and is subject to change without notice—often being a condition of wind and current peculiarities. Even the description of Gorge channels may change and to an extent is contingent upon each individual captain's discretion, particularly in the deeper waters above Bonneville Dam. There is no substitute for constant vigilance and regular updating of information by other sailors.

OREGON SIDE

Rooster Rock State Park (Intermediate). From I-84, take Rooster Rock State Park exit 25. Turn right once you enter the park, and park just to the west of the district parks office and rest rooms near the river.

Rooster Rock does not offer much windsurfing, except in the early spring, late summer, and fall when east winds return to the Gorge. During

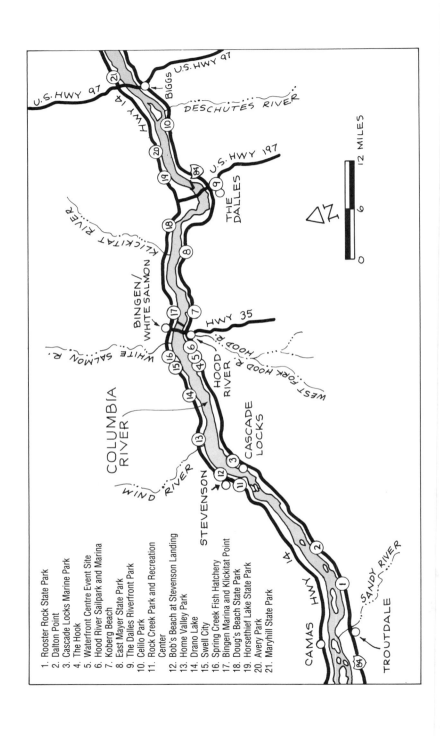

1. Rooster Rock State Park
2. Dalton Point
3. Cascade Locks Marine Park
4. The Hook
5. Waterfront Centre Event Site
6. Hood River Sailpark and Marina
7. Koberg Beach
8. East Mayer State Park
9. The Dalles Riverfront Park
10. Celilo Park
11. Rock Creek Park and Recreation
    Center
12. Bob's Beach at Stevenson Landing
13. Home Valley Park
14. Drano Lake
15. Swell City
16. Spring Creek Fish Hatchery
17. Bingen Marina and Klickitat Point
18. Doug's Beach State Park
19. Horsethief Lake State Park
20. Avery Park
21. Maryhill State Park

west winds, this park can be classified as "beginner." When the east winds are blowing, the park is an enjoyable place to sail, with nice sandy beaches and lots of grass for assembling equipment. Access to the river is not difficult, although a moderately steep drop-off must be negotiated.

Barges customarily use the middle to far side of the river. Watch out for two wooden jetties that protrude from the beach.

An entrance fee is charged during summer weekends and holidays.

Dalton Point (Intermediate). Dalton Point is located at milepost 29.5, 2 miles west of Multnomah Falls, and is accessible only on I-84 westbound. If eastbound on I-84, reverse directions at the Multnomah Falls parking area.

Dalton Point is a nice, one-acre park maintained by Oregon State Parks. Windsurfing can be excellent during east winds, usually early spring, late summer, and fall. During west winds, Dalton Point can be classified "beginner."

Parking is superb and paved. Plenty of grassy, shady areas are present for rigging equipment. The park has no facilities such as picnic areas or camping grounds.

Access to the river could not be easier—just use the boat ramp. Hardly any beach exists, and what does is mostly covered by weeds and large boulders and is somewhat difficult to reach by land.

The barge channel is on the far side of the river. Watch for rocks and boulders when dismounting your board. Park in designated parking areas, not on the boat ramp, and assemble and dry your gear on the grass. Accommodate boat owners by using the ramp only to enter and leave the water.

Cascade Locks Marine Park (Intermediate). From I-84, take Cascade Locks exit 44, and continue straight (east) from the exit, through downtown, 0.6 mile to a left turn marked "Information Center." Once inside the park, turn right and follow signs to "Marina" and "Windsurfing Area" at the far east end of the park.

The Cascade Locks Marine Park is a lovely, shaded, multiple-use park that includes ample parking and picnicking facilities. The bad news is that the windsurfing area is the worst-maintained section of the park and has the poorest access to the park facilities.

Currently, the parking area for windsurfers is adequate but unpaved and dusty. The park's grassy areas are too far away to easily use for rigging. The 200-foot-long beach is sandy with gravel. It is separated from the parking area by a steep, short embankment.

The park is well situated to take advantage of good west-wind conditions. The current is moderate.

Barges use the middle of the river. The current tends to increase in velocity 0.5 mile downstream and works against a disabled sailor who tries to return to the launching site. Also look out for the sternwheeler *Columbia Gorge*, which visits several times each day.

The Hook (Intermediate). From I-84, take Hood River City Center exit 63. Turn north, follow the road to the Waterfront Centre Event Site, and then turn west and follow the road through an industrial area to where the road turns to gravel. Continue west to the end of the gravel/dirt road.

The Hook is located across from the Spring Creek Fish Hatchery but near shore offers some protection from the large waves, strong winds, and fast current. The wind is also buffered by nearby Wells Island, which creates a complete wind shadow for 150 yards east of the island. Stay away from Wells Island to avoid the wind shadow and so as not to disturb a valuable great blue heron rookery and Canada goose nesting sites on the island. Plenty of relatively protected water is found from the Oregon shore to the north side of Wells Island and in the pond south of the berm that leads to The Hook. The full force of the river and the wind begin once you leave the Wells Island wind shadow and enter the middle of the river.

Ample but crowded parking exists at The Hook. Rigging has to be done on the dusty parking area. No facilities exist except a few portable toilets. Access to the water is down a steep embankment of riprap. At the west end of The Hook there are a few narrow paths down the embankment.

This area is very crowded in the spring and summer. River access is difficult, and subsurface rocks can easily snap an ankle of a sailor who carelessly dismounts from his or her board.

Barges use the middle of the river but shade toward the Washington side.

Waterfront Centre Event Site (Intermediate). From I-84, take Hood River City Center exit 63. Drive north from the exit to the site.

This site, which opened in 1990, should help relieve some of the crowding at nearby sites. As the name implies, it was particularly designed to accommodate large competitive events. For obvious reasons, look for other places to sail when events are scheduled here.

The site is located roughly halfway between The Hook and the Hood River Sailpark and Marina. It features a very large gravel parking lot and a narrow grass strip along the river. Launching is from three artificial ramps at the base of a rocky bank. In 1991, wooden bleachers were built to accommodate the crowds that come to view the competitions held here, and improvements to the ramps are in the works.

Most of the barge traffic in this area is closer to the Washington shore, although sometimes barges are moored on the Oregon side, just downstream from the event site.

Hood River Sailpark and Marina (Intermediate). From
I-84, take the White Salmon/Government Camp exit 64. Turn left under
the freeway overpass. Fifty yards later, turn left at the "Columbia Gorge
Sailpark/Marina" sign and follow signs to the "Sailpark/Beach," 0.5 mile
from the port entrance.

The Hood River Marina is one of the most popular windsurfing
sites—for both participants and spectators—in the Columbia Gorge. Fortunately, it is large enough and sufficiently developed to accommodate the
crowds that it attracts.

Enough parking exists, although the most convenient spaces, located
above the beach, fill up early in the day. The port has established a drop-
off and loading zone across from the large grassy area in the center of the
park, however, so no one has to walk far with his or her gear. The temporary loading zone, as well as a prohibition on alcohol and parking in restricted areas, is regularly monitored and enforced by port personnel.

The park has excellent day-use facilities, including food vendors and
rest rooms supplemented by portable toilets. A large, well-maintained,
grassy rigging area is close to the beach.

Sailing off the marina is excellent and accommodates a wide range of
expertise. The wind and current are generally weaker and the river is wider
than at Swell City, the Spring Creek Fish Hatchery, or The Hook, and
novices can stay within the protected confines of the marina itself. Flat
water exists immediately upriver from the beach. Some wave action, usually a chop, is created at the mouth of Hood River downstream and adjacent to the sizable beach. The river bottom and beach are sandy, with
some stones.

The riverfront of the marina is an excellent place to learn to water-
start because it tends to be shallow, especially in the west or downriver
portion. Be very cautious of beginning sailors when sailing through this
area, which is used for lessons by instructors from the local windsurfing
stores and schools.

The primary hazard associated with Hood River is caused by the large
number of windsurfers with a mixed variety of skills. Observe rights-of-way
and slow down when nearing the beach, especially on the downriver section. Watch out for the current from the Hood River, particularly in
spring and early summer, which can hamper a sailor's return to the beach.
Also watch out for shallow water over a large sandbar; ask locals about its
exact location.

Barges pass close to the Washington side.

Koberg Beach (Intermediate). Koberg Beach, 1 mile east of
Hood River, is located at a rest area accessible only to westbound traffic on
I-84. If eastbound on I-84, take Mosier exit 70, then double back 2 miles
to Koberg Beach, identified only by a "Rest Area" sign at milepost 66.
Park at the far west end of the rest area.

Windsurfing near Spring Creek Fish Hatchery

Parking at Koberg—which is mostly paved—is more than adequate. The relatively uncrowded water can make Koberg a pleasant place to sail. Plenty of sandy areas exist for assembling equipment, but there's not much grass. Rest rooms are the only available facilities. Access to the river is excellent, and a very nice sandy beach is located at the western portion of the rest area.

Because the river is narrower than at Hood River, the current is considerably stronger, as are the winds. Upriver visibility at Koberg is very limited because of a large rock outcropping—Stanley Rock—that extends into the river.

Barges use the middle of the river but are relatively close to shore because of the narrow channel. Barges entering the area from upriver may be hidden by Stanley Rock until the last moment.

East Mayer State Park (Expert). From I-84, take Rowena exit 76, drive north, cross the railroad tracks, and then turn east and drive 0.8 mile to the park.

This recently developed state park offers good parking and rigging spaces and modern facilities.

The beach is small but sandy, while the majority of the riverfront consists of flat rock outcroppings. Winds are often of high velocity, and waves are very large.

Barges use the middle of the river.

The Dalles Riverfront Park (Beginner). From I-84, take City Center/The Dalles exit 85, turn north, and then turn right a few yards past the westbound exit ramp and follow the road down into the large parking lot.

The Dalles Riverfront Park is an excellent site for beginning high-wind windsurfers, since it is located at the bottom curve of a hook in the Columbia River where winds are generally lighter than found upriver or downriver. An additional benefit is that the prevailing west winds blow sailors back in the direction of the sandy beach. The same bend in the river also slows the force of the current. Finally, to add further security to the novice sailor, a series of small islands serve as barriers to the barge channel where stronger currents and winds are found.

Lawns provide plenty of space to rig equipment, and a good-sized beach is present.

Note that this park is closed from November 1 to Memorial Day weekend to protect wildlife habitat.

Barges use the middle of the river, outside of the island barriers.

Celilo Park (Intermediate). From I-84, take exit 97, Celilo Park/Deschutes Park.

Celilo Park is an eight-acre, well-shaded, and grassy, pretty park maintained by the U.S. Army Corps of Engineers. The park has modern rest rooms and pleasant picnic areas. Good parking exists, and rigging can be done almost anywhere on grass in the park (watch for goose deposits). Access to the river is excellent, whether at the boat ramp at the far west side of the park or at numerous other riverfront locations. The beach is partly sand, but mostly rocky. Be courteous to local Indians who fish here; avoid areas near their nets.

Very good wind conditions exist at Celilo, but the current is strong. This is a nice location for intermediate-level sailors to practice waterstarts because the wind tends to blow them back to shore: start at the upriver end of the park and do not venture out to the barge lanes and faster current.

Barges are especially hazardous at this location because they pass very close to the Oregon shore. Upriver visibility is obscured by land, so barges coming downriver in the fast current are particularly dangerous and often unexpected.

WASHINGTON SIDE

Rock Creek Park and Recreation Center (Beginner).

From the west end of the city of Stevenson, turn north on the East Second Street extension. Continue 0.25 mile to the Rock Creek Park and Recreation Center and park at the west end of the parking lot near a "Picnic Area Parking" sign. Rock Creek Park has a relatively large lake that is protected from the Columbia River's currents and stronger winds. Only 4 to 5 feet deep (depending on the river level) with a sandy, muddy bottom, the warm lake is an excellent area to learn to sail high winds. The wind usually blows the beginning sailor back to the beach. Several islands can make the winds a bit tricky in sections of the lake.

More than sufficient paved parking places exist close to the launch area by the picnic shelter. The entire park is grass, which makes it ideal for rigging. Watch out for goose deposits, however.

The park has nice picnicking amenities, modern rest rooms, and great playground facilities for kids.

The only hazards at this park—other than the goose deposits—are much broken glass and a bottom that consists more of mud than sand in places. Wear protective footwear, such as tennis shoes.

Bob's Beach at Stevenson Landing (Intermediate). In the town of Stevenson on Hwy 14, proceed to the foot of Russell Avenue, the location of Stevenson Landing. The park is located just downstream from Stevenson's dock for the sternwheeler Columbia Gorge.

Ample parking exists. Several picnic tables and a grassy rigging area are present. Launching is from a rocky beach.

More commercial traffic exists at this site than at other sites upriver. The sternwheeler dock, which extends into the river approximately 50 yards and is located upriver and adjacent to the site, also can be an obstacle.

Barges tend to use the middle of the river.

Home Valley Park (Intermediate). From Hwy 14 at milepost 50.1, approximately 5 miles east of Stevenson and just east of the Wind River bridge, turn toward the river at the Home Valley Park sign. Once inside the park, the road forks. The left fork leads to an overnight camping area, and the right fork leads to the windsurfing site.

A large sandy beach is located at the west end of the park and a smaller sandy beach is in the park's center. Parking spaces are abundant, as are rigging areas. Access to the river is excellent. The river is somewhat narrower here than downriver, and waves are moderately sized. The current is slower than normal. Home Valley is an unusually good location during east winds, since it is located at the east end of a long, straight stretch of the river.

Barges generally are found on the Oregon side of the river.

Drano Lake (Beginner). From Hwy 14 at milepost 57.3, follow the signs to "Boat Launch/Historic Marker." Drano Lake is located at the mouth of the Little White Salmon River midway between Home Valley and White Salmon.

Drano Lake is a medium-size lake approximately 2 miles long and 0.25 mile wide. The lake is fully protected from the Columbia River, although river access is possible by sailing under the bridge at the west end of the lake.

Adequate parking exists around the boat ramp. Access to the lake is excellent. Rigging must be accomplished in the parking lot as no grass exists. No facilities other than seasonal portable toilets are found.

Winds are lighter at Drano Lake than at Home Valley. East-wind sailing is also particularly good at Drano Lake; west winds are partially buffered by a steep hillside. Drano Lake is considerably less crowded with other windsurfers than Home Valley.

This lake has several unique hazards. As at Dalton Point, conflicts with fishermen and other boaters can occur around the boat ramp. Anglers use the lake to fish as well as to gain access to the river. Windsurfers should be considerate of fishermen and other users and should not use the ramp to rig or to dry sails. Conflicts with anglers are most prevalent during the spring (May and June) salmon runs and summer (late July and August) steelhead runs.

Drano Lake is also speckled with short wood pilings occasionally used to tie up log rafts—especially in the western section of the lake—and "deadheads" (partially floating logs) also pose a hazard. The U.S. Fish and Wildlife Service apparently is in the process of removing the wood pilings.

Swell City (Expert). On Hwy 14 at milepost 61.1, Swell City is located midway between Drano Lake and the Hood River/White Salmon bridge. Parking can be found on the south side of the highway. A parking fee has been charged for the past few years.

Swell City is one of the most popular—and crowded—windsurfing locations in the Gorge. Parking is ample but jam-packed. Rigging is usually relegated to the parking area or to the rocky and graveled slopes immediately above the cobbly beach.

Winds are excellent at Swell City, usually 5 to 10 miles per hour stronger than at the Hood River Marina just 3 miles to the east. The beach at Swell City consists of a protected cove approximately 100 yards long. Outside of this protected area, the wind and current increase dramatically. Waves are very large at Swell City, caused in part by its location at the western terminus of a long, straight section of river where the full velocity of the wind meets the countervailing, strong current.

Access to the river from the parking area is excellent, and this short distance—combined with the river and wind conditions—makes Swell City one of the premier windsurfing viewing sites in the Gorge. Unfortunately, no facilities other than seasonal portable toilets exist at this location.

Exercise care when entering and leaving the parking area, which is usually crowded with people and gear. Traffic moves very quickly on this section of Highway 14.

The greatest river hazards at this location—besides the strong wind, current, and large waves—are caused by the number of windsurfers using the river. Observe rights-of-way and look before you jump or jibe. In the

Windsurfing at Mosier

protected cove, watch for rocks just below the surface. Stay away from Indian fishing nets that are often found just offshore and immediately downriver of Swell City.

Barges usually use the middle of the river, but shade toward the Washington shore to a degree.

Spring Creek Fish Hatchery (Expert).

On Hwy 14 at milepost 61.5 is Spring Creek Fish Hatchery's entrance, located 0.5 mile east of Swell City.

Parking is limited and may become more so. Strictly observe all "no parking" signs, and never block the access road to the hatchery. There are some small grassy areas for rigging, and the river is only a few yards from the parking spaces. No beach exists, however, and the riverbanks consist of large boulders or riprap. The embankment is short but steep, and launching can be extremely difficult into the full force of wind, waves, and current.

Sailing conditions approximate those found at Swell City: strong wind, large waves, and fast current. The parking area has no facilities.

Barges pass in the middle of the river, shading a bit to the Washington shore.

Bingen Marina and Klickitat Point (Intermediate).

On Hwy 14 at milepost 66.7, turn south on Maple Street in Bingen. Cross the railroad tracks and take the first left, onto Marina Loop Road. Follow this paved road 1 mile east until you come to the Bingen Marina. Turn right, pass the park and the marina itself on your left, and then drive south and east to the windsurfing area at Klickitat Point.

This recently developed park offers plenty of parking and lawns for rigging. River access is via several sandy paths down a steep embankment of riprap.

The wind is generally stronger here than at Hood River, and the current is faster. Windsurfers should exercise special caution to avoid log rafts and loose, partially submerged logs, or "deadheads," which are common.

Barges pass through the middle of this relatively narrow section of river.

Doug's Beach State Park (Expert).

On Hwy 14 at milepost 78.9, Doug's Beach is located a few miles east of Lyle. Parking can be found on the south shoulder of the highway.

Parking is ample but crowded and can be hazardous when turning into or out of spaces (which is true of all shoulder parking on Highway 14). The Burlington Northern tracks must be crossed on foot while carrying gear, so exercise caution. A 100-yard walk toward the river leads to the launching area. Although a few improvements have been made in recent years, this site was still relatively unimproved at the time of publication.

Doug's Beach offers some of the best expert sailing in the Gorge. Winds and waves are very large at this location, and consequently the site is extremely popular and usually crowded. A small, 100-foot sand beach exists and an even nicer one is located directly across the river in an inaccessible portion of Mayer State Park.

Barges can be particularly dangerous at this location because they pass close to the Washington side and can be partially obscured by a point of land.

Horsethief Lake State Park (Beginner).

From the intersection of US 197 and Hwy 14, turn east on Hwy 14, drive 1.7 miles, and then turn right into the park at milepost 85.2. Follow the park road toward the Columbia River, and park in the main parking area (to the east) or at the boat launch (straight ahead).

Because the lake is not connected to the Columbia River, barges and river currents are not problems. The wind often blows heavier here than at The Dalles, approximately 8 miles west. A wind shadow exists near the park (north) side and far west portion of the lake, and the wind tends to swirl at the easternmost section of the lake. Strongest winds are found near the railroad embankment.

Most beginners find themselves eventually blown across the lake to the riprapped embankment. Struggling up the riprap can be difficult (and exhausting), as is the long walk alongside the railroad tracks. Keep a very close eye out for trains if you find yourself in this situation because, while a train will be visible for a sufficient distance, it is very difficult to hear in a strong wind. Have your partner meet you with the car where the park road runs into the tracks.

Avery Park (Intermediate).

On Hwy 14 at milepost 89.5, approximately 4 miles east of Horsethief Lake State Park, follow the "Avery Boat Ramp" signs down a long gravel road and across a lighted railroad crossing.

This small park is operated by the U.S. Army Corps of Engineers. Twelve overnight camping spaces are present at Avery, but except for portable toilets and a few picnic tables, the park is undeveloped and extremely hot and dusty in the spring and summer. There is no drinkable water.

Access to the rocky beach is easy almost any place along the park, but is best at the boat launch at the western end. The Corps is contemplating improving river access for windsurfers immediately west of the railroad crossing. Parking is simple and not crowded, and plenty of sandy space is available for rigging. Sailing is very good at Avery: winds are strong and the current is moderate. Better-than-average-size and regularly proportioned waves are also present.

Be considerate of the needs of Indian and sport fishermen, who frequently use the boat launch and campground, and especially avoid the traditional Indian fishing platform west of the campground.

Barges can be quite dangerous at Avery because they usually pass close to the Washington shore, between the launching area and Brown's Island.

Maryhill State Park (Expert). On Hwy 14 at milepost 100,

Maryhill State Park is located just east of the Sam Hill Memorial Bridge. The park is very well-identified by road signs. Park at the large, modern rest-room facilities at the southern end of the parking lot.

Maryhill State Park is one of the Gorge's most popular parks, and the popularity is well-deserved due to its superb facilities. Abundant rigging spaces are found on the park's lawns, and river access is easy. Extensive windsurfing improvements to the current park facilities are planned west of the existing campgrounds.

The best place from which to launch is immediately downstream from the swimming area (where windsurfing is prohibited). A nice, gently sloping, pebbly beach eases launching. The river is exceptionally wide at Maryhill, but the current is strong. Very large waves are not uncommon, and the west winds can roar—often when little wind exists elsewhere.

Besides the expert weather conditions, the river's width and strong current can be hazardous at Maryhill. If you break down away from shore, you face a very long swim in a fast current and may quickly find yourself several miles downstream.

Barges use the middle of the river.

FURTHER READING

Gorge Publishing, Inc. *Northwest Sailboard's Gorge Guide.* Published annually.

LaRiviere, John R. *Boardsailing Oregon.* Menasha Ridge Press, 1989.

MBA. *3.5 Windsurfing Guide to the Gorge.* Published annually.

◆

CANOEING AND KAYAKING

By Philip N. Jones

The Columbia River offers a unique paddling experience for canoeists and kayakers. Large expanses of open water, strong winds, tidal influences, river currents, dramatic scenery, large hydroelectric projects, and commercial shipping traffic all add up to a type of paddling not found anywhere else.

This chapter is intended to acquaint the reader with open-water paddling on the Columbia River in the Gorge. The discussion focuses on the use of canoes and kayaks under the unique conditions found in the area. The closing section of the chapter lists all of the boat ramps and hand-launch sites in the Gorge.

Paddling on the Columbia is only for those accustomed to rough water. Paddlers whose experience is limited to calm waters should look elsewhere, in the interest of their own safety.

Although paddling in the Gorge has some inherent dangers, a careful, educated approach can minimize those dangers. The reader is encouraged to approach boating in the Gorge in a cautious manner, preferably accompanied by more experienced paddlers, until sufficient experience allows independent judgments about safe conditions and techniques.

Preparation

CONDITIONS

Although the Gorge is hemmed in by cliffs and steep hillsides on both the Oregon and Washington sides, the waters of the Columbia generally must be classified as open water, rather than the typical river paddling found, for example, on the Willamette River. While a newcomer to the area might conclude that the same canoes suitable for paddling on the Willamette are suitable for the Columbia Gorge, one trip on the Columbia will demonstrate that the Columbia is more similar to the waters of Puget Sound or the fjords of Vancouver Island. The primary culprit for that dis-

Kayak kiting near Cape Horn

tinction is the notorious wind of the Gorge. Even during the relatively mild summer months, strong west winds blow in the Gorge three days out of four.

Wind. The effect of wind on water is a function of fetch and wind speed. Fetch is the distance across a body of water over which the wind blows. Since winds invariably blow through the Gorge, rather than across it, long fetches are the norm, and rough water is the result. When strong river currents flow in opposition to the wind (which is typical in the summer months), the roughness of the water is magnified, since the effect of the opposing current flowing is the same as if the wind had increased in speed.

The strong winds of the Gorge, well known to windsurfers, can be used to aid paddlers. Since the wind blows upstream three days out of four in the summer, a tail wind is usually present when paddling upstream. The most assistance is obtained through the use of a small sail or, more commonly, a kite. During periods of strong winds, a kite-aided kayak can make steady progress against very strong currents, even against the swift currents present during spring freshets. (Although any kind of kite will do, sea kayakers favor collapsible drogue or parafoil kites of the Jalbert design, since that design combines a strong pull with ease of launching. A parafoil of 8 to 10 square feet is adequate for a single kayak, while 13 square feet is desirable for a double boat.)

Tides. Tidal influences also come into play, since the Columbia is tidal below Bonneville Dam. Although the effect of the tide decreases as one moves upriver, a strong ebb tide can add significantly to the already strong current of the river.

The action of the tide can be used to some advantage. On the lower Columbia, say near Cathlamet, the incoming tide (ebb tide) actually causes the river to flow upstream. Although such a complete reversal is less common in the Gorge, an ebb tide can slow the force of the river's current, allowing an easier upstream journey than when the tide and the river current are working together.

Currents. For paddlers lacking the luxury of a car shuttle, the complex currents of the Gorge can often be used to return to their starting point without fighting a strong current. The normal current of the river can be used to speed the journey downstream, and then the return journey can be accomplished with a little help from eddies. Eddies are created by the current and irregularities of the shoreline, which result in small sections of water that are actually moving upstream, against the regular flow. Obviously, they are found close to shore. Even if a true eddy cannot be found, slow-moving or still water can often be found close to shore, since the fastest portion of a river is located where the water is deepest, and thus the shallow areas are usually comparatively slow-moving.

EQUIPMENT

Because of the potentially rough conditions in the Gorge, paddling on the Columbia is often more akin to paddling on salt water than on fresh water. Although sea kayaks are most suitable for open, rough water on the Columbia, canoes are also used, particularly on protected sloughs or by paddlers experienced on open waters.

Canoes and kayaks have two primary differences. Obviously, the front and rear decks of a kayak are covered, while canoes are usually open. In rough water, covered decks are nearly essential to keep the boat, its occupant, and cargo dry. The second difference is that a kayaker sits on a seat that is only 1 or 2 inches above the bottom of the boat, while a canoeist sits about 1 foot above the bottom of the boat or, in rough water, kneels on the bottom of the boat. Either way, the kayaker has a lower center of gravity, and thus is more stable. That stability is of relatively little importance on smooth water, but becomes significant on rough water.

The disadvantage of the kayak seat is that it offers only one semi-comfortable position, while a canoeist can find relief on a long trip by alternating between sitting and kneeling.

The lower seating in a kayak is very important in the windy conditions found in the Gorge, since the body of a sitting or kneeling canoeist acts like a small sail. In addition, the canoe itself catches the wind more than a kayak, since canoes lack the drooped bow and stern of kayaks. As a result, a canoe makes very slow progress against a head wind compared to a kayak, and has much more difficulty in a crosswind.

Canoes are not without their virtues, however. Canoes have greater volume for carrying cargo, and accommodate bulky items that could never fit beneath the decks of a kayak. Canoes can also carry more than two passengers, a rare feat for a kayak, and the higher sitting position of a canoeist gives somewhat greater visibility.

Whether traveling by canoe or kayak, paddlers in the Gorge should outfit their boats with safety in mind.

Sea Kayaks. The sea kayak is usually the most appropriate boat to use. Sometimes called a touring kayak, the sea kayak is dissimilar from a whitewater kayak in nearly every way. Although both generally are made from fiberglass or occasionally plastic, sea kayaks are large and bulky compared with their smaller whitewater counterparts. Since the primary design criterion for a sea kayak is the ability to track (that is, to hold a straight course in strong winds and currents), sea kayaks are long and have a flat bottom. In contrast, a whitewater boat is designed to maneuver quickly, and thus is short and its hull is rockered (the bottom profile of the hull is curved upward like a rocking chair). Sea kayaks are also much larger in volume, in order to carry gear on multi-day trips, while whitewater boats can carry relatively little cargo.

In general, sea kayaks fall into two categories, **narrow** and **wide.** The British have always preferred very narrow boats, and several of those types of boats are available, often from British or Canadian manufacturers. Those boats are 20 to 23 inches wide at their widest point, and thus lack the stability provided by a beamier boat. Due to the tipsiness factor, the narrow boats demand a high level of skill to keep them upright. The advantage of a narrow boat, however, is its speed or "ease of paddling."

The beamier boats are generally 23 to 26 inches wide. The wide beam offers stability for novice paddlers, security while fishing or taking pictures, and much greater cargo capacity. The disadvantages of the wider boats are slow speed and difficulty to roll following a capsize.

Of the two types, the wide boats appear to be most popular in the Northwest, with 23- or 24-inch boats most commonly seen. Both narrow and wide boats are available in models that vary in length from 15 to 19 feet, with 16 and 17 feet most common.

Sea kayaks are also available in **two-person models** that are generally about 30 inches wide and 18 to 21 feet long. Most of these boats employ individual cockpits for each paddler, as opposed to a single large cockpit for both passengers. The double boats are generally faster than the single boats, and are usually quite stable.

The final category of sea kayaks consists of **folding boats** that use wooden or aluminum frames and hulls made of rubber and canvas or nylon. Despite their ability to fold into compact packages, folding boats are remarkably seaworthy. Although more expensive and less durable than their fiberglass counterparts, they have the advantage of easy storage and transport.

Sea kayaks can also be divided into those that employ **rudders** and those that require that all steering be done with **paddles.** Those that have rudders often utilize foot pedals and cables to control the rudder. In general, all double boats have rudders, while none of the narrow single boats do. Many of the beamier single boats have rudders, but the popularity of rudders on single boats seems to be fading.

Canoes. When choosing a canoe, look for features that will serve in rough open waters. Boats described as whitewater canoes are usually designed for river use. Although they deal well with rough water, they track poorly, since maneuverability is important on a whitewater river. Flat water boats, on the other hand, track well, but do not handle rough water well. The best canoe for use on the Columbia, however, combines the tracking ability of the flat water boat with the rough-water capabilities of the whitewater boat. As a result, it will be relatively long (17 or 18 feet) and have a pronounced keel, both of which improve tracking. For the same reason, it should also have little or no rocker. In order to avoid taking on water in rough conditions, it should be relatively deep (have a high "freeboard").

Flotation Devices. Of primary importance is flotation in the event of a capsize. With kayaks, flotation is provided by internal bulkheads, by waterproof flotation bags, or by both.

Internal bulkheads are fiberglass or foam walls permanently installed in the kayak to keep water out of the bow and stern. Waterproof hatches are provided on the upper decks so that the bow and stern can still be used for storage. Some paddlers are reluctant to rely on bulkheads for flotation and carry flotation bags even in boats equipped with bulkheads. **Flotation bags** are usually heavy plastic bags, often shaped to fit into the ends of the kayak, that are inflated (in advance) to prevent the boat from being filled with water in the event of a capsize. For overnight trips, flotation bags are available that can be filled with gear prior to inflation.

Since canoes are generally open boats, flotation bags are the only available form of flotation. Some paddlers use large inner tubes, while others purchase vinyl bags designed specifically to fill the hull of a canoe. In either event, the flotation device must be carefully secured. When looking

Kayaking near Beacon Rock

for flotation equipment, open-water paddlers will find themselves looking at whitewater equipment and learning from experienced whitewater kayakers and canoeists.

In any type of boat, personal flotation devices—**lifejackets**—are absolutely essential. On the open waters of the Columbia Gorge, they should be worn at all times, with no exceptions.

Clothing. Clothing should be selected with the unpredictable weather of the Gorge in mind. A wet suit should be worn during cold weather and strongly considered at all other times. During the summer, a wet suit is very uncomfortable, and thus conventional paddling clothing is usually used, but paddlers should never forget the serious consequences of a capsize in mid-river, regardless of the season. It is often said that a person without a wet suit has a 50 percent chance of surviving 50 minutes in fifty-degree water.

SAFETY CONSIDERATIONS

Hypothermia. The possibility of death from hypothermia should be kept in mind by every paddler in the Gorge. Proper clothing, careful paddling, and knowledge of proper treatment of hypothermia are all essential to open-water paddling. For the beginner, those skills should be acquired in a more forgiving environment before venturing out onto the Columbia.

Commercial Traffic. Paddling on the Columbia offers some unique dangers in the form of heavy commercial traffic, especially barges. The Columbia is a major shipping artery, and dozens of tugs and barges use the river every day, including weekends and holidays. Particularly when traveling downstream, tugs and barges can approach with a great deal of speed, yet they maneuver very slowly. In addition, barges often block the forward view of the crew of the tug. They are difficult to hear as they approach, and they stop very slowly. They have the right-of-way in the shipping channel, which is marked on NOAA charts numbered 18531, 18533, and 18355.

All of this means that tugs and barges command a great deal of respect. Never paddle in the shipping lanes (or anywhere else in the Gorge, for that matter) without keeping a constant watch in all directions for approaching boat traffic. The presence of windsurfers or anchored fishermen is not cause for complacency; both are very adept at scurrying out of the way at the last minute, leaving unsuspecting paddlers face-to-face with a speeding grain barge.

The danger is particularly acute where visibility is limited by islands or cliffs. In the narrow, twisting channel at the upstream end of Bradford Island near Bonneville Dam, for example, tugs and barges can appear with little warning.

In addition, tugs and barges also throw off huge wakes. Keep a respectable distance from them at all times. And never, ever paddle between a tug and the barge it is towing.

Parking. Be very careful when parking or carrying boats near highways and railroad tracks; both environments are very dangerous. Respect private property and "No Parking" signs; abuse of access privileges only makes matters worse.

Dams and Locks. The dams and locks of the Gorge present their own dangers. When paddling near locks—never a good idea in the first place—be aware that the locks may open very quickly to reveal a barge exiting with a great deal of speed. The sensation is thrilling, to say the least.

Contrary to the popular belief that only motorized craft longer than 14 feet may legally use the locks, boats of all sizes and shapes are permitted. Canoes, kayaks, and even swimmers have been locked through at both Bonneville Dam and The Dalles Dam. For at least two reasons, however, paddlers should think twice before using the locks. First, every time a boat is locked up or down at Bonneville or The Dalles, a huge quantity of water is used that might otherwise be available for power generation. Second, the locks can be very dangerous due to other craft, strong currents, and turbulence. Unlike the relatively tame locks on the Willamette at Oregon City, the locks at Bonneville Dam and The Dalles Dam are very high and extremely large, and thus very turbulent.

If, even after the above warnings, a trip through the locks is still under consideration, carefully review the locks regulations issued by the Army Corps of Engineers. The regulations for Bonneville Dam and The Dalles Dam are contained in 33 CFR 207.718. Those regulations can be found in Volume 7 of the *U.S. Coast Pilot* published by NOAA, available at libraries and nautical stores.

When approaching locks, stay close to shore, well away from any currents associated with any nearby spillways or powerhouses, and well away from any tugs and barges that might appear suddenly. Above all, never paddle into the lock entrance area (between the entrance wing walls) without express instructions from the lockmaster, to avoid the possibility of suddenly being squashed by an unseen barge about to enter or exit the locks. At each of the locks, the required procedure (if you lack a two-way radio capable of operating on channel 14, or a mobile telephone) is to locate the pull-cord signal station, or the intercom, marked by large signs at the extreme end of the entrance wing walls. Never proceed beyond that point without talking to the lockmaster and receiving express instructions to enter the entrance area. The instructions may come over the intercom, by bullhorn, or through light signals. However, make certain that the green light you see is intended for you, not a tug and barge about to overtake you. Never share the locks with large craft such as barges unless instructed to do so by the lockmaster. Generally, the lockmaster will not permit small craft to share the locks with barges unless the barges are secured to the wall of the locks to keep the barge from shifting its position. If the barge is carrying hazardous chemicals, no other craft will be permitted in the locks until the barge has locked through.

Commercial vessels have priority to use the locks. If commercial traffic is heavy, the locks may be closed to recreational boats, or a long wait may be required. Portages are usually difficult or impossible.

The locks at Bonneville Dam differ from the rest of the locks along the Columbia, including those at The Dalles Dam. Completed in 1938, the Bonneville locks are much smaller than the others on the river and usually require that large sets of barges be broken up prior to passage. The newer locks at The Dalles and other dams accommodate the sets of barges without alteration. In addition, the newer locks have modern diffusion systems that eliminate much of the turbulence associated with filling and

Navigational locks at Bonneville Dam

emptying the locks. At Bonneville, the trip through the locks is normally very turbulent and probably too dangerous for small craft. However, the lockmasters at Bonneville have the ability to slow the flow of water when small craft are in the locks.

As of this writing, new locks are being constructed at Bonneville immediately south of the present locks. The new locks will be similar to the newer locks at The Dalles and the other upstream dams, thus eliminating the need to break up large sets of barges. The old locks will remain in place and will continue to be functional.

Places to Paddle

The most popular section of the Columbia among flat-water paddlers is the western end of the Gorge, partly due to its easy access from Portland and partly due to the dramatic landscape and numerous waterfalls. For example, a popular one-day paddle is from Dalton Point, near Multnomah Falls at rivermile 133.5, to Rooster Rock State Park, at rivermile 128.5, or to the boat ramp near Corbett, at rivermile 126.5. In addition to providing views of Multnomah Falls and Crown Point, the trip gives paddlers a chance to cross over to the Washington side and visit the huge cliffs known as Cape Horn. Depending on the water level, those cliffs drop directly into the water, and usually offer kayakers an opportunity to paddle into small caves formed by overhangs. Exercise caution when paddling near Cape Horn, however, since the shipping lanes pass very close to the cliffs.

To help paddlers and windsurfers plan trips on the Columbia River, listed below are about four dozen boat ramps and hand-launch sites within the Gorge. The sites are listed from west to east, with the Oregon shore listed first, followed by the Washington shore.

The sites fall into four categories: public boat ramps, many of which are located in public picnic areas or campgrounds; public parks without boat ramps but with water access; private marinas, boat ramps, and windsurf sites open to the public for a fee; and other hand-launch sites, such as areas along highways where cars may be parked and boats launched with relative ease. The list is intended to include every public boat ramp in the Gorge and every park that provides hand launching, but other "unofficial" hand-launch sites are described where parks and boat ramps are lacking along particular stretches of the river or when hand launching appears relatively easy. Although numerous other hand-launching sites can be found throughout the Gorge along the highways that follow the river, their use is generally limited by the steepness of the terrain and the unavailability of parking.

Several of the sites listed below are used by windsurfers. If a site is noted as a popular windsurfing site, expect large crowds and limited parking, particularly on windy spring and summer weekends.

Nearly all of the listed sites are on the Columbia itself, but a few are on tributaries or on lakes created when highway or railroad grades have separated bays from the mainstream Columbia. Launching sites on such lakes are listed only if water traffic can pass under bridges to reach the river. Sites on tributaries are listed only if they are located near the mouth of the tributary and accessible by small nonmotorized craft. In a few cases, ramps located on tributaries can be used for access to the Columbia, but the current (seasonal or otherwise) on the tributary may not permit boaters to return to the ramp. If in doubt, inspect the area in advance.

An attempt has been made to enable boaters to locate the launching

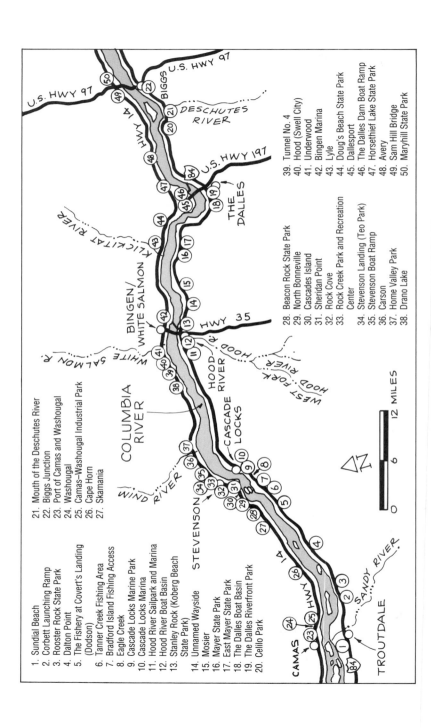

1. Sundial Beach
2. Corbett Launching Ramp
3. Rooster Rock State Park
4. Dalton Point
5. The Fishery at Covert's Landing (Dodson)
6. Tanner Creek Fishing Area
7. Bradford Island Fishing Access
8. Eagle Creek
9. Cascade Locks Marine Park
10. Cascade Locks Marina
11. Hood River Sailpark and Marina
12. Hood River Boat Basin
13. Stanley Rock (Koberg Beach State Park)
14. Unnamed Wayside
15. Mosier
16. Mayer State Park
17. East Mayer State Park
18. The Dalles Boat Basin
19. The Dalles Riverfront Park
20. Celilo Park

21. Mouth of the Deschutes River
22. Biggs Junction
23. Port of Camas and Washougal
24. Washougal
25. Camas–Washougal Industrial Park
26. Cape Horn
27. Skamania

28. Beacon Rock State Park
29. North Bonneville
30. Cascades Island
31. Sheridan Point
32. Rock Cove
33. Rock Creek Park and Recreation Center
34. Stevenson Landing (Teo Park)
35. Stevenson Boat Ramp
36. Carson
37. Home Valley Park
38. Drano Lake

39. Tunnel No. 4
40. Hood (Swell City)
41. Underwood
42. Bingen Marina
43. Lyle
44. Doug's Beach State Park
45. Dallesport
46. The Dalles Dam Boat Ramp
47. Horsethief Lake State Park
48. Avery
49. Sam Hill Bridge
50. Maryhill State Park

sites both from public highways and from the water. The latter is usually much more difficult than the former, and often requires careful observation and close attention to nautical charts or topographic maps. With each launching site is shown the approximate rivermile at which the ramp is located. The rivermiles measure the length of the river from its mouth to the point in question. Although the NOAA nautical charts and the USGS topographic maps both purport to use statute miles (as opposed to the longer nautical miles), the two do not always show the rivermiles in the same locations. When the charts and maps disagree, the NOAA chart rivermile is shown first, with the USGS map rivermile shown after a slash. Since the distances are approximate, and since future editions of maps may vary, other navigational aids should be used in addition to the rivermiles listed.

Whether using a boat ramp, a public park, or a hand-launching site, be courteous to windsurfers and other users, as well as to local residents and businesses. With the increasing popularity of boating and windsurfing in the Gorge, continued access to the river may be limited if boaters abuse the right to park cars and launch boats from some areas.

OREGON SIDE

Sundial Beach (Rivermile 120). From I-84, take exit 17. Turn north off Marine Drive onto Sundial Road at the west end of the Troutdale Airport. A privately owned boat ramp is located at the north end of Sundial Road. A fee is charged for its use. From the water, the ramp is directly under several power lines, just west of the mouth of the Sandy River.

Corbett Launching Ramp (Rivermile 126.5). From I-84, take exit 22. This boat ramp and small parking area are located at Corbett Station, immediately north of the exit. From the water, the area is easily recognized by the freeway overpass and on-ramps; it is also marked by a light.

Rooster Rock State Park (Rivermile 128.5). From I-84, take exit 25. This large park has extensive beaches, plus a boat ramp and floating docks in a lagoon at its west end. An admission fee is charged on weekends and holidays during the summer. When approaching the lagoon from the Columbia, the entrance is about 0.25 mile west of Rooster Rock. During periods of low water, the slough between the lagoon and the Columbia is dry.

Dalton Point (Rivermile 133.5). This boat ramp is accessible only to westbound traffic on I-84 near milepost 29. The ramp is located on a small point about halfway between Multnomah Falls and Phoca Rock. Eastbound traffic can reach Dalton Point by making a U-turn at the Multnomah Falls rest area.

The Fishery at Covert's Landing (Dodson) (Rivermile 140.25).

From I-84, take Ainsworth State Park exit 35 and proceed 0.3 mile east. This privately operated marina and campground includes a boat ramp.

Tanner Creek Fishing Area (Rivermile 144/144.5).

From I-84, take exit 40 and follow the signs past the fish hatchery to the public fishing area. Boats may be hand launched from this area just west of the mouth of Tanner Creek. The best launching is near the west end of the parking area. From the water, the area is marked by triangular orange marker 94, directly across from the Hamilton Island boat ramp.

Bradford Island Fishing Access (Rivermile 145/145.5).

From I-84, take Bonneville Dam exit 40 and follow the signs toward the visitor center. After crossing the powerhouse, bear left past a viewpoint/parking area and follow the road to the fishing access. Boats may be hand launched from the north side of the downstream end of Bradford Island.

Eagle Creek (Rivermile 146/146.5).

From I-84, take exit 41 and then follow the signs toward the Overlook Park picnic area. Boats may be launched in the mouth of Eagle Creek, directly underneath the freeway and railroad bridges. From the water, the mouth of the creek is just southeast of the upstream end of Bradford Island. Watch carefully for barge traffic when paddling through the narrow passage between Bradford Island and the Oregon shore.

Cascade Locks Marine Park (Rivermile 148.5/148.75).

From I-84, take exit 44 or 47. Boats may be hand launched just downstream from the historic site of the Cascade locks. The locks are now flooded, but carry a strong current. When approaching the park from upstream, pass through the old locks, then keep to the left after leaving the locks.

Cascade Locks Marina (Rivermile 149/149.25).

The Port of Cascades Locks maintains a boat ramp and marina near a visitor center 0.25 mile upstream from the old locks. The entrance to the marina is immediately east of a passenger dock used by the sternwheeler *Columbia Gorge*. A small beach, located just east of the marina, is popular with windsurfers. Watch carefully for other watercraft.

Hood River Sailpark and Marina (Rivermile 169.25).

From I-84, take exit 64, turn north and then west, drive past the boat basin, the visitor center, and the museum, and then drive north along the jetty to the beach. Public parking and a gravel beach are located at the north end of the jetty forming the Hood River Boat Basin. From the water, the beach is immediately east of the mouth of Hood River. This crowded public park is extremely popular with windsurfers.

Hood River Boat Basin (Rivermile 169.5).

From I-84, take exit 64. A public boat basin, a boat ramp, and a dock are located immediately northwest of the exit, between the mouth of the Hood River and the Hood River Bridge over the Columbia.

Stanley Rock (Koberg Beach State Park) (Rivermile 171).

Located near I-84 milepost 66, this wayside is accessible to westbound traffic only. Small boats may be hand launched from either the west end of the park by portaging a short distance to a beach, or from the east end of the park on a rocky shore. The two launching sites are at each end of the large outcropping known as Stanley Rock; the beach is on the west end, and the rocky shore is on the east end. From the water, the park is directly across the river from Bingen and is easily recognized by Stanley Rock and by overhead power lines.

Chicken Charlie Overlook (Rivermile 173.75).

This undeveloped wayside near I-84 milepost 68 southwest of Eighteenmile Island can be used for launching small craft. Access is available only from the westbound lanes of the freeway. This wayside was named after a former resident of Eighteenmile Island.

Mosier (Rivermile 174.75).

From I-84, take exit 69, turn south, take the first left (Rock Creek Road), and then drive 0.2 mile to a bridge over seasonal Rock Creek. Immediately west of the bridge, turn left on a rough road that follows the dry creekbed under a railroad bridge to a parking area. Boats must be carried under the freeway to the launching site. This recently developed windsurfing site is owned by the city of Mosier, but at the time of publication it was being maintained by the Rock Creek Boardsailing Association, which charges a small fee to help maintain the site.

Mayer State Park (Rivermile 181.25).

From I-84, take exit 76 and drive west on Hwy 30 (the Rowena Crest scenic loop) for about 0.5 mile, then follow signs to a bridge back over the freeway. A boat ramp gives access to Salisbury Slough, which opens into the Columbia. The entrance to the slough is 0.5 mile east of a point with a light. At the point,

174 ◆ COLUMBIA RIVER GORGE

the river is very narrow and the resulting currents can be considered dangerous.

East Mayer State Park (Rivermile 182). From I-84, take exit 76. From the north side of the Rowena interchange, drive north and across the railroad tracks, and then turn east 0.8 mile to the park. This popular windsurfing park is located at the community of Rowena, about 1 mile east of the main section of the park.

The Dalles Boat Basin (Rivermile 190). From I-84, take exit 85. Located immediately northwest of the exit, this public marina includes a large modern boat ramp and public rest rooms. The ramp is not actually in the basin, but immediately east of it. The boat basin is just east of a city wharf.

The Dalles Riverfront Park (Rivermile 190.25). The city of The Dalles has developed a very large waterfront park east of The Dalles Boat Basin, with particular emphasis on windsurfing. It is closed from November 1 to Memorial Day weekend due to wildlife habitat.

Celilo Park (Rivermile 202.25/201). This large park, operated by the Army Corps of Engineers, includes a boat ramp at its west end, providing access to the river through a small bay. The entrance to the bay is marked by a light, and is directly across the river from a water tank at the town of Wishram. Stay well away from any Indian fish nets.

Mouth of the Deschutes River (Rivermile 204.5/204). The mouth of the Deschutes has no freeway access. From I-84 eastbound, take Celilo Park exit 97; from I-84 westbound, take Biggs Junction exit 104. From both exits, the old highway can then be followed to two state parks: Heritage Landing Park on the west side of the river's mouth and Deschutes River State Park on the east side. Boats can be hand launched from either park; the park on the west side also has two launching areas, one a ramp for boats on trailers and one a hand-launching area for rafts and smaller craft. (A Deschutes River Pass must be purchased before launching watercraft on the Deschutes River; the passes are available from most sporting goods stores.) From the parks, the Columbia can be reached by paddling north under three bridges. From the water, the bridges are located off the south channel of the Columbia as it passes Miller Island.

Biggs Junction (Rivermile 208.5/207.5). From I-84, take exit 104. Just east of a grain elevator, less than 0.5 mile west of the Sam Hill Bridge (US 97), a small unimproved park and a primitive boat ramp are located just off the westbound on-ramp. Plans call for this park to be substantially improved and renamed the Biggspeed Windsurfing Park.

Paddling at Cape Horn

WASHINGTON SIDE

Port of Camas and Washougal (Rivermile 121.5).
From Hwy 14 in Washougal, turn south on Second Street, turn right on Front Street, and follow it 0.5 mile to a large parking area and a boat ramp. Commercial boat facilities are also available. The ramp is about 1 mile east of the upper end of Lady Island.

Washougal (Rivermile 122.75).
From Hwy 14 in Washougal, turn south on Fifteenth Street to an undeveloped hand-launch site immediately west of an industrial facility marked by two large tanks.

Camas–Washougal Industrial Park (Rivermile 123).
From milepost 17 on Hwy 14 in Washougal, turn south on Thirty-Second Street to Index Street, and then follow Index to a gravel road at its west end. From the end of the gravel road, boats can be carried over a dike to a hand launch. This site may be hard to find from the water, but it is near a small peninsula 0.5 mile upstream from an industrial facility with two large tanks.

Cape Horn (Rivermile 132.5).
From milepost 26.5 on Hwy 14, turn south on Cape Horn Road, follow it 1.5 miles to a railroad crossing, and then turn left to a rocky beach, where boats may be hand launched. The site is 0.5 mile east of the upstream end of a railroad tunnel.

Paddling past Beacon Rock

Skamania (Rivermile 140.5). From milepost 32.9 or 33.5 on Hwy 14, turn south on Skamania Landing Road. A small boat ramp is located near the east end of this road that loops through the community of Skamania. The ramp is just south of a small bridge, at the back of a bay 1 mile west of Beacon Rock.

Beacon Rock State Park (Rivermile 141.5). At milepost
34.2 on Hwy 14 (about 0.5 mile west of Beacon Rock), turn south on Beacon Rock Moorage Road and follow it to a campground with two boat ramps and a large dock. The facilities are located north of the lower end of Pierce Island, a Nature Conservancy preserve.

North Bonneville (Rivermile 144/144.5). From milepost 38.5
on Hwy 14, turn south on Dam Access Road and follow it southwest for about 1 mile to a boat ramp on Hamilton Island, directly across from the mouth of Tanner Creek and triangular orange navigational marker 94. Beyond the boat ramp is an extensive public access area where boats may be hand launched. Similar public access areas can be reached by driving northwest on Dam Access Road toward the new, second powerhouse. (No boats are permitted above the toe of Cascades Island, the island created by the construction of the second powerhouse.)

Cascades Island (Rivermile 145.75). Drive across the second
(north) powerhouse from Hwy 14 to a rocky beach at the fishing area at the toe of the island. Boats can be hand launched. The current can be very strong near Cascades Island. No boats are permitted above the toe of Cascades Island.

Sheridan Point (Rivermile 147.5). From milepost 41.1 on Hwy
14, park at a turnout and carry your boat across two sets of railroad tracks to a rocky shore. This site is less than ideal, but is one of the few possibilities on the Washington side immediately upstream from Bonneville Dam. Stay well away from the upstream side of the dam.

Rock Cove (Rivermile 149.75). From milepost 43.5 of Hwy 14,
turn north to reach an undeveloped park on a tiny peninsula. Boats may be hand launched. The Columbia can be reached under two bridges at the east end of the lake.

Rock Creek Park and Recreation Center (Rivermile
149.9). From the west end of Stevenson, turn north on East Second Street. This park is located on the northeast shore of Rock Cove. The Columbia can be reached under two bridges at the east end of the lake.

Stevenson Landing (Teo Park) (Rivermile 150.5). At the
foot of Russell Avenue in Stevenson are a small picnic area and a hand-launch site. The park also has a prominent dock with a gangplank for the sternwheeler *Columbia Gorge*, but the dock is not suitable for small craft. Immediately downstream from the park is Bob's Beach, a popular windsurfing site.

Stevenson Boat Ramp (Rivermile 150.75). In Stevenson, turn south on Russell Avenue and proceed three blocks to Cascade Avenue; follow it east to a public boat ramp and a parking area near the mouth of Kanaka Creek, 0.25 mile east of the dock at Stevenson Landing.

Carson (Rivermile 154.75). From milepost 49.6 on Hwy 14, turn north on Old Hatchery Road and drive 0.4 mile to a boat ramp and a floating dock. The boat ramp is just inside the mouth of the Wind River, between Carson and Home Valley. Access to the Columbia is under a railroad bridge and a highway bridge.

Home Valley Park (Rivermile 155.25). From milepost 50.1 on Hwy 14, turn south. The park is located 0.7 mile east of the mouth of the Wind River. The best launching is from a small cove at the west end of the park.

Drano Lake (Rivermile 162.25). This large lake is located at the mouth of the Little White Salmon River. It has a boat ramp on the north side of the highway/railroad causeway at milepost 57.3 on Hwy 14 near a historical marker. Access to the Columbia is under a bridge at the west end of the lake at rivermile 161/162.

Tunnel No. 4 (Rivermile 164.75). At milepost 59.6 on Hwy 14 (immediately east of Tunnel No. 4), a small rocky beach offers a hand-launch site on the east side of a promontory. (The reference to Tunnel No. 4 on the USGS topographic maps has been incorrectly placed on Tunnel No. 3.)

Hood (Swell City) (Rivermile 166). A rocky beach and a parking area are at milepost 61.1 on Hwy 14, 0.5 mile west of the entrance to the Spring Creek Fish Hatchery, across and slightly upstream from Ruthton Point on the Oregon side. This site, known as Swell City, is very popular with windsurfers; at the time of publication, an access fee was being charged.

Underwood (Rivermile 168.25). At milepost 63.4 on Hwy 14, on the west bank of the mouth of the White Salmon River, just inside the Highway 14 bridge, is the Big White Salmon Indian Fishing Site, which includes a boat ramp. It is operated by local Indians whose permission should be obtained before launching boats or parking cars. An alternative is to hand launch on the shore of the Columbia several hundred feet west of the bridge, on some riprap occasionally used by windsurfers.

Bingen Marina and Klickitat Point (Rivermile 172). From milepost 66.7 on Hwy 14 in Bingen, turn south on Maple Street and fol-

On an island off Beacon Rock

low it 0.7 mile east to the picnic area and marina. A boat ramp and a large floating dock are located in this boat basin at the east end of Bingen. From the water, the entrance to the boat basin is marked by two lights. Boats may also be hand launched at Klickitat Point, a windsurfing park just west of the entrance to the boat basin.

Lyle (Rivermile 180.75). From milepost 74.9 on Hwy 14, immediately east of the bridge over the mouth of the Klickitat River, turn south on a dirt road and follow it 0.3 mile east to a boat ramp, formerly a landing for the ferry to Oregon. Directly across the river is Mayer State Park. Because the river is quite narrow, very strong currents are common in the vicinity of Lyle and the state park.

Doug's Beach State Park (Rivermile 183.75). At milepost 78.9 on Hwy 14, 3 miles east of Lyle, is this hand-launch site, popular with windsurfers. A moderate portage is required. From the water, it is marked by a light and navigational marker 57A.

Dallesport (Rivermile 189.5). From milepost 82.2 on Hwy 14, turn south on Dallesport Road and follow it south for 2.7 miles. (Or turn east on Dallesport Road off US 197 0.3 mile north of The Dalles Bridge and follow it east for 1.6 miles.) Then drive south 0.5 mile on Old Ferry Road to a boat ramp located near The Dalles Airport. The ramp is directly across the river from The Dalles public wharf and a grain elevator.

The Dalles Dam Boat Ramp (Rivermile 192). From US 197, turn east 0.3 mile north of The Dalles Bridge. A paved boat ramp and a small dock are located immediately upstream from the locks at The Dalles Dam. When approaching the ramp from the water, stay close to the north bank to find the ramp near the entrance to the locks. Do not enter the locks area without instructions from the lockmaster.

Horsethief Lake State Park (Rivermile 194.5/194). At milepost 85.2 on Hwy 14 is the entrance road to the park. This large state park contains two boat ramps, one on Horsethief Lake and one on the Columbia. The ramp on the Columbia is located on a small point just west of Horsethief Lake. Horsethief Lake has no water access to the Columbia.

Avery (Rivermile 198/197.5). From milepost 89.7 on Hwy 14, turn south to this picnic area and boat ramp, located directly north of Brown's Island. Boats can also be launched at a small point 0.5 mile west of the boat ramp. Auto access is via the road to the boat ramp.

Sam Hill Bridge (Rivermile 209/208). Boats may be launched at several points along a dirt road leading west from the north end of the Sam Hill Memorial Bridge.

Maryhill State Park (Rivermile 210/209). This large state park includes a boat ramp 1 mile east of the Sam Hill Bridge. The entrance to the park is near the north end of the bridge.

FURTHER READING

Jones, Philip N. *Canoe Routes: Northwest Oregon.* The Mountaineers Books, 1982.

◆

WHITEWATER KAYAKING

By Ed Newville

Whitewater kayaking is a relatively new sport to the Pacific Northwest and an obscure sport in general. The icy rivers may seem uninviting to most people, but those willing to give the sport a try find a great variety of recreational kayak runs within 1 or 2 hours of the Portland metropolitan area. Partly due to this variety, kayaking has been experiencing an increase in popularity in the Portland area within the last 10 years.

Traditionally, most whitewater kayaking activity in the Portland area centered on the highly visible and easily accessible stretches of the Sandy and Clackamas rivers. Kayakers share these well-known rivers—which for the most part represent class III rapids of moderate difficulty—with rafters, canoeists, and numerous fishermen in drift boats or hip boots. As kayaking has grown in popularity and the average skill of local boaters has increased, boaters have sought out and discovered other attractive and more challenging runs on less obvious whitewater rivers. Several of these—representing some of the best kayaking runs in the region, ones that far surpass those on the other, more well-known Portland-area rivers—enter the Columbia River in the Columbia River Gorge. These runs are located on the Wind and White Salmon rivers on the Washington side of the Columbia Gorge, and on Hood River on the Oregon side.

These runs are highly prized for their scenic value. The boater who pauses between rapids for a slow look around often finds the sheer basalt walls covered with the lush growth of ferns and wildflowers. In certain places, cold-running springs shoot out from between the layers of the rock canyon walls and shower directly down on the river below. These hanging botanical gardens and springs are well hidden and generally unknown. The narrow canyons through which these rivers flow can totally isolate the river from nearby farms and roads. This unspoiled solitude, open mainly to those who travel down the river in small boats, can be quite profound.

It is hoped that people will always be able to enjoy making their way in small boats down the challenging whitewater of these rivers. All of these kayak runs, especially the narrow canyons of the White Salmon and West Fork of the Hood rivers, have been threatened by dams or water diversion projects at one time or another. The experience of boating these unique rivers could never be found on rivers elsewhere in the region. It would be a truly great loss to have small hydroelectric projects silence these fine rapids now flowing in their picturesque, basalt-lined canyons.

Preparation

Several topographic factors make these kayaking runs on Gorge tributaries unique. Two high peaks—Mount Adams and Mount Hood—closely flank the Columbia River to the north and south as the river cuts its course through the Cascade Range. These tributaries, which collect the runoff and snowmelt from those high peaks, must drop to the level of the Columbia in the short distance of 15 or 20 miles. This steep gradient, often a drop in excess of 100 feet per mile, creates large, powerful rapids too violent and congested with boulders for drift boats, open canoes, and, at times, even rubber rafts, but those rapids are perfect for sturdy, maneuverable kayaks. Also, unlike challenging sections of other Cascade rivers, where the steepest gradient is normally found far upstream near the headwaters at high elevations, the Gorge tributaries often have their steepest gradients in their lower reaches. In making the final plunge into the Columbia River Gorge, the Wind and White Salmon rivers have cut deep, narrow canyons with very steep gradients through hard basalt rock. These small gorges form constricted powerful rapids often demanding a very high degree of skilled technique from whitewater boaters. They represent challenging whitewater runs on par with the highest standards of the sport. Portland area residents are lucky to have such whitewater gems so close to home.

The low elevations of these runs (the put-in is usually no more than 1,000 feet in elevation) also means that they can be paddled even during the midwinter season. Unlike other higher-elevation runs that depend on the coming of warm spring weather to thaw frozen rivers and open access roads, problems with snowed-in roads or iced-over water are rare on these runs. With the introduction of sophisticated clothing such as dry suits and nylon pile underwear, boaters paddle these rivers even in midwinter in relative comfort. And oftentimes it is during that season when, due to constant heavy rains, these runs are at their best.

RIVER SKILLS

With one or two exceptions, all of the described kayak runs in the Columbia Gorge, even at moderate water levels, require advanced–intermediate to expert boating skills. Persons new to the sport of kayaking and those needing to brush up on their skills should start out on more open class II rivers such as the lower Sandy River below Dodge or Oxbow Park before tackling most of the runs described here. Only after a boater has mastered the art of precise maneuvering through complex rapids is he or

Knucklegrinder, upper White Salmon River (photo by Ed Newville)

she encouraged to seek out these challenging kayak runs.

Even greater caution is urged when the water levels in these rivers reach a high level. During the high water of the first few weeks of the spring runoff, or any time after a steady downpour of rain, all of these runs may be significantly more difficult and dangerous than normal. Relatively inexperienced boaters should avoid trying these runs for the first time during those times.

Skills Classification. Beginner: One who knows the basic strokes and can handle a kayak in smooth water. **Novice:** One who can effectively use all basic whitewater strokes, can read whitewater and negotiate easy rapids with assurance, and can attempt an Eskimo roll with at least partial success in smooth water. **Intermediate:** One who can negotiate rapids requiring sequential maneuvering and use of eddy turns, and can reliably Eskimo roll under most conditions. **Advanced:** One who has the ability to safely run, with complete control of the kayak, difficult and complex rapids requiring precise maneuvering; one who has a completely reliable Eskimo roll even in extremely turbulent water. **Expert:** One who has, in addition to mastery of all whitewater skills, wide experience on many rivers and the ability to rescue other kayakers having difficulty.

RIVER CONDITIONS

River Gradient and Difficulty. Information on the gradient of a river can assist the boater in an assessment of its difficulty. The average gradient in feet per mile is listed for each of the described runs. Remember that the listed gradient is an average; hence, in certain sections the gradient may be significantly greater.

The tributaries of the Columbia River entering in the Columbia Gorge are normally of moderate volume—about 1,000 to 2,000 cubic feet per second. Under these circumstances, when the gradient is less than 50 feet per mile, class II and class III rapids may be present; between 50 and 100 feet per mile, class III to class V rapids are found; and above a gradient of 100 feet per mile, many class IV to class V rapids are present, with possible mandatory portages of unrunnable falls or obstructions.

The difficulty of any particular rapid varies with the water level. Also, rivers of steeper gradient (those in excess of 100 feet per mile) increase in difficulty much more dramatically with additional water than rivers of lesser gradient. Any kayak run should be approached with a great deal of caution during periods of high runoff, especially on rivers with a steep average gradient. For example, the White Salmon River above B Z Corner is almost always boated after the river level has significantly dropped from the high-water stage of spring or early summer.

River and Rapids Classification. Class I: Water suitable for beginners and novices. Moving water with a few small riffles and small regular waves; passages clear. **Class II:** Water suitable for intermediates. Water with easy rapids of medium difficulty; clear, wide passages; channels obvious without scouting. Some maneuvering is required around occasional boulders. **Class III:** Water suitable for advanced–intermediate and advanced kayakers. Water with numerous large, irregular waves; rocky, narrow passages often requiring considerable maneuvering; rocky drops up to 3 or 4 feet high. Certain rapids may require advance scouting from shore. **Class IV:** Water suitable for advanced and expert kayakers. Water with long, powerful rapids, dangerous rocks, boiling eddies; constricted passages requiring precise and difficult maneuvering; sharp, powerful drops up to 6 or 8 feet high. Scouting from shore is mandatory on first run; rescue conditions are difficult. **Class V:** Water suitable for expert kayakers only. Water with extremely difficult, almost uninterrupted, very violent rapids requiring complex maneuvering under extremely difficult conditions; very large, turbulent, powerful drops in excess of 10 or 12 feet high. Advance scouting is mandatory; rescue ropes and personnel should be in position when at all possible. **Class VI:** Water with difficulties of class V carried to extremes; clearly impossible or nearly so; extreme hazard to life and limb. Suitable, if at all, only for teams of expert paddlers at favorable water levels and only after careful study, with experienced rescue personnel in position.

For a complete discussion of river safety and kayaking techniques, refer to the excellent text of *Wildwater,* listed at the end of this chapter.

Whitewater Runs

In the following descriptions of the kayak runs, a range of water flow in cubic feet per second (CFS) and corresponding classification of difficulty are listed as a recommendation of when the river is runnable. Regard these ranges as only an approximation. An optimum level is also listed. This is not necessarily the level at which the run is at its easiest. Rather it is the approximate water level at which fully competent boaters, very familiar with the river, most enjoy doing that particular run. There is simply no substitute for a person's own judgment in an assessment of his or her ability, on a given day, to safely paddle a river at a particular level of flow.

A general description of each run is followed by gauge information. A gauge is merely a measure of the depth of the river at a particular point, which is then translated into water volume, which is expressed in CFS. After gauge information, directions to the put-in are given, then the run is described, and, finally, directions to the take-out are given.

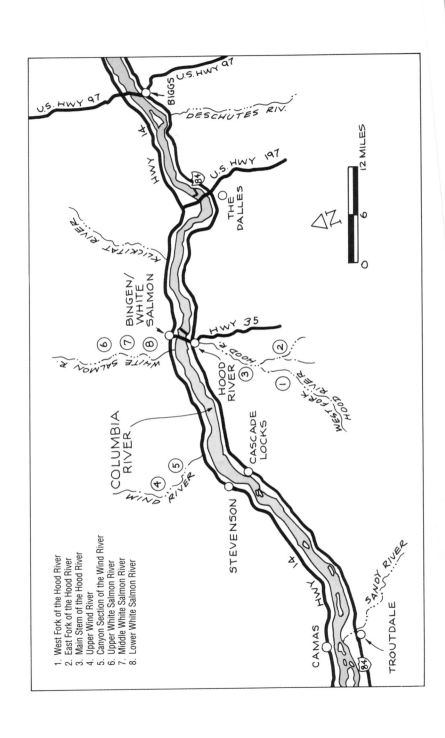

1. West Fork of the Hood River
2. East Fork of the Hood River
3. Main Stem of the Hood River
4. Upper Wind River
5. Canyon Section of the Wind River
6. Upper White Salmon River
7. Middle White Salmon River
8. Lower White Salmon River

OREGON SIDE

◆ WEST FORK OF THE HOOD RIVER

Put-in: Branch Creek at White Bridge Park
Take-out: Confluence of the East and West forks
Distance: 5.5 miles
Gradient: 90 feet/mile
Volume and difficulty: 1,200 CFS* + ; class IV
Optimum: 2,000 CFS*
Portages: 2 falls
* measured at Tucker Bridge

The West Fork of the Hood River is a fine run for whitewater enthusiasts. It begins as a clear, broad mountain stream flowing through deep woods well hidden from any roads or homes. Numerous play waves and holes are present, especially in the last 2 miles of the run where the river enters a small, twisting gorge.

Although Mount Hood provides a good deal of snowmelt, this source of runoff is quickly extinguished in early spring. Frequently the run is at its best after heavy winter rains or a sudden thaw. The Tucker Bridge gauge, located well below the confluence of the East and West forks, is the best indication of when the two upstream forks are runnable. The West Fork may carry anywhere from one-third to two-thirds of the total reported volume under certain conditions.

A gauge is also located just upstream from the West Fork Bridge just above Punchbowl Falls. Although an overgrown trail leads down to this gauge, the gauge is normally only read during the run itself—usually in an attempt to further procrastinate before running Punchbowl Falls. When this gauge reads less than 4 feet, the pace of the river is moderate and the Punchbowl is often run. One can take out on the exposed concrete adjacent to the main chute, examine the drop, and decide whether to bypass or run it. When the gauge reaches 5 to 6 feet, the trail leading up from the gauge is a good place to take out instead of running further. At high water levels it is extremely difficult to eddy out and carry around the falls after paddling past the gauge; the concrete shelf next to the main chute is then buried under a swift current. Caution: another concrete shelf at the base of the drop extends out from the left shore—even at high water levels, you must run the powerful main chute.

From I-84, exit at Hood River and drive south to the town of Dee. At Dee, turn right, following signs toward Lost Lake and Lolo Pass. Park at White Bridge Park, about 6 miles past Dee. Although not plowed for snow, the road to the put-in is passable during most of the winter. The put-in is at 1,200 feet.

From the put-in, there are many class III boulder gardens and an oc-

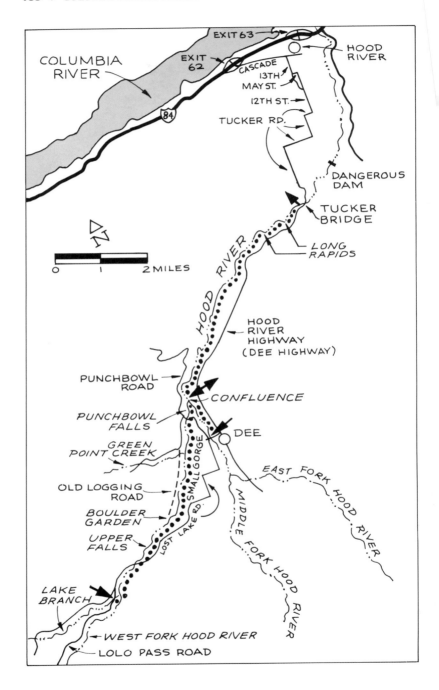

Whitewater, West Fork of the Hood River (photo by Ed Newville)

casional trickier drop. About 3 miles from the put-in, 1 mile or more downriver from the Lost Lake Road bridge, is the former site of Upper Falls, once a challenging drop but now a fish ladder that must be portaged on the left.

Below the fish ladder, the river narrows and the pace picks up. About 1 mile downstream is the most difficult rapid on the run—a long boulder garden sweeping to the left. At higher water levels, the boulder garden becomes a maze of good-sized holes and pour-overs. This drop can be scouted with difficulty from the right. The river twists through a small gorge for the remaining 2 miles. Here the river is "pool and drop" with many good play spots. Small eddies abound, even at high water levels. Watch for the West Fork Bridge just above Punchbowl Falls. At low river levels, the Punchbowl can be scouted and portaged from the concrete shelf alongside the main chute (see gauge information above). At high river levels, this shelf is buried underwater and it is necessary to take out well before the lead-in to the Punchbowl. The main chute can be run, after a thorough reconnaissance, but note that this chute, which flows over an 8-foot ledge, is extremely powerful even at a low level of flow. While no one has been injured here, many paddlers have taken nasty swims after bouncing backward into the plunging falls. Check for logs frequently trapped at the base, and have throw ropes ready. The confluence with the East Fork is just downstream.

Driving directions to the take-out at the confluence are given in the description for the main stem of the Hood River.

◆ EAST FORK OF THE HOOD RIVER

Put-in: Paper mill at Dee
Take-out: Confluence of East and West forks (the run is usually
    continued to Tucker Bridge)
Distance: 1 mile
Gradient: 120 feet/mile
Volume and difficulty: 800–1,000 CFS*, class III + ; greater than
    1,000 CFS*, class IV
Optimum: 1,200 CFS*
Portages: None
* measured at Tucker Bridge

For those with good class IV boating skills, this short section of the
East Fork is the favored beginning of a run down the main stem of the
Hood River to Tucker Bridge. No separate gauge information is available
for this branch of the Hood River. At times this fork appears to carry about
one-third of the total flow of the main stem, and at other times the volume
appears to be as much as two-thirds.

From I-84, exit at Hood River City and drive south to the town of
Dee. Put in near the paper mill.

The gradient is much steeper in this section than in the main stem,
and the river is confined to a small, twisting canyon. Several short—but
sweet—sharp drops of 4 or 5 feet are found before the river joins the West
Fork in a final plunging rapid.

For those who decide to take out at the confluence, driving directions
to the confluence are given in the description for the main stem of the
Hood River.

◆ MAIN STEM OF THE HOOD RIVER

Put-in: Confluence of the East and West forks
Take-out: Tucker Bridge
Distance: 6 miles
Gradient: 66 feet/mile
Volume and difficulty: 800–1,200 CFS, class III + ; greater than
    1,200 CFS, class IV
Optimum: 1,500 CFS
Portages: None

This enjoyable, moderately difficult stretch of river is just a few minutes' drive south from the town of Hood River. The run begins at the confluence of the East and West forks of the Hood River. Those forks follow
sharp, twisting courses through narrow canyons until they merge. At that
point, the river eases its pace and widens out, and the main stem of the
Hood River proceeds toward the Columbia River in long, sweeping turns

A drop on the West Fork of the Hood River (photo by Ed Newville)

bordered by forests and orchards.

A gauge is located under the Tucker Bridge at the take-out. The reading is available from the River Forecast Center in Portland (phone 503-249-0666). A gauge reading of 4.5 equals 1,200 CFS, one of 6.5 equals 3,000 CFS.

To reach the put-in at the confluence, from I-84, take Hood River City Center, exit 63 and drive south on 12th Street and Tucker Road, which eventually crosses the Main Stem at Tucker Bridge (the take-out) and then leads to the town of Dee. At Dee, turn west, then turn north after crossing the East Fork. One mile farther, just before crossing the West Fork, turn north onto a dirt road near the east end of the West Fork Bridge. The river is 500 feet down a trail. Punchbowl Falls can be scouted during the shuttle from a trail on the west side of the falls. The trail leads to a wooden staircase that descends to the concrete fish ladder below.

The climax of this run is provided by a long, unnamed set of rapids about 1 mile before the end of the run. This eighth-mile section is distinctly more difficult than the earlier sections of the river and requires continuous maneuvering to avoid rocks and pour-overs. At higher river levels, the water flushes through with tremendous speed, forming long sets of 4-foot waves with an occasional powerful hole to trap the unwary. These rapids begin at the head of a long island, which is passed on the right. After the island, easier rapids that are visible from the road lead to the take-out on the right just upstream from Tucker Bridge. Although the river continues to look inviting below the bridge, a dangerous dam is only 1 mile downstream. Take out.

WASHINGTON SIDE

◆ UPPER WIND RIVER

> Put-in: Bridge 0.5 mile north of Carson Fish Hatchery on Paradise Creek Road
> Take-out: Bridge at Stabler
> Distance: 8 miles
> Gradient: 32 feet/mile
> Volume and difficulty: 600+ CFS; class II
> Optimum: Unknown
> Portages: 3–4 log jams

Thoughts of the Wind River conjure up visions of its powerful, racing drops in the canyon below Stabler. It is somewhat anomalous that upriver from these class V rapids, the river takes on the characteristics of a mature, meandering lowland river. In this "upper" section, the river crisscrosses the broad valley floor at a leisurely pace, and the small basalt canyons one

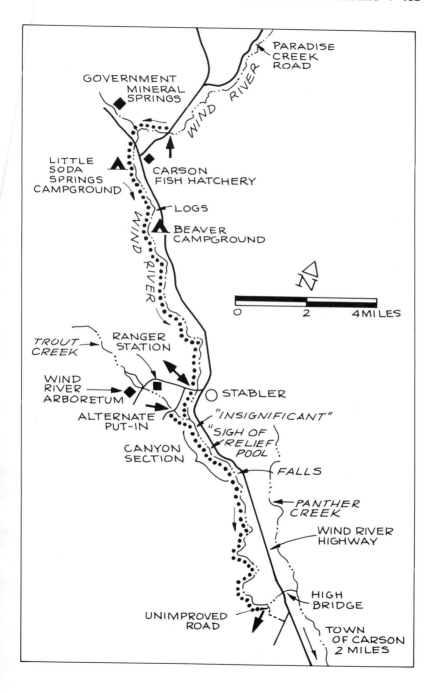

PARADISE
CREEK
ROAD

WIND RIVER

GOVERNMENT
MINERAL
SPRINGS

LITTLE
SODA
SPRINGS
CAMPGROUND

CARSON
FISH HATCHERY

LOGS

BEAVER
CAMPGROUND

WIND RIVER

N

0   2   4 MILES

TROUT
CREEK

RANGER
STATION

WIND
RIVER
ARBORETUM

○ STABLER

ALTERNATE
PUT-IN

"INSIGNIFICANT"

"SIGH OF
RELIEF"
POOL

CANYON
SECTION

FALLS

PANTHER
CREEK

WIND RIVER
HIGHWAY

HIGH
BRIDGE

UNIMPROVED
ROAD

TOWN
OF CARSON
2 MILES

encounters here have little in common with their relatives just downstream.

No gauges are presently maintained on this section of the Wind River. See gauge information for the class V canyon section of this river.

From Hwy 14 milepost 47.9 in Carson, drive north on the Wind River Highway to Carson National Fish Hatchery. At the fork, take a right and put in at the Paradise Creek Road Bridge 0.5 mile farther north.

This upstream run is recommended as a very scenic alternative to the more demanding class V section. This is a run for persons who, on a given day—for one reason or another—decide they prefer the subtler impressions found on quieter mountain streams.

Several large log jams are present on this section of the river. As they lie in relatively quiet water, however, they present no real danger or difficulty to bypass.

For directions to the take-out at the bridge at Stabler, see the directions to the put-in for the canyon section of the Wind River.

◆ CANYON SECTION OF THE WIND RIVER

Put-in: Bridge at Stabler
Take-out: Old Detour Road, 0.5 mile upstream from High Bridge
Distance: 6.5 miles
Gradient: 80 feet/mile, overall; 125 feet/mile, 2-mile canyon section
Volume and difficulty: 600–1,200 CFS, class IV +; greater than 1,200 CFS, class V
Optimum: 1,500 CFS
Portages: None

This challenging section of the Wind River is a premier whitewater run for advanced boaters. It is a very popular winter run, as the conditions are fairly mild and at least adequate water is practically guaranteed. The elevation at the put-in is only 900 feet.

The most difficult rapids are in the 2-mile canyon section near the start of the run. Here the rapids are very strong and nearly continuous. The volume of the river, however, is usually large enough to allow for a great deal of improvisation. In fact, the complexity of the rapids—requiring an ability to quickly read demanding whitewater—*demands* a healthy degree of improvisation. In addition, the river can be safely paddled at very high river levels by those having the requisite technical bigwater skills. At high flow levels, large boulders and major drops create some truly impressive holes. An unanticipated swim at this level is, however, relatively forgiving for a river of this level of difficulty. While no one relishes the idea of a helpless swim downriver while submerged well below the surface most of the time, the Wind River generally lacks the ugly un-

Rough water on the Wind River (photo by Ed Newville)

dercut ledges, logs, or mandatory portages that would make such a mistake much more serious on other expert runs.

All in all, the Wind is a river to be respected, and a place to celebrate one's skills and ability to paddle difficult whitewater—after those skills are honed on less-demanding runs elsewhere. The lower 4 miles of the run, which are class III + or easy class IV water, seem almost anticlimactic. But even here there are many eddies to catch and small holes to surf that give the paddler an opportunity to enjoy being on the river, and to reflect upon a successful run.

The Wind River was first run late in the summer of 1977 by Steve Zack and Bob Blily. Unbreakable plastic kayaks had just arrived upon the scene and a paddler could bash his way down through the rocks with relative impunity. The first exploratory runs were done at very low water levels—perhaps 200 to 300 CFS. During the next few years, subsequent parties ventured forth at increasingly higher levels until eventually the river was being boated at very high flows indeed, when all but the largest boulders were buried beneath the surging flow.

Still, only a relatively small group of people made a practice of paddling the Wind, and the river retained something of a sinister reputation. Then in 1982 a tireless canoeist from Chicago with a lot of time on his hands moved to Portland. Harvey Shapiro logged more than two dozen runs on the river during that winter and the next spring. He was taking everybody down the river who owned a boat and said they could roll, myself included. Though the river inevitably lost some of its mystique as it quickly gained a following, it is still a great run.

No government agency presently monitors the volume of the Wind River. The only gauge on the river, just upstream from the riverside hot springs near the town of Carson, is difficult to reach and is partially destroyed in any case. Records kept by the USGS in 1975 and 1976 show the average flow from November through May to be about 1,500 CFS with numerous periods of high flow well above 2,500 CFS. The river is reliably runnable after the first of the heavy winter rains and remains so well into June.

River runners have developed a crude gauge by reference to a series of logs and a large rock visible on the left side of the river at the take-out. The river is very low, but runnable if all seven of the logs are above the water level. Conditions are considered moderate if three to four logs are visible. If only one or two logs are showing, the river is very high and requires considerable caution. If no logs are visible, the upstream rock is used to gauge the water level, and the river is considered to be very high, a fearsome series of giant waves and huge holes.

From Hwy 14 milepost 47.9 in Carson, drive north on the Wind River Highway to Trout Creek Road. Turn left onto Trout Creek Road and follow it to the bridge (Stabler Bridge). The put-in is west of the Stabler Bridge.

The very skilled may wish to put in on Trout Creek and run the last 0.5 mile of this tributary until it joins the Wind just upstream from the first major rapid—Insignificant. This large creek drops about 150 feet in this 0.5 mile section. This alternate, with tight turns and tiny eddies, is a short class V that can only be run when the Wind is at least a medium flow. Look out for logs that completely cross the narrow stream channel.

From the Stabler Bridge put-in, the river flows quietly through a small canyon with numerous easy warm-up rapids until it is joined by Trout Creek and the volume is increased significantly. The first major rapid—a long one—is around the corner to the left. It is aptly referred to as either "Insignificant" or "Initiation" in comparison to those yet to come. The lead-in is visible from the road. After several lesser rapids, the river is funneled into a chute along its left bank. This drop—named "Climax" or "Ram's Horn"—culminates in a large flushing hole or breaking set of waves, depending on the water level. From the base of Climax, a long boulder garden leads to the first large pool since the beginning of the canyon—the "Sigh of Relief Pool." After this pool, the river turns to the right and several lesser class IV rapids follow in quick succession. One sweeps by a rock wall along the right bank and ends in a series of waves or holes. Another narrows into a chute along the left bank and ends in a pleasant pool. A boulder garden leads to the biggest drop on the river—a riverwide, 6-foot cascade (also known as "Climax" by local boaters). It ends all too soon. Less exhilarating rapids lead to the take-out.

The Old Detour roadhead is the last opportunity to conveniently take out of the river. While pleasant-looking rapids lead off around the bend

Wind River (photo by Ed Newville)

and under High Bridge, they lead to an absolutely unrunnable class VI triple drop near the town of Carson. At this point, the river funnels down to less than 20 yards wide and roars over huge cascades adjacent to a concrete fish ladder. There is a maintained trail down to this spot where a suspension bridge crosses the river directly over the cascades. The trail begins behind the Carson Hot Springs Resort. The 10-minute hike makes an interesting side trip when the river level is high.

The take-out is on Old Detour Road, about 0.5 mile upstream from High Bridge.

◆ UPPER WHITE SALMON RIVER

Put-in: Adjacent to Sunnyside Road just before it intersects the road to Glenwood
Take-out: Bridge at B Z Corner
Distance: 10 miles
Gradient: 100 feet/mile, overall; 145 feet/mile for 2-mile section near Ash Falls
Volume and difficulty: 1,000 CFS* +, class V
Optimum: 1,300 CFS*
Portages: 4 unrunnable falls, 1 dangerous log
* measured on the Underwood gauge

This is an expert kayak run that only in recent years has been run on a regular basis, and then only at moderate water levels. Presently the ten-

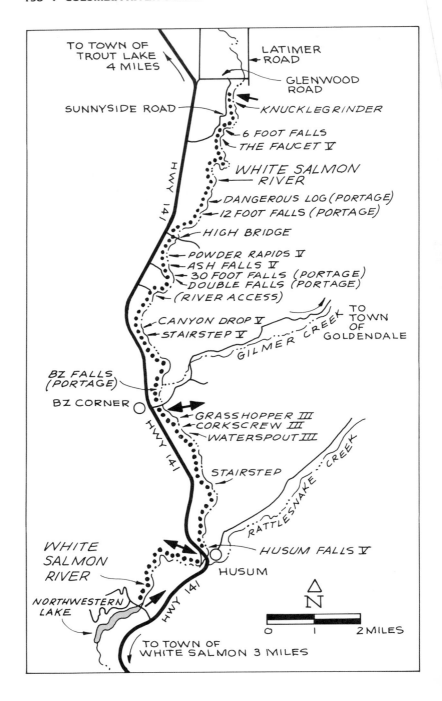

dency is to break the run up into shorter, more manageable sections, although—because the river is mostly confined to a very small canyon—intermediate access is difficult. Abbreviating the run requires bushwhacking up or down steep cliffsides. The entire 10 miles to B Z Corner was completed in a single day by the persons making the first exploratory trips—that effort has seldom been repeated but is certainly feasible for very skilled and confident boaters. The margin for error on this challenging and serious run is not great. Dozens of sharp class IV drops and several class V rapids of considerable difficulty will be found; certain waterfalls must be portaged and others can be run; and there is a distinct need to anticipate a quick rescue by setting ropes before certain drops are run. All of this guarantees a very long day for paddlers undertaking the entire 10-mile run to B Z Corner. First-timers on the river need to do a good deal of scouting and careful eddy hopping.

Bill Gray, Dave Axelrod, John McCracken, and Jens Housley made the first descent of this section of the White Salmon River at 1,300 CFS (a very healthy volume) on May 18, 1980. Coincidentally, Mount St. Helens—about 30 miles distant—erupted while the group made the run. Skies darkened by millions of tons of volcanic ash added dramatic special effects and intensified the tension felt by the group during this exploratory descent. The group named Ash Falls for the volcanic fallout dropping during the run. While the special effects are not likely to be repeated for subsequent parties, certainly all boaters on their initial foray onto this challenging run will experience a trepidation not unlike that of the original party.

The Underwood gauge is located near the point where the White Salmon enters the Columbia River—hence the reading is considerably higher than the actual flow at the put-in well upstream. The reading is available from the NOAA tape recording in Seattle (206-526-8530). The gauge is downstream from a hydroelectric generating facility at Northwestern Lake. Under "normal" conditions, the level of the lake is held constant and the facility releases the same amount of water as enters the reservoir daily. However, at best, the gauge reading is only roughly indicative of the volume of the river upstream.

In addition, many underground springs enter the White Salmon River, especially in the section below Ash Falls. Late in the summer, these springs significantly increase the total volume of the river. During this time, it may be possible to boat a lower portion of the 10-mile run when the water level is inadequate for starting at the Sunnyside Road put-in.

To reach the put-in from Hwy 14 in Bingen, turn left and follow Hwy 141 north to Sunnyside Road. Follow Sunnyside Road to just before it intersects with the road to Glenwood.

The run begins in a slow-moving pool visible from Sunnyside Road paralleling the river. The first drops are formed when the river begins to cut a narrow channel into the basalt bedrock. Knucklegrinder (IV), less than a boat-length wide, marks the beginning of the difficult rapids. Below this rapid, sheer basalt cliffs confine the river to a narrow, twisting gorge punctuated by sharp, powerful drops. After the first several drops in the gorge, the rock walls recede for several hundred yards, then close again to loom high overhead. Several more class IV drops follow in quick succession. Beyond a stream of water, falling from the overhanging canyon wall directly into the river below, is the first runnable falls—a 6-foot-high cascade that can be scouted and easily portaged on the left. Several more powerful, short drops follow immediately below the falls.

One hundred yards downstream from a wooden bridge crossing overhead is The Faucet (V)—a 20-foot-high falls. It can be run off the green spout of water to the right of a large log sticking straight up in the falls. The falls can be inspected from either the right or left shore, but it can only be portaged on the right. The exit eddy on the right is no more than 12 feet above the falls itself and is quite small—at very high water, it may not be there at all. Room for recovery or rescue after running The Faucet is short, as another powerful class IV rapid begins just 80 yards downstream. The next and final rapid in this gorge is a tricky, twisting staircase of five or six closely connected short drops covering about 100 yards. After this series of ledges, the canyon opens and the pace eases. The next 2 miles are easy class III.

Just after the canyon again narrows, there is a dangerous log wedged across the river. This log, partially obscured in the whitewater, can be difficult to see from upstream. Portage it on either side. Downstream from the log a few hundred yards is another mandatory portage—a 12-foot falls curving off to the left that funnels itself into a stump sticking up at the base of the falls. Eddy out and portage this one on the left. The tempo builds again from this point, especially after passing under the green truss bridge over the river; tricky class IV drops follow thereafter in close succession. A steep trail on the right just below the high bridge leads up to the road, for those whose energy is flagging. Ropes are usually needed here for pulling the boats up.

A mile below the bridge, where the river turns sharply to the left, is Powder Rapids (V). This long and powerful rapid is one of the few visible from Highway 141. The group who made the first descent of the river compared paddling this rapid at high water to "skiing deep powder." Scout it on either side. After Powder Rapids, the numerous short, powerful drops increase in size. Ash Falls (V), a very powerful 12-foot cascade 0.25 mile downstream, should be carefully scouted and run only with rescue ropes at hand. The falls are easily portaged on the left. More often than not, the tremendous boil and backwash foil boaters' best-laid plans for a successful run. Swimmers and floating equipment tend to recirculate repeatedly back into the falls. Little Ash Falls—a sharp, constricted 6-foot plunge—lies 30 yards downstream.

One hundred yards ahead, after another short drop and a fast-moving

White Salmon River (photo by Ed Newville)

pool, lies an unrunnable 30-foot falls—a mandatory portage. Most boaters use an awkward portage on the left up over rocks and into a steep ravine; some prefer to portage on an airy ledge on the right above the falls. In either case, put in again after passing a second, smaller falls 80 yards downstream. After several more drops, another unrunnable 30-foot double falls must be portaged on the left. On the right, a short, easy trail leads up to a logging road on the canyon rim at this point.

The next 2 miles until Canyon Drop are considerably easier. However, in two places the river narrows into a tight class IV drop with undercut rocky borders. These drops, which deserve scouting, have destroyed at least one kayak. The first is known as "Spider Man" for the tendency to find oneself up against the undercut wall on river right. The next is an innocent-looking slot called "The Green Gash." Enter this drop with a slight angle to the left; there is a serious depression against the wall on the river right that tends to recirculate swimmers back into the drop. The beginning of Canyon Drop (V) can be recognized by the obvious approach of violent rapids between narrow rock walls as the river turns to the right and drops out of sight—eddy out on the right. This intimidating rapid can be previewed while peering down from the remains of a burned-out log bridge. A private dirt road leads to Highway 141 from this point, but it is closed to public use. It should be used only when necessity excuses the trespass. Canyon Drop and the rapid immediately following—Stairstep (V)—are not easily portaged.

Those two rapids are perhaps the most difficult and certainly the scariest rapids on the river. They require precise maneuvering around holes and boulders that funnel the boater toward potential collisions with the sheer rock canyon wall. Even during the very low flows of August and September, these two rapids are still very powerful and tricky. During the winter and spring, when the river volume is high, these rapids approach the limits of sane kayaking for experts familiar with the river. Look these drops over well.

Several class IV drops follow after the canyon. The second major drop appears less than a mile below the first; scout on the left. Although this drop is not as technical as the first, the penalty for a swim here is much more severe, for less than a few hundred yards downriver lies a 14-foot waterfall. The falls are recognized by a sweeping right turn in the river and should be portaged on the right. At least one boater has inadvertently run this falls upside down and backward. A terrorizing thought at best. Boaters can either launch off the cliff, vertically 14 feet, or attempt to enter their boats in a small eddy just down river, not an easy feat. From here on, a boater can finally relax and reflect on a successful run. The next mile or more of the river is pleasant class III. Just before the end of the run, there are a few more class IV drops, and then a dubious 10-foot falls—B Z Falls—that should be portaged, although some paddlers choose to run it. After going over the falls, most of the water bounces off the left side of the canyon wall and is thrown violently back to the right. The falls lie 100 yards downstream from a water diversion powerhouse. The eddies on the right above the falls are small, and the current moving to the falls is very swift. Although these eddies are not especially difficult to catch, the proximity of the falls can be unnerving—more than one boater has inadvertently rolled over in the current, recovered too slowly, missed the last eddy, and then been swept over B Z Falls. Thankfully, no one has been injured. The portage around B Z Falls follows the ledge above the river on the right until it is possible to scramble down a gully back down to the water.

B Z Corner is just 0.25 mile downstream. Take out under the bridge immediately after the last rapid and climb up a steep but well-worn trail on the left to Highway 141 above.

To reach the take-out at B Z Corner, from Hwy 14 in Bingen, turn left and follow Hwy 141 north to B Z Corner. Take out at the bridge at B Z Corner.

◆ MIDDLE WHITE SALMON RIVER

Put-in: Bridge at B Z Corner
Take-out: Just above the bridge and falls at Husum
Distance: 4 miles
Gradient: 45 feet/mile
**Volume and difficulty: 800–1,300 CFS*, class III; greater than
    1,300 CFS*, class IV**
Optimum: 1,200 CFS*
Portages: None
* measured at the Underwood gauge

This is the most popular section of the White Salmon River for boaters with intermediate skills. The numerous rapids are still confined within narrow canyon walls, but the gradient is much less than in the section above B Z Corner. An ability to maneuver through whitewater with some precision is still required, as several of the drops lie hidden around small bends in the river.

The river runs in a small canyon with lush vegetation growing from the walls and is seemingly quite isolated from the surrounding farmland. The numerous springs that enter the White Salmon above B Z Corner keep the water level sufficiently high on this section to allow a run throughout most of the summer. Even in August, when rivers elsewhere have long since dwindled to small trickles, there will be many small play waves and holes here.

See the gauge information for the upper White Salmon River.

For directions to the put-in at B Z Corner, see the directions to the take-out for the upper White Salmon River. Boaters usually begin this run by putting in just upstream from the rapid below the bridge at B Z Corner. This long rapid, with a few holes to upset the unwary, is more powerful than those downriver. It can easily be bypassed if desired. Boaters may put in on the west side of the river after paying a small fee for use of the maintained path. Rubber rafts belonging to private parties, as well as the rafts of several commercial outfitters, are lowered down to the river on a cable system from this point. There is also a steep, unimproved fishermen's path starting near the east end of the bridge that leads down to the opposite side of the river.

Grasshopper, Corkscrew, and Waterspout are some of the named class III rapids that are within the first mile of this run. About 1 mile before Husum, the canyon walls recede, the pace eases considerably, and the river meanders through open farmland.

Take out on the right bank, well above Husum Falls, at a small dirt ramp. Husum Falls—about a 10-foot pour-over—is run on occasion by kayaks and rafts; a portage is highly recommended. To reach the take-out at Husum, from Hwy 14 in Bingen, turn left and follow Hwy 141 north to Husum. Take out just above the bridge and falls at Husum.

◆ LOWER WHITE SALMON RIVER

Put-in: Bridge at Husum
Take-out: Northwestern Lake
Distance: 3 miles
Gradient: 25 feet/mile
Volume and difficulty: 800–1,200 CFS, class II+
Optimum: 1,000 CFS
Portages: None

This is a good run for novice boaters. It requires some maneuvering around boulders protruding in small, rocky drops. The rapids are mostly clustered together within the first mile of the run. After that point, the river drifts slowly to Northwestern Lake through picturesque forests.

See the gauge information for the upper White Salmon River run.

Put in just below Husum Falls. See the directions to the take-out on the middle White Salmon River run. Take out at the boat ramp on Northwestern Lake. The park concessionaire charges for the use of this landing. To reach the take-out at Northwestern Lake, from Hwy 14 in Bingen turn left and take Hwy 141 north through White Salmon. About 7 miles from Hwy 14, turn left to Northwestern Lake.

FURTHER READING

Garren, John. *Oregon River Tours.* 6th ed. Garren Publishing, 1991.

North, Douglass A. *Washington Whitewater.* The Mountaineers Books, 1992.

Tejada-Flores, Lito. *Wildwater.* The Sierra Club, 1978.

Willamette Kayak and Canoe Club. *Soggy Sneakers Guide to Oregon Rivers.* 2d ed. 1986.

◆

BICYCLING

By Philip N. Jones

What kind of roads are best for bicycling? Some riders prefer lonely back roads, narrow and winding, but devoid of traffic. Others prefer steep mountain roads, where legs get the maximum workout and scenery is majestic. Still others prefer the straight and flat, where miles disappear effortlessly.

An abandoned section of the Columbia River Highway, now the Starvation–Viento Trail

The Columbia Gorge offers all of those kinds of roads, if you know where to look. The main highways that traverse the length of the Gorge are often straight and flat, offering the fastest route from one end of the Gorge to the other. Side trips up tributary valleys offer steep mountain roads and lonely farm roads. And the incomparable Columbia River Highway offers cycling on a unique historic road preserved from the days of the Model T.

But cycling in the Gorge is not all beautiful scenery, lonely roads, and historic highways. Many of the roads are narrow and, in places, dangerous. Many are heavily trafficked, and the persistent winds of the Gorge can stop even the most powerful pedalers. During the winter, the Gorge can be as icy as a freezer. The geography of the Gorge often severely limits alternative routes. Unlike the flat Willamette Valley, with its many farm roads often laid out in a grid pattern, or the rolling plains of eastern Oregon, the Gorge is a confining place to bicycle, since the steep cliffs and river canyons have long limited the dreams of road builders.

The purpose of this chapter is to acquaint the reader with the opportunities and limitations of riding in the Gorge. After a brief overview of riding conditions and recommended equipment, a few suggested rides are presented, but readers are encouraged to study local road maps and branch out on their own, looking for roads not often found by motorists or other cyclists.

Bicycle trips in the Gorge can generally be divided into two categories: east–west rides through the Gorge, and scenic diversions into the tributary valleys. In general, the east–west highways follow level routes along the Columbia, while the side trips are hilly adventures into the foothills and mountains of the Cascade Range, although both of those observations have their exceptions.

Preparation

MAJOR HIGHWAYS IN THE GORGE

Two major highways run the full length of the Gorge. On the Oregon side, Interstate 84 (formerly Interstate 80 North) begins in Portland and passes through Troutdale, Cascade Locks, Hood River, The Dalles, and Biggs before heading off to eastern Oregon and eventually joining I-80 near Salt Lake City. It is a modern limited-access freeway; only 37 exits are available in its 86-mile passage through the Gorge. (Appendix B consists of a list of those exits.)

In Oregon, bicycle riding is permitted on interstate freeways except within the Portland metropolitan area. In the Gorge, all of Interstate 84 is open to cycling, since Troutdale exit 17 marks the eastern edge of the restricted zone.

Many riders detest freeway riding, preferring the slow-paced quiet of back roads. However, Interstate 84 is clearly the fastest route from one end of the Gorge to the other. The shoulders are generally wide and free of gravel, and the roadway is unbelievably level, especially considering the awesome terrain of the Gorge. The roar of high-speed traffic a few feet away may limit the aesthetic experience of cycling through the scenic grandeur of the Gorge, but for many the speed makes up for the unpleasant distraction.

The other route through the length of the Gorge is Highway 14 on the Washington side of the Columbia. It begins in Vancouver, Washington, and passes through several small towns—including Camas, Washougal, North Bonneville, Stevenson, Bingen, and Maryhill—before extending east to Pasco and Kennewick. An older, two-lane road, Highway 14 is much less traveled than Interstate 84. For those seeking to avoid the rush of the freeway, Highway 14 is the only other choice for a continuous route through the Gorge. It has several of its own drawbacks, however. Its shoulders are often narrow or even nonexistent. The climb up over Cape Horn (25 miles east of Vancouver) is exhausting, although the view from the top is stunning. And the seven highway tunnels east of Stevenson are very narrow, even though they are thankfully short.

A third alternative exists, but can only be used for two sections of the Oregon side. That third alternative is the Columbia River Highway, the aesthetically dramatic road described in an earlier chapter. Originally built in 1915, it was the first road through the Gorge. When Interstate 84 was constructed in the early 1950s, the central section of the Columbia River Highway was, regrettably, destroyed although a few small sections remain. Only the western section (from Troutdale to John Yeon State Park) and the eastern section (from Mosier to The Dalles) are intact. Today those two remaining sections are popularly (and justifiably) known as the scenic highway. They are narrow, hilly, extremely winding, and (in the case of the western section) heavily trafficked, but the surrounding landscape and aesthetic design far excel that of Interstate 84 or Highway 14.

Highway 14 and the two intact sections of the Columbia River Highway are among the rides described at the end of this chapter. Interstate 84 is not described in detail—riders contemplating a trip through the Gorge on Interstate 84 should consult the list of exits in Appendix B and any decent road map. Little else is needed. Although the 100-mile route through the Gorge on Washington Highway 14 is described below, no map or mileage log is provided, since the route follows Highway 14 for the entire distance.

A detailed description of a 338-mile ride up and back on both sides of the Gorge, utilizing Highway 14, Interstate 84, and the Columbia River Highway in addition to some back roads, is contained in *Bicycling the Backroads of Southwest Washington*, listed at the end of this chapter.

When planning a ride through the Gorge, a little imagination in route planning goes a long way. Although only two highways run the length of the Gorge, and the scenic highway traverses only two sections of the Gorge, those three choices can be mixed and matched, particularly since three bridges cross the Columbia in the Gorge, allowing riders to switch from one side of the river to the other. The bridges are located at Cascade Locks (the Bridge of the Gods), Hood River, and The Dalles. In addition, Interstate 205 crosses the Columbia on the Glenn Jackson Bridge just west of the Gorge, while the Sam Hill Memorial Bridge crosses the river between Maryhill and Biggs at the east end of the Gorge.

Of these five bridges, only the Glenn Jackson Bridge, with its wide bike path located between the northbound and southbound lanes, was designed for safe cycling. The other bridges are narrow two-lane roads, and can be dangerous to cyclists. Some have relatively low guard rails. Some of the bridges are not paved, but instead are constructed of perforated steel. As a result, the moving water below and the exposure are both readily apparent to cyclists, an effect that can be quite unnerving.

At the time of publication, both the Hood River Bridge and the Bridge of the Gods charged a toll, although the Hood River Bridge did not charge cyclists.

Nevertheless, the bridges offer cyclists a degree of flexibility. For example, a ride east through the Gorge might begin in Troutdale and follow the Columbia River Highway up over Crown Point, past Multnomah Falls to John Yeon State Park. From there, one could complete the trip to the east end of the Gorge on Interstate 84 or, by continuing east on Interstate 84 for only 7 miles, one could cross over to the Washington side on the Bridge of the Gods. The route could then be completed on Highway 14, or the rider could return to the Oregon shore at Hood River or The Dalles. A return at Hood River would require 5 miles of freeway riding before the Columbia River Highway could be rejoined at Mosier (although the abandoned section of the Columbia River Highway between Hood River and Mosier may someday be reopened for bicycle traffic).

When planning such a mix-and-match ride, choose the route carefully. For example, the seven narrow tunnels of Highway 14 are all located east of Stevenson, and the west ends of Highway 14 and the Columbia River Highway are both hilly, as is the section of the Columbia River Highway between Mosier and The Dalles.

In contrast to the highways that traverse the length of the Gorge, the side valleys offer back roads not heavily traveled by motor traffic. A few of the side valleys contain major highways (such as Oregon State Highway 35 in the Hood River Valley). Some of those side valleys offer rolling farm roads to explore, particularly the Hood River Valley with its extensive orchards, or the White Salmon River Valley in Washington. But one should expect many hills to climb and descend, as the routes follow the rivers that originate high in the mountains.

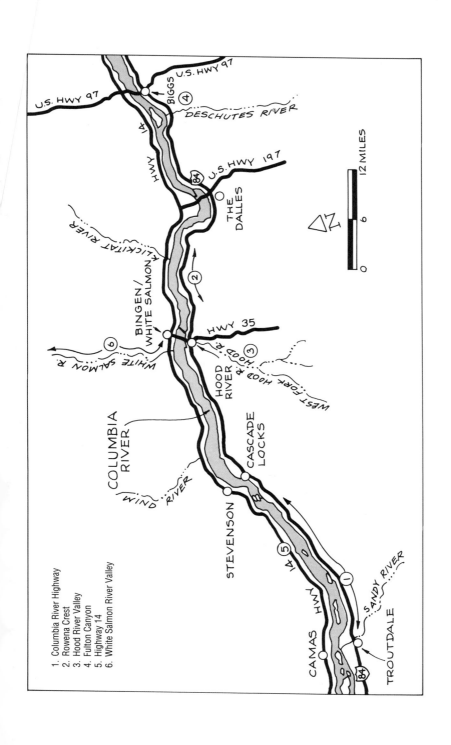

1. Columbia River Highway
2. Rowena Crest
3. Hood River Valley
4. Fulton Canyon
5. Highway 14
6. White Salmon River Valley

U.S. HWY 97

U.S. HWY 97

BIGGS

④

DESCHUTES RIVER

HWY 97

U.S. HWY 197

84

THE DALLES

KLICKITAT RIVER

②

BINGEN/
WHITE SALMON

HWY 35

⑥

WHITE SALMON R.

③

HOOD
RIVER

HOOD R.

WEST FORK HOOD R.

COLUMBIA
RIVER

CASCADE
LOCKS

WIND RIVER

84

STEVENSON

14 ⑤

14 ⑤

CAMAS HWY

SANDY RIVER

①

84

TROUTDALE

N

0   6   12 MILES

WEATHER

Weather should be taken into account when planning a ride. During summer months, westerly winds blow through the Gorge three days out of four. Obviously, a west-to-east ride benefits from those winds, while an east-to-west ride is hindered. If east winds come up during the winter, they often bring frigid arctic air into the Gorge from eastern Washington and Oregon. The chapter on weather describes the wind conditions of the Gorge in some detail. In general, weather being experienced elsewhere in the Northwest is often magnified in the Gorge.

EQUIPMENT

Equipment should be chosen carefully. A lightweight, expensive bike is not required, but one in good working order is essential. Bike shops are few and far between in the Gorge, and many of the hills of the Gorge are so long and steep that good tires and brakes must never be overlooked. A blowout or a brake failure on a long descent is a serious affair.

Mountain-bike riders can find gravel roads to ride by reviewing Forest Service maps, but the routes described in this chapter are all paved and suitable for road bikes with narrow rims and tires.

Gearing must be chosen with the route and load in mind. A quick ride along Interstate 84 with a light load could easily be done with the gearing found on almost any bike, since the level route will not require extra-low or extra-high gears. On the other hand, a scenic tour up some of the side valleys with a heavy load requires very low gears, particularly for those in less than perfect shape. Some riders believe that a low gear of 40 inches is sufficient for such rides, while others would prefer to go as low as 30 inches. For a more detailed discussion of gearing choices in particular, and choosing equipment in general, several good bicycling books are available. See the listing at the end of this chapter.

Rides

Six recommended rides are described below. They are listed from west to east on both the Oregon and the Washington side. They vary in length from the 100-mile ride from Vancouver to Maryhill on Highway 14 to the 9.8-mile ride from Mosier to Rowena on the eastern section of the Columbia River Highway. With the exception of the route on Highway 14, all are relatively short rides designed to be completed in a day or less; the average length of the day rides is only 37 miles, a distance that even inexperienced riders can cover in a day.

Each trip description is preceded by an information block that describes the starting point and points of interest along the way, plus lists the distance covered, the cumulative elevation gain, the recommended time of year and the recommended starting time, and the estimated time needed to cover the route. Each trip description is followed by a mileage log.

When selecting a ride, use the distance covered and the cumulative elevation gain as the best measure of the effort required to complete the route. As a general rule of thumb, allow about 1 hour to cover every 10 miles, assuming you would like to stop along the way for sightseeing, lunch, et cetera.

OREGON SIDE

◆ COLUMBIA RIVER HIGHWAY

Start: Lewis and Clark State Park, near Troutdale, just south of I-84 exit 18
Distance: Up to 49.8 miles
Terrain: Hilly
Cumulative elevation gain: 1,900 feet
Time of year: Any season, except during freezing conditions
Starting time: 9:00 A.M.
Allow 6 hours

When the Columbia River Highway opened in 1915, it was acclaimed as both an engineering marvel and an aesthetic masterpiece. The story of its design and construction is told in an earlier chapter.

This ride covers the intact western half of the highway, starting near Troutdale, slowly climbing up over Crown Point, and then descending to near water level, to pass at the feet of many of the Gorge's spectacular waterfalls. Along the way, it visits eight state parks, including the Vista House at Crown Point, and crosses several historic highway bridges.

Although the entire western section of 24.9 miles is described as an out-and-back trip of 49.8 miles, it can be shortened by a U-turn at any point, or the ride could be started at any of the parks or waterfalls along the highway. For example, the climb over Crown Point can be avoided by starting at Latourell Falls, just east of Crown Point.

One caution: the Columbia River Highway was designed for Model Ts. It is narrow, twisting, and, on sunny days, populated by tourists paying more attention to the scenery than to the road. Ride carefully.

0.0 Lewis and Clark State Park (day use only; water available). Leave the parking lot and turn left. Follow this road past the Troutdale bridge at 0.3 mile and the Stark Street bridge at 2.9 miles.
3.3 The entrance to Dabney State Park is on the right (day use only;

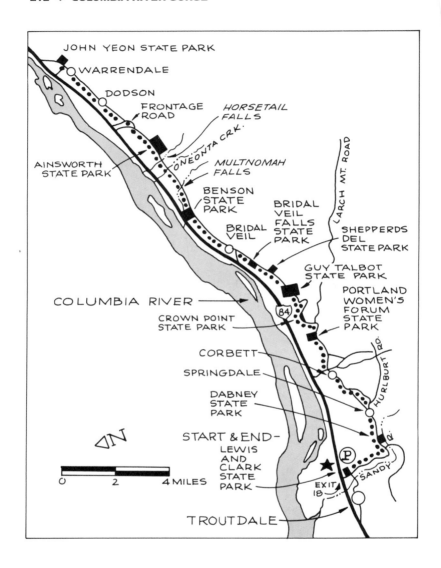

water available).

4.6 Springdale. Bear right, following the signs to Crown Point.

4.8 Bear left at the intersection with Hurlburt Road.

6.3 Corbett.

8.8 Portland Women's Forum State Park (day use only; water available). Probably the most famous view of the Gorge is available from this

The descent from Crown Point

park located at Chanticleer Point.

9.2 Intersection with Larch Mountain Road. Bear left.

10.0 Crown Point State Park, consisting of the Vista House. The highway curves around the front of Vista House, then drops (at a 5 percent grade, the maximum permitted by Samuel C. Lancaster, the designer of the highway) through a series of Lancaster's graceful 100-foot-radius curves.

12.4 Latourell Falls day use area, part of Guy Talbot State Park (water available). Walk your bike up a short path for a full view of the falls. Also note the craftsmanship of the highway bridge over Latourell Creek. It is probably the only braced spandrel concrete arched bridge in the state, and one of the first built in the United States.

Multnomah Falls

13.7 Shepperds Dell State Park (day use only; water not available). A short path at the east end of the bridge gives excellent views of the bridge and Shepperds Dell Falls.

14.7 Bridal Veil Bridge. This small bridge is supported by its solid railings rather than supported from below, to allow clearance for the three log flumes and the small dam that once lay beneath it.

15.3 Bridal Veil. Continue east on the Columbia River Hwy, rather than turning left to the freeway.

17.9 Wahkeena Falls, part of Benson State Park.

18.5 Multnomah Falls, the highest in Oregon at a combined height of 620 feet (store; water available). On both sides of the falls, the highway traverses steep ground on concrete viaducts.

20.8 Oneonta Creek. The present highway bridge was built in 1948 to replace the original 1914 bridge, which is now used as a wayside. Note the evidence of the tunnel to the east, which was closed when the new bridge was built.

21.1 Horsetail Falls.

21.6 Ainsworth State Park picnic area. An overnight camping area is located at mile 23.8 (water available).

22.4 Intersection with I-84. Turn right, following the signs toward I-84 eastbound. A short section of the scenic highway was destroyed by the construction of this interchange.

22.7 Turn right onto Frontage Road. At mile 22.8, Frontage Road rejoins the old alignment of the Columbia River Hwy.

23.1 Dodson. The large barn on the south side of the road was built circa 1870. Above it sits a basalt formation known as St. Peters Dome.

24.0 Warrendale.

24.9 John Yeon State Park (day use only; no water available). East of this point, the scenic highway was destroyed by the construction of I-84. This is the eastern end of this ride. Make a U-turn and proceed west, retracing the route back to Lewis and Clark State Park.

49.8 Lewis and Clark State Park. End of ride.

◆ ROWENA CREST

Start: Mosier (I-84 exit 69)
Distance: 9.8 miles
Terrain: Very hilly
Cumulative elevation gain: 600 feet
Time of year: Any season
Starting time: 2:00 P.M. or earlier
Allow 2 hours

Rowena Crest is the most prominent viewpoint on the eastern section of the Columbia River Highway. A lofty 700 feet above the Columbia

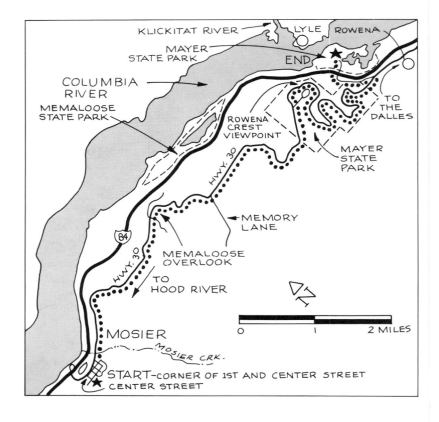

River, Rowena Crest offers commanding views up the river toward The Dalles and across the river to the mouth of the Klickitat River and the town of Lyle. In the foreground, the Rowena Loops of the Columbia River Highway wind their way down from Rowena Crest to the community of Rowena.

Like the graceful curves of the highway beneath Crown Point on the western section of the highway, the Rowena Loops are typical of the careful craftsmanship demonstrated by Samuel C. Lancaster when he designed the Columbia River Highway. Earlier proposals to build a highway through the steep terrain of the Gorge had employed unacceptably steep grades and sharp curves, but Lancaster's design employed a roadbed that never exceeded a slope of 5 percent and never used a curve of less than a 100-foot radius. Where others would have used steep grades and hairpin turns to negotiate the cliffs below Rowena Crest, Lancaster employed the graceful S-curves (the Rowena Loops) so easily viewed from the crest.

Other features of the highway are also evident on this short ride. Watch for the cement mileposts installed along the highway in 1991, replicas of the original mileposts erected in 1915. Near Rowena Crest, the highway is lined by carefully crafted stone railings, typical of the attention to detail shown throughout the length of the highway. In Mosier, the route crosses the Mosier Creek Bridge, an early example of the arched concrete bridges that would soon bring fame to their designer, Conde B. McCullough. He served as state bridge engineer from 1919 to 1938, and is particularly remembered for the magnificent arched bridges he designed on the Oregon coast in the 1930s.

The Rowena area is not just noted for the preservation of the Columbia River Highway. It is also noted for a Nature Conservancy preserve, named for former governor Tom McCall and dedicated to the preservation of the many wildflowers that occur on Rowena Crest.

This ride begins in the town of Mosier, rides up the gentle slope to Rowena Crest, then drops down through the Rowena Loops to the tiny community of Rowena and a riverfront park, Mayer State Park. The ride can be done in either direction, although the eastern section (the Rowena Loops) is the steeper of the two. The ride is described as a one-way trip, which requires a car shuttle. (Although riding on the freeway back to Mosier is legally permissible, it cannot be described as pleasant. In contrast, a two-way ride on the Columbia River Highway is quite pleasant, if strenuous. A lunch break at Mayer State Park helps riders recover from the climb up to the crest and catch their breath after the exhilarating drop through the loops.)

0.0 Corner of Center Street and Hwy 30 in Mosier, near an undeveloped city park. Proceed east on Hwy 30.

0.2 Hwy 30 crosses Mosier Creek on a 1920 reinforced concrete arch bridge, designed by C. B. McCullough. A short trail leads upstream to Mosier Creek Falls.

2.9 Watch for an inconspicuous turnout on the north side of the highway; just a few feet north is Memaloose Overlook, offering grand vistas of the Columbia.

6.5 Turn right at a sign pointing to Rowena Crest Overlook. On the north side of the road is Tom McCall Preserve at Rowena Plateau, a Nature Conservancy preserve dedicated to the protection of the wildflowers of Rowena Crest.

6.6 Rowena Crest Overlook, part of Mayer State Park. Views of the upper Gorge. To the east, the Rowena Loops of the Columbia River Hwy wind down to the river. Across the Columbia, the town of Lyle stands next to the mouth of the Klickitat River. Return to Hwy 30.

6.8 Turn right onto Hwy 30.

7.0 The stone railing of the Columbia River Hwy is interrupted by one of the original observatories. As the highway drops down through the

Rowena Loops, watch carefully for loose gravel on the roadway.

9.0 Turn left, following signs to East Mayer State Park.

9.7 After crossing over I-84 and railroad tracks, turn right into the park.

9.8 Mayer State Park. End of ride.

◆ HOOD RIVER VALLEY

Start: Waucoma Park in Hood River, at the corner of 13th and State streets (I-84 exit 63)
Distance: 42 miles
Terrain: Flat to moderately hilly
Cumulative elevation gain: 3,000 feet
Time of year: Spring, summer, or fall
Starting time: 10:00 A.M.
Allow 4 to 5 hours

The Hood River Valley is known for its fruit orchards, views of the north face of Mount Hood, and snow-fed mountain streams. This ride begins in the town of Hood River and travels up the valley, halfway to Mount Hood, before looping back to Hood River. Along the way, it stops at several parks, passes through miles of orchards, crosses several mountain streams, and offers numerous views of Mount Hood and even a few of Mount Adams, across the Columbia to the north.

This is a particularly good ride to take in the spring, when the orchards are in full bloom. The blossoms are usually at their best in late April; Hood River's annual blossom festival is often held the last Sunday in April. Another good time to visit the area is in the fall, when many of the farmers operate fruit stands along the route.

The route visits four small parks. The first, Panorama Point County Park, is aptly named for its view of the valley, its orchards, and Mount Hood. Situated on a small knoll just 3 miles from Hood River, it is an excellent destination for a very short ride.

The other three parks are Waucoma Park in Hood River, Oak Grove Park in the community of Oak Grove, and Tucker Park along the banks of the Hood River. The latter, a secluded park offering picnicking and camping, is a fine spot for lunch.

Several variations can be made to this route. For a shorter ride, the map shows several points—particularly near the town of Odell—where shortcuts can be taken.

To the south, some interesting lava beds can be visited by riding west from Parkdale (mile 21.7) on Lava Bed Road.

On the west side of the loop, Punchbowl Falls (not to be confused with the smaller, better-known Punch Bowl Falls on Eagle Creek) can be visited by turning west at the community of Dee (mile 27). When Punchbowl Road is reached, follow it north for about 1 mile. The falls can be

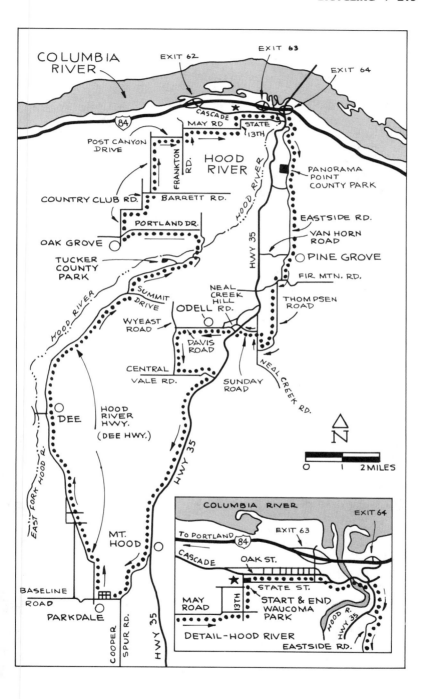

viewed just downstream from a bridge over the West Fork of the Hood River.

Another diversion, this one east of the route, may become available in the near future. By continuing straight, rather than turning right, at mile 1.1, the route of the 1915 Columbia River Highway can be followed east toward Mosier. Unfortunately, the road is now gated, since two highway tunnels were closed and filled with rubble in the 1960s. However, the tunnels have been studied for possible reopening for bicycle and pedestrian use. If they are reopened, cyclists will be able to follow the historic highway from Hood River to Rowena, and then on to The Dalles, without having to use Interstate 84.

Almost all of the roads on this route are lonely farm roads. Although shoulders are nonexistent, traffic is very light. In a few sections, notably on Highway 35, traffic can be heavy and fast. Although those sections are brief, ride carefully.

0.0 Waucoma Park, at the corner of State and Thirteenth streets in Hood River. Ride east on State Street.

0.7 State Street joins Hwy 30. Continue east on Hwy 30, but watch carefully for traffic.

1.0 Hwy 30 crosses the Hood River on a new bridge, built in 1982 to replace a 1918 bridge that had been the largest on the Columbia River Hwy.

1.1 Turn right onto Hwy 35. The shoulder is very narrow, so ride carefully.

1.4 Turn left onto Eastside Road, following signs to Panorama Point.

3.0 Turn right into Panorama Point County Park (day use only).

3.2 Panorama Point. After enjoying the views, return to Eastside Road.

3.4 Turn right (south) onto Eastside Road.

5.6 Eastside Road curves to the southwest.

5.8 Bear left on Eastside Road at an intersection with Van Horn Road in the community of Pine Grove.

6.6 Turn right at a T-intersection with Fir Mountain Road (Moore Road).

6.7 Turn left (south) onto Thomsen Road. Eventually, Thomsen Road curves to the west.

8.8 Turn right (north) onto Neal Creek Road.

9.3 Turn left (west) onto Sunday Road.

9.8 Turn left onto Hwy 35. Watch carefully for traffic.

10.0 Turn right onto Davis Road at a sign pointing to Odell.

10.8 When the arterial turns right (north) to the town of Odell, continue straight (west), following a sign pointing to Dukes Valley.

11.6 Turn left (south) at an intersection with Wyeast Road.

13.0 Turn left at a T-intersection with Central Vale Road.

14.0 Turn right onto Hwy 35. Since Hwy 35 has a moderate amount of traffic, ride carefully.

Hood River Valley from Panorama Point

19.2 When Hwy 35 enters the community of Mount Hood (store), turn right onto Cooper Spur Road at a sign pointing to Parkdale.

21.1 Turn right onto Baseline Road, following a sign pointing to Parkdale and Dee.

21.7 In Parkdale, follow the arterial when it curves right (north), following signs to Dee.

24.3 The route passes a store.

27.0 The community of Dee.

31.0 At a Y-intersection with Summit Drive, bear left, following signs toward Hood River.

32.8 Turn left into Tucker County Park (camping, picnicking, water available, rest rooms). This attractive county park is located along the main branch of the Hood River.

33.2 Return to the main road and turn left (east).

34.6 Turn left onto Portland Drive.

36.7 Community of Oak Grove. Turn right (north) onto Country Club Road. One block south is Oak Grove County Park, formerly a schoolyard. The schoolhouse is still standing, but is now a private residence.

37.4 Follow Country Club Road when it turns right (east).

38.7 Although the arterial continues east on Barrett Road, turn left (north), following Country Club Road. At mile 37.9, it turns north, and at 38.4 it turns east again.

39.2 Turn right onto Post Canyon Drive. (The perfectly symmetrical peak visible to the north is 2,755-foot Underwood Mountain, on the Washington side of the Gorge.)

40.0 Turn left (north) at a T-intersection with Frankton Road.

40.2 Turn right (east) onto May Road.

41.7 Turn left onto Thirteenth Street.

41.9 Turn right onto State Street.

42.0 Turn left into Waucoma Park. End of ride.

◆ FULTON CANYON

Start: Deschutes River State Park, on Hwy 206 east of The Dalles. From I-84, take exit 97, then drive east to the park.
Distance: 32.5 miles
Terrain: Hilly
Cumulative elevation gain: 1,900 feet
Time of year: All year
Starting time: Before noon
Allow 3 hours

This ride, at the extreme eastern end of the Gorge, is wholly within Sherman County, a sparsely populated wheat-farming area with a total population of about 2,500 in its 831 square miles. That's less than three people per square mile.

This ride starts at the mouth of the Deschutes River and climbs steep Fulton Canyon to Wasco, then descends Scott Canyon to the town of Rufus on the Columbia. The route then follows the old highway to Biggs Junction and then to the mouth of the Deschutes.

The few towns in Sherman County are tiny. Its county seat, Moro, has a population of less than 300. This ride visits three other Sherman County communities—Rufus, Wasco, and Biggs Junction. Of the three, Wasco has the most population, about 400.

Sherman County hasn't always been that small. At the turn of the century, the county was a thriving region, with a plethora of businesses serving the wheat ranchers. Today, the once-bustling towns are sleepy little burgs. But all is not lost; being an economic backwater has meant that many of the historic structures of Sherman County are still standing.

The town of Wasco is typical. Once served by the railroad, Wasco was an important grain shipper. Now the railroad is gone and the tracks have been torn up, but the original brick buildings, many unoccupied, still stand in tribute to a busier era.

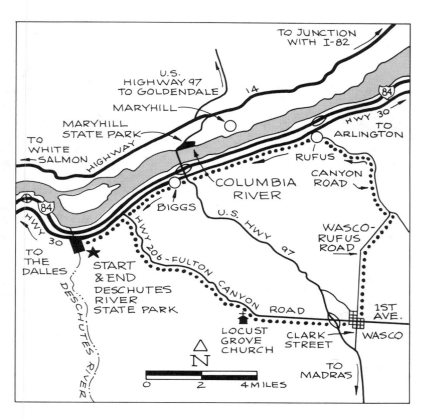

0.0 Deschutes River State Park day use area. Leave the park and turn right (east) onto Hwy 30.

1.9 Turn right on Hwy 206 (Fulton Canyon Road). The next 4 miles are steep and winding.

8.3 Locust Grove Church. Built in 1895, this small church was last used in 1914. Unfortunately, the building is now in private hands and is used as a barn.

12.1 Intersection with US 97. Continue east on Fulton Canyon Road.

12.8 Fulton Canyon Road enters Wasco and becomes First Avenue. A city park (water available) is on the right. This quaint town is characterized by several historic brick buildings, many with faded advertisements painted on their sides. Although the railroad once passed through Wasco, the tracks were removed years ago.

12.9 At the corner of First and Clark, turn left (north) and follow the signs toward Rufus.

Locust Grove Church

13.1 Continue straight, rather than turning left toward US 97 and The Dalles.
14.0 Views of Mount Hood and Mount Adams. At 21.1 first glimpses of the Columbia River to the north.
22.5 When the road enters Rufus, it curves to the north and becomes Main Street.
22.6 Rufus (store, cafe). Turn left at an intersection with First Street. This becomes Hwy 30; continue west.
25.9 Stonehenge Memorial is visible on the bluffs across the Columbia.
27.0 The Sam Hill Memorial Bridge is visible downstream, leading to the Washington town of Maryhill and Maryhill State Park. To the west, Mount Hood rises above the Oregon side of the Gorge.
27.8 Biggs (store, cafe). Continue west through an intersection with US 97.
30.6 Fulton Canyon Road is on the left. Continue west on Hwy 30.
32.3 Turn left into Deschutes River State Park.
32.5 Day use area. End of ride.

WASHINGTON SIDE

◆ HIGHWAY 14

Start: Various points
Distance: Up to 103 miles
Terrain: Mostly moderate; some long hills
Cumulative elevation gain: 3,300 feet
Time of year: Spring through fall
Starting time: 8:00 A.M.
Allow 1 to 3 days

Washington state Highway 14 runs the entire length of the Columbia River Gorge, from Vancouver to Maryhill. Along the way, it visits several small towns, including Camas, Washougal, North Bonneville, Stevenson, Bingen/White Salmon, and Lyle. The road is narrow, lacks shoulders, and passes through seven narrow tunnels. Nevertheless, for experienced cyclists able to deal safely with such conditions, it is an excellent way to see the Gorge.

For most riders, this is a 2- or 3-day ride. Although racers or marathon riders could complete the route in a day, little time would be left to enjoy the spectacular scenery and points of interest. Some of those include Fort Vancouver National Historic Site, the spectacular views from Cape Horn, Beacon Rock State Park, the north shore visitor center at Bonneville Dam, Horsethief Lake State Park, Maryhill Museum and State Park, and Stonehenge Memorial.

For overnight riders, a few campgrounds are available along the route. In addition, bed-and-breakfast inns have sprung up in many of the small towns, taking much of the suffering out of bike touring.

Stores and restaurants are available in the towns mentioned above, as well as in several of the smaller communities.

Unfortunately, the Washington side of the Gorge is relatively devoid of parks. Developed state parks, for example, number only three (Beacon Rock, Horsethief Lake, and Maryhill), although undeveloped windsurf sites (such as Doug's Beach) have now been acquired by the state. In contrast, the Oregon side of the Gorge boasts sixteen state parks.

Neither a detailed mileage log nor a map are provided here, since the route simply follows Highway 14, although back roads can be used in the western end of the Gorge to avoid the heavy, high-speed traffic in the vicinity of Vancouver, Camas, and Washougal.

If you start in downtown Vancouver, the route is 102.3 miles to the Sam Hill Memorial Bridge at the eastern end of the Gorge. However, several alternate starting points could be considered. For example, the route could start in Portland and cross over to Highway 14 via the modern new bike path on the Glenn Jackson Bridge of Interstate 205. Other alternate starting points include Fort Vancouver National Historic Site or the town of Camas. The route can also be ridden from east to west, rather than west to east, although summer winds favor the latter direction of travel.

The western section of the ride is definitely hilly, as it climbs 800 feet over Cape Horn, the prominent cliffs across the river from Bridal Veil, Oregon. The central section is comparatively flat, while the eastern section is a mixture of rolling hills that slowly regain the same 800-foot elevation reached at the summit of Cape Horn. The final 2 miles, however, are a near-vertical drop from the high bluffs of the Columbia Hills to Maryhill State Park and the Sam Hill Memorial Bridge.

◆ WHITE SALMON RIVER VALLEY

Start: Daubenspeck Park in Bingen, on Hwy 14 at milepost 66.7
Distance: 62.9 miles
Terrain: Hilly
Cumulative elevation gain: 2,100 feet
Time of year: Spring through fall
Starting time: 10:00 A.M.
Allow 6 hours

This ride runs the gamut from the shores of the Columbia River to the high plateau at the foot of Mount Adams. Along the way, the route follows a steep mountain river popular with whitewater kayakers (see the chapter on canoeing and kayaking) and visits several small towns. In the background stands majestic Mount Adams, at 12,307 feet the second-highest peak in Washington.

The ride starts in Bingen, near the Columbia, but climbs quickly to its twin sister, the town of White Salmon, just 1 mile up the hill. Both towns show signs of ersatz alpine chalet-style architecture, an attempt to imitate villages along the Rhine, such as Bingen, Germany. More genuine varieties of architecture are found later on the route. Look for old barns and Victorian farmhouses.

The towns quickly give way to evergreen hillsides and the deep canyons of the White Salmon River Valley. As the route climbs to the high plateau, those landscapes in turn give way to open pine forests, then scrub trees and orchards, and eventually farmland, while the roads turn from winding mountain routes to straight farm roads.

The northeastern section of the route passes through the Conboy Lake National Wildlife Refuge, a huge preserve dedicated to migratory ducks and geese. The best season to view the birdlife is from late February through April, when hordes of dusky Canada geese are present.

Carry drinking water, since few sources can be found along the way.

0.0 Daubenspeck Park, at the corner of Willow Street and Humboldt Avenue on the west end of Bingen. Ride east on Humboldt Avenue.

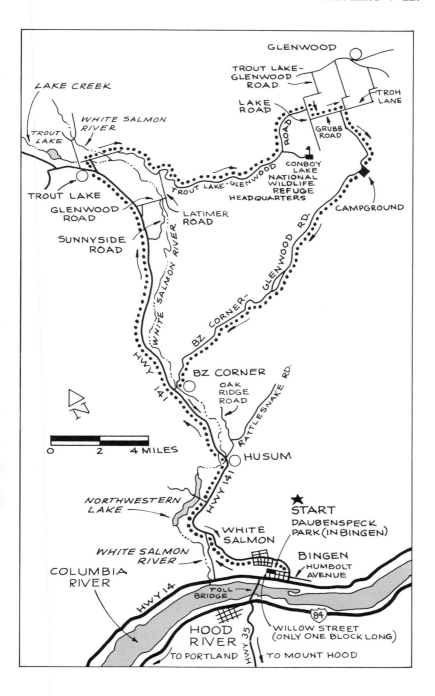

GLENWOOD

TROUT LAKE-
GLENWOOD
ROAD

TROH
LANE

LAKE CREEK

WHITE SALMON
RIVER

LAKE
ROAD

ROAD

GRUBB
ROAD

TROUT
LAKE

CONBOY
LAKE
NATIONAL
WILDLIFE
REFUGE
HEADQUARTERS

TROUT LAKE

TROUT LAKE-GLENWOOD

CAMPGROUND

GLENWOOD
ROAD

LATIMER
ROAD

SUNNYSIDE
ROAD

GLENWOOD RD.

WHITE SALMON RIVER

BZ CORNER-

HWY 141

BZ CORNER

RATTLESNAKE RD.

OAK
RIDGE
ROAD

N

0   2   4 MILES

HUSUM

NORTHWESTERN
LAKE

HWY 141

★
START
DAUBENSPECK
PARK (IN BINGEN)

WHITE
SALMON

WHITE SALMON
RIVER

BINGEN

HUMBOLT
AVENUE

COLUMBIA
RIVER

84

HWY 14

TOLL
BRIDGE

HOOD
RIVER

HWY 35

WILLOW STREET
(ONLY ONE BLOCK LONG)

TO PORTLAND

TO MOUNT HOOD

0.3 Turn left (north) onto Oak Street (Hwy 141).

1.5 White Salmon.

3.3 Follow Hwy 141 when it turns right at an intersection with Boyer Road.

6.9 A left turn at this intersection leads to a public park on Northwestern Lake (camping, store, picnicking), a reservoir formed by a dam on the White Salmon River.

8.9 Husum (store, cafe). Stay left, on Hwy 141.

12.9 B Z Corner (store, cafe). Stay left, on Hwy 141.

17.4 Trout Lake (store). Bear right, following a sign pointing to Glenwood. The road passes over the cascades of Trout Lake Creek.

17.6 Turn right onto an unmarked paved road marked by a sign pointing to Glenwood.

28.7 A gravel road on the right leads 1 mile to the headquarters of the Conboy Lake National Wildlife Refuge.

31.4 Turn right at a T-intersection with Lake Road.

31.9 Follow the arterial as it turns left and becomes Grubb Road.

32.9 Turn right onto an unmarked paved road.

36.5 The route passes a public campground, part of the wildlife refuge.

50.0 B Z Corner (store, cafe). Turn left onto Hwy 141.

54.0 Husum (store, cafe).

61.4 White Salmon.

62.6 Bingen. Turn right onto Humboldt Avenue.

62.9 Daubenspeck Park at the corner of Humboldt Avenue and Willow Street in Bingen. End of ride.

FURTHER READING

Bridge, Raymond. *Bike Touring: The Sierra Club Guide to Outings on Wheels.* Sierra Club Books, 1979.

Jones, Philip N. *Bicycling the Backroads of Northwest Oregon.* The Mountaineers Books, 1984. (2d ed., co-authored with Jean Henderson, due 1992.)

Woods, Bill, and Erin Woods. *Bicycling the Backroads of Southwest Washington.* 3rd ed. The Mountaineers Books, 1992.

PHOTOGRAPHY

BY STEWART HARVEY

It's not surprising that the spectacular geology of the Columbia River Gorge is a magnet for the camera. Since the opening of the Columbia River Highway in 1915, people have flocked to the Oregon side of the Gorge by the thousands, bringing cameras by the hundreds. The results have been thousands of pictures of waterfalls, basalt columns, and foliage. Most of the photographs, of course, have been made by hikers, tourists, and Sunday drivers, to whom the Gorge is a lush, colorful landscape replete with deep green ferns, white wake-robin trillium, bleeding heart, yellow bells, blue dicks, purple parsley, and gallons of cascading water. It's a weekend photographer's paradise, and a place where serious artists on both sides of the river have found a rich resource for personal response.

EARLY PHOTOGRAPHY IN THE GORGE

The waterfall and hiking areas of the southern shore are but a small portion of what has been a visually stimulating region for photographers of all levels for more than 120 years. Pioneer photographers have been drawn to Rooster Rock, the Grand Cascades, Celilo Falls, Castle Rock (now Beacon Rock), Maryhill, and Multnomah Falls since the 1860s. Their legacy has been a series of fine and sensitive statements about the Columbia River landscape, and a surprisingly relevant resource for contemporary image makers.

In those days, travel in the Gorge was arduous and photography equipment heavy. The "serious" photographer had to produce negatives at whatever size the finished prints were to be made, and so cameras were large. The common sizes would take 8x10- or 11x14-inch glass negatives, but a landscape photographer making prints to adorn an office wall or for display in a gallery might haul around a "mammoth" camera capable of taking 18x22-inch glass plates. Not only were the cameras huge and heavy, but developing their "wet plate" negatives had to be done on the spot, requiring a portable processing tent. It meant that an entire wagonload of equipment was necessary to produce even a single print. The pioneer photographer might take a steamboat to The Cascades (renamed Cascade Locks in 1878) and then board the Oregon Pony (a short-track portage locomotive that carried passengers around the Grand Cascades to another steamboat), or he might strike out by wagon along trails that would be considered crude at best. It took lots of willpower and a strong back.

The most significant of the early photographers, and one of the best, was Carleton E. Watkins, who photographed the Gorge in 1867 and again in the winter of 1884–85. He was one of a small but important band of pioneer landscape photographers such as Frank J. Haynes, William Henry Jackson, and Timothy O'Sullivan, who were the first to bring photographs of the great scenic areas of America to an eager, worldwide audience. Their work in introducing the public to the great wonderlands of Yosemite Valley and the Yellowstone country paved the way for our national parks and wilderness reserves, and it is a testament to the grandeur of the Columbia Gorge that Watkins, Haynes, and Jackson each included it in their itinerary of national treasures.

Watkins' wonderfully luminous prints depict a river basin already impacted by the relentless pursuit of commerce. In fact, he took relatively few "pristine views" of nature. Instead, in many of the images, small boats or steamships navigate the windswept waterway, sawmills spew smoke, and pitch-roofed homesteads dot hillsides logged bare. Everywhere, there is the railroad with its deep roadbeds blasted or tunneled through the basalt, and its webwork trestles cutting across inlets. Watkins' work illustrates, as does the work of Oregon photographers Issac Grundy Davidson, Oscar and Fred Kiser, and Benjamin A. Gifford, one of the unique and frustrating features of the Gorge—that it has been unalterably stamped by the presence of commerce. Unlike the wilderness areas that formed the Yellowstone, the riverboats, wagon portages, and settlers had beaten even the earliest photographers to the Gorge. It was the gateway to the Willamette Valley from the time of the first settlers, and thus photographers have all been faced with the choice of trying to judiciously avoid all traces of human presence in their photographs or, like these early photographers, incorporating the human presence as part of what the Gorge is all about.

Actually, the Columbia River Basin is not a visually homogeneous environment. The ecology shifts from thick, moist forests with picturesque waterfalls on the Oregon side to the rolling hills of the Washington side and the high-desert sage and barren, wind-scoured rock formations of the eastern regions. Each of the early photographers seems to have settled into depicting their own special interest. Of course, Multnomah Falls and the other waterfalls made famous on stereopticon views and Cartes-de-Visite were favorite subjects, but many of the early photographers found the unique geological features of the Gorge photographically fascinating. Indeed, making "records of the rocks" has been one of the great themes of Columbia Gorge photography. James G. Crawford and Issac Grundy Davidson were two of the nineteenth-century Oregon photographers whose work reflects a concern for the quality and texture of geological forms. These and later "celebrants" of rocky places would often make a series of views of a single formation in an attempt to capture the elusive complexity of an area developed by relentless geological forces.

The rich diversity of the Gorge has attracted photographers of widely varied sensibilities. In the late 1800s, Lily White and her friends, Sarah H. Ladd and Maude Ainsworth, all members of the fine-art-oriented Photo-Secession, sailed up and down the length of the Gorge in Lily's palatial houseboat, the *Raysark*. From this unique offshore vantage, the women were able to create wonderfully atmospheric views that celebrated the river in its changing moods and shifting light. The pictorial tradition was in full flower at the turn of the century, and many of the early photographers made placid pastoral views of the Gorge area that included such commonplace elements as grazing sheep or a lone fisherman in a rowboat.

The research of Terry Toedtemeier, who in 1984 assembled the Portland Art Museum's comprehensive 153-piece exhibition, "Wild Beauty: Photography of the Columbia River Gorge 1865–1915," and who is considered one of the state's leading authorities on the history of Columbia Gorge photography, provides some invaluable and fascinating information on these pioneer photographers. One interesting fact was that Lily White's *Raysark* was incredibly elegant, featuring four furnished staterooms, a galley, and a darkroom complete with running water. In contrast, both in style and content, was the work of Gifford, whose work described the role man had come to play in the look of the Gorge environment. Gifford was a documentarian who was interested in capturing the moment, and often his images depended on a split second, when a new ship might be plunging off its skids at the Celilo boatworks or as a blast of dynamite cleared the rail grade at Mosier. In many ways, the delicate landscapes of White, Ladd, and Ainsworth contrast greatly with the rigorous Gifford documents of man's subjugation of the Gorge, and the two bodies of work taken together illustrate the opposite ends of depicting the Columbia Gorge photographically.

Most photographers have had to view the Gorge in broader and more complex terms. Formed by volcanic action and great floods, and then modified by the needs of pioneer navigation, the Columbia River Gorge is a wonderwork of catastrophic erosion and gouged-out rights-of-way for the railroad and highway systems. It is neither simply a unique geological specimen nor a beautiful, pristine wilderness untouched by the hand of man (something it probably hasn't been for centuries); rather, it is a conglomeration of ecologies and formations, some of which are natural in origin and others manmade. The contemporary photographer either must work very hard to create the illusion that the area is "unspoiled" by the artifacts of civilization and commerce, or else incorporate the natural and manmade as being part of the same dynamic whole.

This is not a radical departure from traditional standards of West Coast landscape photography. In fact, Terry Toedtemeier found that the prevailing notion that West Coast landscape photography involves pristine environments is pretty much a twentieth-century preoccupation. He points out that of the more than 350 "mammoth" images produced by Carleton Watkins in 1867 and 1884–85, only two are absolutely devoid of any evidence of man's presence. An interesting historical aside is that even though Watkins worked in the wet plate process requiring processing in the field, he still produced more images than the four other "mammoth" plate photographers (Haynes, Jackson, McAlpin, and Lamb) who followed him—put together—and they had the advantage of the newer gelatin dry plates.

When the Columbia River Highway opened in 1915, it was hailed not only as a significant engineering achievement, but also as a provider of the most accessible and breathtaking views of the Gorge in its history. Thousands of tourists flocked to the Gorge for picnics and Sunday drives, most armed with a camera. The result has been an avalanche of snapshot and postcard-type pictures of Multnomah Falls and the like. One avid collector of Columbia River postcards boasts a cache of more than 15,000 different cards. Small wonder that the serious contemporary photographer finds making fresh images of the Gorge more than a little bit frustrating. Photographically, both in terms of aesthetics and technical matters, the Columbia Gorge is as challenging as any of the great scenic areas.

THE DIVERSITY OF THE GORGE

In truth, there are probably as many ways to approach photographing the Gorge as there are photographers to approach it. My own work usually involves both the natural and man-made. I'm especially fond of the Columbia River Highway and the way it's become something of an artifact in its own right. For me the remains of that beautifully sculptured roadway blend so perfectly with the character of the Gorge as to be inseparable. The worn and weathered structure of the Shepperds Dell bridge, the crumpled stairway at Oneonta, or the abandoned diner at Dodson all seem as much an integral part of the Gorge's evolution as the volcanic formations, and I've been striving to unite them visually for a number of years. Most of the other photographers I've talked to have developed their own visual themes, or at least have concentrated their energies on selective environments.

Stu Levy is concerned with photographic areas in the Gorge that are endangered by progress. Our first workshop together involved taking a dozen or so people to some of our favorite Gorge locations. The day ended on a high note at a small but elegant set of sand dunes just east of The Dalles on a hillside above Interstate 84. The dunes were geologically unique in an area so far from the ocean, and wonderful to photograph. Stu returned a few months later to find that the highway division of the Oregon Department of Transportation had "stabilized" the dunes by covering them with a "mineral blanket" of crushed rock. It was a great loss to photographers and robbed the people of Oregon of a geologic jewel. "I've realized," says Stu, "how fragile and easily lost some of those unique features of the Gorge are, and I want to record as much of the detail and beauty of these special places as I can before they are gone forever."

Stu photographs in what must be called the classic black-and-white tradition made famous by Edward Weston and Ansel Adams. He and many other serious photographers of the natural scene use large negative cameras that are able to render the landscape in great detail. This type of photography emphasizes formal compositions and crisp, sharp-focused subject matter. Its counterpart in color photography would best be represented by people like Ray Atkeson or Christopher Burkett, to mention only two of a large number. Large-format photography also places a great emphasis on technical excellence, in terms of both the exposure and development of materials and the making of finished prints.

TECHNICAL PROBLEMS

The Columbia Gorge is a technically demanding subject that challenges all skill levels of photography. One of the major challenges to successful photography in the waterfall areas of the Gorge is achieving proper exposure. With its steep walls, thick forests of Douglas fir, and hillsides blanketed with ferns and mosses, the Gorge presents an amazingly wide divergence of luminance. Because the Oregon waterfall region faces north, the sun most often backlights the subject or cuts through the upper portion of the rock faces. The resulting gap between meter readings in the deep shadows and bright rocks or sky might be ten or twelve f-stops. Since most films are only capable of rendering a range of seven f-stops between shadow and highlight values, the photographer must often settle for inky shadows without visible detail, blown-out highlights, or both. Very accomplished black-and-white photographers can handle such a situation by employing Ansel Adams' Zone System techniques, but color photographers have fewer exposure controls, and all of it requires patience, study, and practice.

A problem that affects the weekend and backpacking photographer is the relative lack of light in the dense forests of the waterfall region. The situation is compounded by the needs of most landscape images for sharp focus throughout the scene, which requires the use of a small aperture and thus an exposure time that is beyond hand-held steadiness. With a large-format camera focused on a close subject, the exposure might be several seconds or even several minutes in length. For this kind of photography, a sturdy tripod is a must, but many hikers find it simply too much extra weight. There are, of course, many lightweight tripods on the market, but most are too rickety and not well made. The serious Gorge photographer must take much more equipment than is comfortable for a hike, but that's the only way to really master the situation. Even 35mm gear gets very heavy after a few hours on the trail. I find it helpful to think of Carleton Watkins hauling a box of 18x22-inch glass plates in the same area more than 100 years ago. It helps a little, but not enough.

PLANNING A PHOTO TRIP INTO THE GORGE

A reasonable approach to making successful photographs in the Gorge is to plan each excursion carefully. Be realistic about the purpose of the trip. If it's really a hike with family and friends, then hauling a ton of photo equipment along is just going to burden everyone. You'll be faced with holding up everyone's progress while you make pictures or being left behind. A better idea for a hike is to take a small auto-focus camera, or even a lightweight 35mm system, and use the camera as a sketchbook. Make records of potential subjects, and enjoy the hike. You can then return with your serious equipment at another time when the purpose of the trip is photographs, not hiking.

Another part of planning is to identify, if you can, the principal subject matter you are after. That's not always possible, and you do have to leave yourself open to subjects of opportunity, but often you should have a definite location in mind when you start out, and even a general idea of the anticipated results. Knowing this can help you make informed selections of lenses and film, as well as of accessory items; it can also help you decide what to leave home. Many photographers have the problem of not taking every piece of gear they own on every excursion. That can lead to photographer burnout, and worse—lost equipment. Cars are often broken into in the Gorge, and extra gear left in the car is an open invitation. More to the point, taking too much of the wrong gear can get in the way of making photographs. We've all seen the overequipped "serious" photographer struggling to find the right lens while the snapshooters were blazing away and, often as not, getting the best shots.

THE NARROW VIEW

Planning the outing and concentrating on a limited subject matter can overcome many of the technical and aesthetic problems that are part of working in the Gorge. One of those problems is the scale of the Gorge. Few vantage points really yield anything like an overview of the Gorge. Crown Point and the view from the Portland Women's Forum State Park are the two most accessible views on the Oregon side, but the remainder of the waterfall area is pretty much obscured. A few nice views can be found on the Washington side, but in general a compelling perspective of the Columbia River Gorge as a whole is difficult to translate photographically. Most of the time, photographs are taken looking up at a waterfall or a rock

Shooting at Multnomah Falls (photo by Joe Walicki)

formation, which tends to diminish its scale. Working with smaller subjects is easier and is more likely to produce finely crafted results. Smaller areas are also more likely to be lit evenly, and that means greater likelihood of technical success.

Another reason why the limited subject approach works well in the Gorge is because the Gorge has so many different "looks." The brown rolling bluffs of the northern shore contrast strikingly with the thick forests and protruding basalt formations of the southern shore. As we travel east, the terrain shifts again to windblown primitive areas like Memaloose or Rowena Crest, and the plant life changes to more high-desert varieties. By focusing our attention on specific sections of the Gorge, we may be guilty of imitating the fable of the blind men touching different parts of an elephant, but at least we will have our subject somewhat under control and our view will be a personal one. Most of the really successful photographers of the Gorge have developed a rather specific approach and point of view. Terry Toedtemeier works in close to rock formations with black-and-white film and wide-angle lenses. The result, he suggests, "does amplify the subject, revealing its particular details, in a visual context that includes the surroundings. Given that the Gorge abounds in many small geologic features, this method of working close in has proved very success-ful and at times necessary, especially in the often-encountered situation wherein the subject is crowded next to the river's edge or the edge of a cliff." Terry's approach is a good example of how a well-defined visual aes-thetic often works on a practical level as well.

Each photographer needs to spend enough time and energy with his subject in order to achieve visual understanding. All aspects of the photo-graphic process, including film, lens, perspective, and technique, have to be aligned to even attempt to articulate the sensations involved in being there. The atmosphere in the Gorge is truly great; the wind and the heavy, rain-laden skies are as much a part of the Gorge experience as are the cliffs and vegetation. More importantly, each photographer has his or her own personal response to those elements, and that response is what can inform a great photograph of the natural scene. Technique, of course, is never an end in itself, but correctly applied, the right combination of film, format, and lens will resolve the Gorge in terms that are a faithful rendering of the photographer's visual understanding of the place.

The union between aesthetic and technique appears in the work of most successful photographers. Ideally, one informs the other. Stu Levy's tendency to isolate contrasting subjects and backgrounds lends itself per-fectly to his dramatic style of black-and-white printing. The subtle and evocative colors in a Chris Burkett Cibachrome print complement his gentle and reverent approach to nature. In the most revealing images, there has been a successful blending of the photographer's response to sub-ject and the methods of his or her craft. My own experience has been that my equipment must complement the way that I visually respond to the subject. I often use a Widelux or a wide-field camera because with it I can pull together the several and diverse facets of the Gorge into a dynamic whole. To me, it's the way the Gorge seems to be—a series of small mira-cles that comprise a place of singular visual significance.

FURTHER READING

Portland Art Museum. *Wild Beauty: Photography of the Columbia River Gorge 1865–1915.* Exhibition catalog, 1984.

Watkins, Carleton E. *Photographs of the Columbia River and Oregon.* Friends of Photography, 1979.

◆

PARKS AND CAMPGROUNDS

By Kathleen Tyau

Listed below are all of the public parks and campgrounds located in the Columbia Gorge, with a few exceptions. Small city parks and privately owned RV parks are not listed, nor are a few of the windsurfing parks where facilities are so limited as to be of little interest to the general public. The parks that are described as popular with windsurfers are usually very crowded during windy periods in spring and summer.

The parks are listed from west to east, first on the Oregon side, then on the Washington side.

Current information should be verified when planning a visit to parks in the Gorge. For example, many of the parks are closed during the winter months, and available facilities often change from year to year. In addition, the greatly increased use of parks by windsurfers in recent years is resulting in the expansion of existing parks and development of new parks throughout the Gorge.

OREGON SIDE

Lewis and Clark State Park. (Just south of I-84 exit 18, 18 miles east of Portland.) Picnic tables, rest rooms, day use only. This state park lies at the base of Broughton Bluff, the natural landmark that signals the beginning of the Columbia Gorge at the mouth of the Sandy River. A spacious grassy area is available for picnicking and games. The Sandy River can be reached by carefully crossing the highway, where a boat ramp is located. The cliffs above the park are popular with rock climbers, but are dangerous to the inexperienced.

Dabney State Park. (From I-84, take exit 18 and drive south 3 miles on the Columbia River Hwy.) Picnic tables, rest rooms, hand-launch boating, day use only. Dabney State Park is on the east bank of the Sandy River 3 miles south of Lewis and Clark State Park. From picnic tables amidst Douglas fir, visitors to this park may view the river and the tree-covered bluff on the other side.

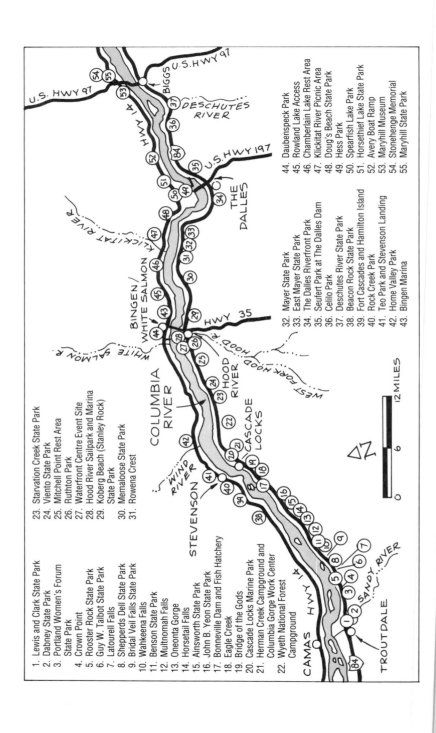

1. Lewis and Clark State Park
2. Dabney State Park
3. Portland Women's Forum State Park
4. Crown Point
5. Rooster Rock State Park
6. Guy W. Talbot State Park
7. Latourell Falls
8. Shepperds Dell State Park
9. Bridal Veil Falls State Park
10. Wahkeena Falls
11. Benson State Park
12. Multnomah Falls
13. Oneonta Gorge
14. Horsetail Falls
15. Ainsworth State Park
16. John B. Yeon State Park
17. Bonneville Dam and Fish Hatchery
18. Eagle Creek
19. Bridge of the Gods
20. Cascade Locks Marine Park
21. Herman Creek Campground and Columbia Gorge Work Center
22. Wyeth National Forest Campground

23. Starvation Creek State Park
24. Viento State Park
25. Mitchell Point Rest Area
26. Ruthton Park
27. Waterfront Centre Event Site
28. Hood River Sailpark and Marina
29. Koberg Beach (Stanley Rock) State Park
30. Memaloose State Park
31. Rowena Crest

32. Mayer State Park
33. East Mayer State Park
34. The Dalles Riverfront Park
35. Seufert Park at The Dalles Dam
36. Celilo Park
37. Deschutes River State Park
38. Beacon Rock State Park
39. Fort Cascades and Hamilton Island
40. Rock Creek Park
41. Teo Park and Stevenson Landing
42. Home Valley Park
43. Bingen Marina

44. Daubenspeck Park
45. Rowland Lake Access
46. Chamberlain Lake Rest Area
47. Klickitat River Picnic Area
48. Doug's Beach State Park
49. Hess Park
50. Spearfish Lake Park
51. Horsethief Lake State Park
52. Avery Boat Ramp
53. Maryhill Museum
54. Stonehenge Memorial
55. Maryhill State Park

Portland Women's Forum State Park. (On the Columbia River Hwy, 1 mile west of Crown Point.) Benches, paved area, no picnic tables or rest rooms. At this small wayside park, one finds a scenic overlook (Chanticleer Point) from which to enjoy perhaps the most famous view of the Columbia Gorge, including Crown Point to the east and Rooster Rock below.

Crown Point. (Eastbound on I-84, take exit 22, drive up the hill to the town of Corbett, then drive east 3 miles on the Columbia River Hwy; westbound on I-84, take exit 28, then drive west 3 miles.) From famous Crown Point, one finds panoramic views of the Columbia Gorge where the Columbia River Highway winds out to a point high above the Columbia River. Majestic Beacon Rock rises prominently on the Washington side of the Gorge, and Rooster Rock juts out below. Located at this site is the historic Vista House, built in 1917 and recently renovated, which now houses an interpretive center, a crafts shop, and rest rooms.

Rooster Rock State Park. (I-84 exit 25.) Rest rooms, picnic tables, large parking lots, day use only, entrance fee during summer months. This large park along the Columbia River is very popular for sunbathing, picnicking, and water sports. Boating facilities consist of a ramp and floating docks in a lagoon at the west end of the park. On the north side, steep stairs and rock paths lead down to a long, sandy beach with a roped-off swimming area. This beach is especially popular with windsurfers when strong winds blow from the east.

Guy W. Talbot State Park. (On the Columbia River Hwy between Crown Point and Shepperds Dell.) Rest rooms, picnic tables, day use only. Guy Talbot State Park lies on a gentle slope in a grove of fir trees above the community of Latourell. This park is easily overlooked, since it cannot be seen from the Columbia River Highway. Stone steps on the south end of the park lead to Latourell Creek and point to several Gorge trails across the highway.

Latourell Falls. (On the Columbia River Hwy, 0.5 mile east of Guy W. Talbot Park.) Rest rooms (on the north side of the highway), parking lot, day use only. Latourell Falls, part of Guy W. Talbot State Park, can be seen south of the Columbia River Highway. A very short paved path leads to a particularly good view of these spectacular 249-foot falls. Trails from the highway extend 0.8 mile to Upper Latourell Falls.

Shepperds Dell State Park. (Eastbound on I-84, take exit 22, then drive east on the Columbia River Hwy for 7.4 miles; westbound on I-84, take exit 28, then drive 1.6 miles west.) Limited wayside parking, no rest rooms or picnic tables. From the east end of the Shepperds Dell Bridge, a short trail leads to the upper part of Shepperds Dell Falls, just a few hundred feet from the highway. Along the trail, one has excellent views of one of the highway's most beautiful bridges, a graceful concrete deck arch built in 1914.

Bridal Veil Falls State Park. (From I-84, take exit 28 and drive west on the Columbia River Hwy 1 mile.) Rest rooms, picnic tables. From the parking lot at this park, a trail winds downhill through the woods a short distance to Bridal Veil Falls. Another trail makes a loop to the north, offering excellent views of the river. Both trails are described in the hiking chapter. At the time of publication, the adjacent town of Bridal Veil and its lumber mill had been purchased by the Trust for Public Land. Plans for the future use of the site had not yet been finalized, but it seems likely that some or all of the site will be converted to park use.

Wahkeena Falls. (From I-84, take exit 28 and drive 2.6 miles east on the Columbia River Hwy.) Rest rooms, picnic tables, parking. On the south side of the highway at this park, Wahkeena Falls dominates the landscape, while across the highway lies a picnic area maintained by the Forest Service.

Benson State Park. (Eastbound on I-84, take exit 30; westbound, take exit 29 and rejoin the freeway going east to exit 30.) Picnic tables, large shelter, parking, hand-launch boating. This shaded park is bordered by Wahkeena Pond and Benson Lake, both of which are suitable for small nonmotorized craft. Closed during the winter.

Multnomah Falls. (I-84 exit 31; or follow the Columbia River Hwy 3 miles east from Bridal Veil.) Restaurant, snack bar, gift shop, rest rooms, day use only. At 620 feet, Multnomah Falls is the highest waterfall in the Columbia Gorge and the fourth-highest in the United States. The falls and Multnomah Falls Lodge may be reached from either the freeway or the Columbia River Highway. The falls are visible from the freeway, the Columbia River Highway, or the trails leading to upper portions of the falls. The Forest Service maintains a small nature center, and leases the lodge to a concessionaire.

Oneonta Gorge. (On the Columbia River Hwy, 0.5 mile east of Multnomah Falls.) Limited wayside parking, no park facilities. This wayside, located on a 1915 bridge, offers a close view of the narrow cleft known as Oneonta Gorge, a designated botanical area. The wayside is popular with photographers and, during warm weather, hikers who hike (and wade) to the south end of Oneonta Gorge for a view of Oneonta Falls. The wayside utilizes one of the original Columbia River Highway bridges, which was bypassed in 1948. Evidence of a 1914 tunnel (now filled with rubble) can be seen just to the east.

Multnomah Falls Lodge

Horsetail Falls. (On the Columbia River Hwy 2.6 miles east of Multnomah Falls.) Picnic tables, parking, access to trails, no rest rooms. This wayside at Horsetail Falls has been rebuilt using stone taken from the old Rocky Butte Jail in Portland.

Ainsworth State Park. (Just west of I-84 exit 35, on the Columbia River Hwy 3.1 miles east of Multnomah Falls.) Rest rooms, camping, picnic sites, limited parking. This park consists of several adjacent sites along the south side of the Columbia River Highway and includes two small picnic areas (one with rest rooms) and a secluded campground.

John B. Yeon State Park. (From Ainsworth State Park, follow signs east to Dodson/Hood River, but just before the road enters the freeway, turn east on Frontage Road and drive past the communities of Dodson and Warrendale to the state park.) The trail to Elowah Falls (3 miles round trip) begins at the west end of the gravel parking area, but this state park provides no other facilities.

Bonneville Dam and Fish Hatchery. (From I-84, take exit 40, drive north under the freeway and railroad bridge, and then follow signs to the fish hatchery.) In years gone by, a large grassy picnic area with playground equipment could be found adjacent to the Bonneville Dam Fish Hatchery. At the time of publication, the area has been engulfed by construction associated with the building of new navigation locks. Other visitor facilities, which have not been disturbed by the construction, include a visitor center, fish-ladder viewing, public fishing access, a gift shop, and several viewpoints of the dam and the original powerhouse.

Eagle Creek. (Eastbound on I-84, take exit 41; westbound, take exit 40, then rejoin the freeway eastbound.) Rest rooms, picnic tables, shelter, camping. North of the Eagle Creek exit is Overlook Park, a picnic area on a bluff above the river at the mouth of Eagle Creek. A paved road leads up to the park, which features stone shelters built in the 1930s. To the south is a campground and day use area maintained by the Forest Service.

Bridge of the Gods. (From I-84, take exit 44, then follow signs toward the Bridge of the Gods.) Rest rooms, day use only. This small park is found at the south end of the Bridge of the Gods. It is often visited by hikers following the Pacific Crest Trail, which utilizes the Bridge of the Gods on its route from Mexico to Canada.

Cascade Locks Marine Park. (From I-84, take Cascade Locks exit 44 and follow the main road into town; watch for the park entrance on the north side of the street; the entrance road leads under the railroad tracks.) Rest rooms, picnic tables, large shelter with a fireplace, camping, boat

Cascade Locks Marine Park

ramp, marina, small windsurfing beach. This park is located at the National Historic Site of the locks built in the 1880s to bypass The Cascades of the Columbia, ancient rapids that were submerged when Bonneville Dam was built in the 1930s. A museum, a visitor center, and a gift shop are at this site, together with the original locks, now flooded by Bonneville Dam. Scenic cruises on the sternwheeler *Columbia Gorge* depart several times daily during the summer from a dock near the visitor center.

Herman Creek Campground and Columbia Gorge Work Center.

(Westbound on I-84, take exit 47; eastbound, take I-84 Cascade Locks exit 44, then follow the road 2.1 miles east through the town of Cascade Locks. Follow Forest Lane north and east 2 miles, crossing the freeway, and then turn left 0.4 mile to the Columbia Gorge Work Center.) Rest rooms, picnic tables, ample parking. Follow the driveway past the Columbia Gorge Work Center 0.3 mile to the campground. A picnic area lies adjacent to the camping area. The Herman Creek Trail 406 starts just west of the campground, or at the work center in off-season.

Wyeth Campground.

(From I-84, take exit 51, then drive 0.25 mile west on Herman Creek Road.) Camping, rest rooms, picnic tables, parking, access to Wyeth Trail (411). This campground, which is maintained by the Forest Service, is located on the south side of Herman Creek Road, near the town of Wyeth.

Starvation Creek State Park

Starvation Creek State Park. (Eastbound on I-84, take exit 55; westbound, take exit 51, then rejoin the freeway eastbound and drive 4 miles to exit 55.) Picnic tables, rest rooms, parking. From the parking lot, a short paved path leads to picnic areas and to Starvation Creek Falls. Across Starvation Creek from the rest rooms, a path leads east to an abandoned section of the original Columbia River Highway, which can be hiked 1 mile east to Viento State Park (see the hiking chapter).

Viento State Park. (I-84 exit 56, 8 miles west of Hood River.) Camping, rest rooms, picnic tables. Viento State Park consists of a campground south of the freeway, as well as a park and campground north of the freeway closer to the river. Each campsite is attractively set off from the others by trees and shrubs. Windsurfers favor this site for its good sailing conditions and camping facilities, so the Viento campground is often full during the summer, especially on weekends. The hike to the river requires a careful crossing over railroad tracks. Just south of the freeway, an abandoned section of the Columbia River Highway can be hiked 1 mile west to Starvation Creek State Park (see the hiking chapter).

Mitchell Point Rest Area. (Eastbound on I-84, take exit 58; westbound, take exit 56, then return eastbound to exit 58.) Parking lot, outhouses. The Columbia River Highway once went through a rock tunnel at Mitchell Point, modeled after the Axenstrasse tunnel in Switzerland, complete with several openings affording views of the river. Unfortunately, the tunnel was destroyed after the freeway was built. Mitchell Point now consists of a scenic viewpoint of the Columbia River. The Wygant Trail follows the road west from the parking lot.

Ruthton Park. (From I-84, take exit 62, then drive west on Westcliff Drive 0.4 mile past the Columbia Gorge Hotel.) Picnic tables, no rest rooms or water, day use only. Ruthton Park is a small county park offering superb views from a rocky bluff overlooking the Columbia River near the historic Columbia Gorge Hotel.

Waterfront Centre Event Site. (North of I-84 exit 63.) This large windsurfing park has few facilities other than a large gravel parking lot and launching facilities for windsurfers.

Hood River Sailpark and Marina. (From I-84, take exit 64, then turn north toward the Hood River Bridge, but turn left just before the marina. Drive past the visitor center and museum and follow the road to the edge of the river; turn right and then drive north to the beach.) Large grassy areas, rest rooms, picnic shelter and tables, jogging path and exercise course, sandy beach, large parking lots crowded with windsurfers. This popular windsurfing site is on the east side of the mouth of the Hood River.

Koberg Beach (Stanley Rock) State Park. (Westbound access only from I-84 at milepost 66; follow the "Rest Area" sign.) Parking, rest rooms, hand launching of small boats, no picnic tables. Just to the east of Hood River, a 140-foot rocky bluff juts out at the edge of the Columbia River, forming Stanley Rock. The riverbank slopes gently south of the park to form a gravel-covered beach. A trail goes up the side of Stanley Rock to a grassy area overlooking the river.

Memaloose State Park. (Westbound access only from I-84 at milepost 73, about 3 miles west of Rowena.) Rest rooms, camping. Memaloose State Park is a rest area and campground located between the freeway and the Columbia River. The park overlooks Memaloose Island, a former Indian burial ground. Some of the picnic tables are protected by windbreaks; others are placed in a recessed, landscaped area.

Rowena Crest. (On Hwy 30 between Mosier and Rowena.) No facilities. This section of Mayer State Park is a spectacular viewpoint immediately west of and overlooking a section of the Columbia River Highway known as the Rowena Loops. The Rowena Crest site also offers views across the Columbia River to the town of Lyle and east to The Dalles. Nearby is the Tom McCall Preserve, a Nature Conservancy project, with excellent wildflowers in season (see the chapters on wildlife and wildflowers).

Mayer State Park. (From I-84, take Rowena exit 76, drive west on Hwy 30 about 0.5 mile, and then follow signs north to the park.) Rest rooms, picnic tables, boat ramp. The park is located on a site overlooking Salisbury Slough and the Columbia River.

East Mayer State Park. (From I-84, take Rowena exit 76, drive north across the railroad tracks, and then turn east in 0.8 mile to the park.) Day use only. Commonly referred to as Rowena Park, this popular windsurfing park has recently been improved with a new parking area and rest rooms.

The Dalles Riverfront Park. (From I-84, take exit 85, turn north, and then drive east to the park.) Picnicking, rest rooms, day use only. Facilities at this large waterfront park have been greatly expanded, due to its popularity with windsurfers. Closed from November 1 to Memorial Day weekend due to wildlife habitat.

Seufert Park at The Dalles Dam. (From I-84, take exit 87, then drive north on US 97. Before crossing The Dalles Bridge, follow signs east to The Dalles Dam.) Day use only. This park is located on the grounds of The Dalles Dam visitor center. Park your car at the center and take the free train ride to the powerhouse. The train stops at three possible picnic sites, but there are rest rooms only at the last two stops.

Celilo Park. (I-84 exit 97.) Picnic tables, rest rooms, boat ramp. Celilo Park is a large riverfront park maintained by the Army Corps of Engineers. This pleasant park consists of a grassy area with a large parking lot. Since Celilo is a designated Native American fishing site, boaters and windsurfers should be careful not to get tangled in submerged fishing nets.

Deschutes River State Park. (Eastbound on I-84, take Celilo exit 97 and drive east on Hwy 30 for 3 miles; westbound on I-84, take Biggs exit 104 and drive west 4 miles.) Camping, lawns, picnic tables, rest rooms, parking. This park is located on both banks of the mouth of the Deschutes River just before it enters the Columbia. The west side (Heritage Landing) consists primarily of a boat ramp and parking for the many boaters that use the Deschutes. The east side is more parklike, with camping and picnic areas.

WASHINGTON SIDE

Beacon Rock State Park. (Hwy 14, milepost 35.) Boat ramp, dock, beach, parking, picnic area, camping, rest rooms. Beacon Rock is a prominent 800-foot rock formation on the Washington side of the Columbia. Visible for miles, it once came close to becoming an Oregon state park. Beacon Rock State Park is now divided into three areas, two of

Beacon Rock Trail

which accommodate campers. The first section can be reached by turning south on Beacon Rock Moorage Road at milepost 34.22 and following the road 0.3 mile to a day use area along the river. Beacon Rock lies just across the bay.

The second area is a wayside on Highway 14 at the base of Beacon Rock, consisting of rest rooms and a few parking spaces. Henry Biddle's 1918 trail up Beacon Rock begins here. The entrance to the third and largest section of the park is located on the north side of the highway at milepost 35. It includes a large parking lot and picnic grounds, the trailhead to Hamilton Mountain, and a campground.

Fort Cascades and Hamilton Island. (From Hwy 14, milepost 38.5, turn south on Dam Access Road. Follow the road for 0.2 mile, turning right and then left into the park.) Parking, rest rooms, historical displays. This park is just east of the town of North Bonneville and west of the second (north) power house of Bonneville Dam. This is a day use park with a shelter and a path leading down to the river. The park has a large grassy area and a few trees but no picnic tables. The Fort Cascades Historic Trail, which begins here, is described in the hiking chapter. Other day use areas are located along the river both east and west of Fort Cascades; most are simply parking areas for fishermen.

Rock Creek Park. (From Hwy 14, milepost 44.2, in Stevenson, turn north on East Second Street and drive 0.25 mile to the park.) Picnic facilities, rest rooms, playground. This park is on the shore of Rock Cove, a bay that has been separated from the Columbia River by the railroad and highway grades.

Teo Park and Stevenson Landing. (Hwy 14, milepost 44.3, in Stevenson at the foot of Russell Avenue.) Picnic sites. Teo Park is located on the Columbia River. The main feature of this site is a boat ramp and dock (the sternwheeler *Columbia Gorge* stops here). The park occupies a small grassy area with a few picnic tables and barbecue grills.

Home Valley Park. (Hwy 14, milepost 50.1.) Parking, rest rooms, picnic tables, camping. This secluded park, with a lovely view of the river, is easy to miss. The entrance lies at the eastern end of the town of Home Valley, at the mouth of the Wind River. The east fork of the park access road leads to a campground, rest rooms, picnic area, and playing field. To get to the swimming beach, follow a short trail from the picnic area. Take the west fork of the access road to reach a small cove and rock-lined beach designated for use by windsurfers. Day-use facilities at this site include outhouses, a grassy rigging area, and parking lot. A trail through a small wildlife refuge begins at this end of the park.

Bingen Marina. (From Hwy 14, milepost 66.7, in Bingen, turn south on Maple Street, cross the railroad tracks, and then drive east 0.7 mile to the marina and park.) Picnic area, rest rooms. This park is located on an inlet of the Columbia River. A floating dock has been installed, as has a boat ramp. Views from the park include Burdoin Mountain to the north. Nearby is Klickitat Point, a recently developed windsurfing site.

Daubenspeck Park. (From Hwy 14, milepost 66.2, in Bingen, turn north one block on Willow Street.) Playground equipment, picnic tables, rest rooms. This city park is located at the west end of the town of Bingen.

Rowland Lake Access. (From Hwy 14, milepost 70.9, turn north on County Road 1230 and proceed 0.5 mile.) Outhouses, parking. This is a small, shady park on the north side of Rowland Lake, about 4 miles east of Bingen. The lake was created when the highway and the railroad tracks crossed a bay of the Columbia River.

Chamberlain Lake Rest Area. (Hwy 14, milepost 74.) Covered picnic tables, rest rooms, parking. This highway rest area sits on a rocky bluff overlooking the Columbia River. From grassy slopes and picnic tables, there is an excellent view of the Oregon side of the Gorge as well as Memaloose Island.

Klickitat River Picnic Area. (From Hwy 14, milepost 75.9, in Lyle, turn north on Hwy 142 and drive north 0.8 mile.) Outhouse, no picnic tables. This rustic, undeveloped picnic area is on the east bank of the Klickitat River in a very scenic area.

Doug's Beach State Park. (Hwy 14, milepost 78.9, 3 miles east of Lyle.) Outhouses. This waterfront park is very popular with windsurfers, so parking may be hard to find on windy days. Pay close attention to posted parking rules. The path to the river requires crossing over railroad tracks. Facilities are currently limited, but may be expanded in the future.

Hess Park. (From US 197, milepost 1.1, just north of The Dalles Bridge, turn east on a gravel road.) Picnic tables. This is a very small and secluded park on a pond just north of The Dalles Dam. The park consists of a few willow trees and a small picnic area.

Spearfish Lake Park. (From US 197, milepost 1.2, just north of The Dalles Bridge, turn east on Dock Road and drive about 1 mile.) Boat ramp, several picnic tables, some with shelters. This is a small park on tiny Spearfish Lake and even smaller Little Spearfish Lake. No fires or motorized boats allowed.

Horsethief Lake State Park. (Hwy 14, milepost 85.2.) Large parking lot, two boat ramps (one on the lake and one on the Columbia), picnic tables, rest rooms. This large state park lies south of the highway along a lake adjacent to the Columbia River. A grove of poplars provides shade in this otherwise sparsely vegetated section of the Gorge. Camping, swimming, and boating are allowed. Closed October through March.

Avery Boat Ramp. (Hwy 14, milepost 89.8.) Picnic tables, camp sites, outhouses, no drinking water. This small waterfront park and campground provides a good view of the Sam Hill Memorial Bridge at Biggs Junction.

Maryhill Museum. (Hwy 14, at milepost 98.8.) Picnicking is permitted on the spacious grounds of this museum. Open 9:00 A.M. to 5:00 P.M. March 15 to November 15. The museum itself is described in the next chapter.

Stonehenge Memorial. (Hwy 14, milepost 102.6.) No facilities. This full-size replica of Stonehenge was constructed between 1918 and 1930 by Sam Hill, the railroad attorney who also built Maryhill Museum and was instrumental in building the Columbia River Highway. Hill wanted to build a monument to the futility of war, and thus dedicated his Stonehenge to the servicemen of Klickitat County who died in World

Stonehenge Memorial

War I. A path leads a few feet down the hill to Sam Hill's grave. The replica is open daily.

Maryhill State Park. (On US 97, 1.5 miles south of the junction of Hwy 14 and US 97, near the north end of the Sam Hill Bridge.) Rest rooms with showers, swimming beach, boat ramp and dock, extensive picnic and camp sites. These amenities attract many families, including windsurfers. This very large park lies along the Columbia River adjacent to the town of Maryhill.

◆

MUSEUMS, VISITOR CENTERS, AND OTHER ATTRACTIONS

By Philip N. Jones

The Columbia River Gorge is rich in history, and most of the cities and towns have made an attempt to preserve some of their historic artifacts and architecture by maintaining museums and historic buildings. Listed below are all of the museums in the Gorge, plus historic houses, churches, and other buildings open to the public, including various visitor centers. The sites are listed from west to east, with the Oregon side listed first, and then the Washington side. Many of the attractions, particularly the smaller ones, are open only on weekends or during the summer months.

OREGON SIDE

Troutdale Railroad Depot. (473 East Columbia Street, Troutdale, OR 97060. For information, phone the Troutdale city hall at 503-665-5175.) This railroad station was built in 1907. In 1976 it was donated to the city of Troutdale and moved a short distance from its original site. The main portion of the depot is used as a small railroad museum by the Troutdale Historical Society.

Harlow House. (726 East Columbia Street, Troutdale, OR 97060. For information, phone the Troutdale city hall at 503-665-5175.) The Harlow House, located in Troutdale, was built in 1900 by Fred E. Harlow, son of the founder of Troutdale, Capt. John Harlow. The house has been maintained in its original condition by the Troutdale Historical Society, and the grounds are part of the city park system.

Vista House. (On the Columbia River Hwy atop Crown Point. Phone 503-695-2230.) Built in 1917, shortly after the Columbia River Highway was completed, this unique building was intended by Samuel Lancaster as an observation point and comfort station on what is perhaps the most

Vista House at Crown Point

spectacular site in the Gorge. Designed by Edgar Lazarus in the Art Nouveau style, the Vista House has been designated as a National Historic Landmark. The main floor contains an information desk and interpretive displays, the basement offers a gift shop, and the second floor observation deck is open.

Multnomah Falls Lodge. (I-84 exit 31. Phone 503-695-2376.) Designed by A. E. Doyle for the city of Portland in 1925 to replace an earlier lodge at the foot of Multnomah Falls, this lodge is now owned by the Forest Service and leased to a concessionaire, which operates a restaurant, a gift shop, and a snack bar. The Forest Service also operates a small nature center.

Bonneville Dam Visitor Center. (I-84 exit 40. Phone 503-374-8820.) This large visitor center is located on Bradford Island, between the dam spillway and the original powerhouse. Exhibits in the center describe history, navigation, and other aspects of the dam. Fish ladders and ship locks are also open to public viewing, although at this writing new locks were under construction. At the west end of the Bonneville complex is a fish hatchery, also open to the public, along with fish viewing ponds. During the summer months, a gift shop is open at the hatchery.

Cascade Locks Historical Museum. (Cascade Locks Marine Park, in Cascade Locks. Phone 503-374-8535.) This museum is housed in one of the locktenders' houses built in 1905 at the site of the old Cascade Locks. Although the house is small, it holds an excellent collection of historical material dealing with steamboat days, railroading in the Gorge, the era of fishwheels, and domestic life at the turn of the century.

Cascade Locks Visitor Center. (Cascade Locks Marine Park, in Cascade Locks.) The visitor center was once the visitor center at Bonneville Dam; when it was replaced, the building was barged to Cascade Locks and returned to use. It now houses a gift shop and is the home base for the sternwheeler *Columbia Gorge,* which provides excursions several times daily during the summer months. The normal itinerary of the boat is a round trip between Cascade Locks, Bradford Island (Bonneville Dam), and Stevenson. The visitor center and the sternwheeler are both operated by the Port of Cascade Locks, P.O. Box 307, Cascade Locks, OR 97014. To make reservations for the sternwheeler excursion, phone 503-374-8619 or 503-374-8427. In Portland, the phone number is 503-223-3928.

The Mount Hood Railroad. (110 Railroad Avenue in Hood River. For reservations or current schedule information, phone 503-386-3556.) This scenic railroad offers excursion rides through the Hood River Valley from its depot in Hood River. Two itineraries are offered. The shorter 17-mile trip takes 2 hours and makes the round trip from Hood River to the town of Odell and back again. The longer trip of 44 miles takes 4 hours and visits Parkdale, in the foothills of Mount Hood.

Port of Hood River Visitor Center. (Port Marina Park, in Hood River, north and west of I-84 exit 64. Phone 503-386-2000 or toll-free 800-366-3530.) This visitor center offers travel information and a display of a large 3-D map of the region.

Hood River County Historical Museum. (West end of Port Marina Park, in Hood River, north and west of I-84 exit 64. P.O. Box 781, Hood River, OR 97031. Phone 503-386-6772.) This surprisingly large and well-designed museum features displays concerning pioneer days and early industry and agriculture of the Gorge and the Hood River Valley.

The Gorge Discovery Center. (To be built at Crates Point, on the Columbia River north and west of The Dalles. For current information, contact the Center at P.O. Box 998, The Dalles, OR 97058. Phone 503-386-2333.)

Original Wasco County Courthouse. (406 West Second Street in The Dalles. P.O. Box 460, The Dalles, OR 97058. Phone 503-296-4798.) This tiny courthouse, built in 1859, once stood on the current city hall site at Third and Court in The Dalles. It was moved at least five times and now serves as a small museum on a site located east of The Dalles City Natatorium (public swimming pool) at the west end of the city, next to The Dalles Area Chamber of Commerce. Its contents include exhibits on Indian culture and the history of The Dalles.

Approaching Bradford Island on the sternwheeler Columbia Gorge

Surgeons Quarters at Fort Dalles (Fort Dalles Museum).
(15th and Garrison in The Dalles. P.O. Box 806, The Dalles, OR 97058.
Phone 503-296-4547.) Built in 1856, this house is Oregon's oldest example of Gothic Revival architecture. It is the only building surviving
from Fort Dalles, a military compound operated between 1850 and 1867,
and is now operated as a museum.

Old St. Peter's Church. (Third and Lincoln streets in The Dalles.
P.O. Box 882, The Dalles, OR 97058. Phone 503-296-5686.) This 1897
Catholic church is an outstanding example of Gothic Revival architec-

ture. Its 176-foot red-tile steeple towers over the downtown area of The Dalles. The interior is equally splendid, with 40-foot vaulted ceilings, thirty-four stained-glass windows, and several statues. No longer used as a church, it is open for public viewing and for weddings or other gatherings.

St. Paul's Chapel. (Union and Fifth streets in The Dalles. Phone 503-298-4477.) This church, built in 1875, still boasts its original pews in a Carpenter Gothic interior. The Episcopal diocese of eastern Oregon uses the building as its headquarters and for a weekly service Wednesdays at noon. Nearby, in The Dalles City Park, the Victor Trevitt House is undergoing restoration.

The Dalles Visitor Information Center. (901 East Second Street, The Dalles, OR 97058. Phone 503-296-6616 or 800-255-3385.) This information center is located in a former woolen mill at the east end of The Dalles. Among the available information are brochures describing walking tours of the historic district and driving tours of The Dalles area.

The Dalles Dam Visitor Center. (North and east of I-84 exit 87, in The Dalles. Phone 503-296-9778.) In addition to a display on the history of the dam and the surrounding area, a free train ride is offered to the dam, where tours may be taken.

WASHINGTON SIDE

Bonneville Dam–North Shore Visitor Center. (Second powerhouse and Cascades Island. East of North Bonneville, Washington. Phone 509-427-4281.) The second powerhouse, completed in 1982, is the newest addition to the Bonneville Dam complex. Visitors are permitted to tour the powerhouse to view the generating turbines, fish ladders, and other facilities. The sheer size of the building and its equipment is striking. A short trail leads to a viewpoint. Cascades Island, the island created when the new powerhouse was built, can also be visited.

Bridge of the Gods Visitor Information Center. A small visitor information center is located on Hwy 14, just east of the north end of the Bridge of the Gods.

Skamania County Historical Society Museum. (Columbia Street and Vancouver Avenue in Stevenson. P.O. Box 396, Stevenson, WA 98648. Phone 509-427-5141.) Located in the Courthouse Annex in Stevenson, just north of the library, this museum features displays on local history, including logging, steamboats, and railroads in the Gorge. The museum is planned to be incorporated into a Columbia Gorge Interpretive

Center (see next entry) to be constructed west of Stevenson, at the west end of Rock Creek Cove.

Columbia Gorge Interpretive Center. (Proposed to be built west of Stevenson, at the west end of Rock Creek Cove. P.O. Box 396, Stevenson, WA 98648. Phone 509-427-8211.) At the time of publication, some of the items intended to be displayed in the new center were temporarily on display in a former Masonic Hall at 150 Northwest Loop Road in Stevenson, one block east of the Stevenson Library. In Stevenson, turn north on Columbia Street, then turn east on Vancouver Avenue one block to the temporary museum.

Gorge Heritage Museum. (Corner of Maple and Humboldt in Bingen. P.O. Box 394, Bingen, WA 98605. Phone 509-493-3228.) This Methodist church, built in 1911, is now a small museum with displays on the history of the Gorge and early domestic life and commercial affairs in the Gorge.

The Dalles Dam. (East of US 197, 0.3 mile north of The Dalles Bridge.) Although the primary visitor facilities for The Dalles Dam are on the south side of the river, the north end of the dam offers public viewing of the navigation locks, the fish ladders, and the dam spillway. The north side complex also offers grand views of The Dalles Bridge.

Maryhill Museum. (On Hwy 14 2 miles west of US 97. P.O. Box 23, Maryhill, WA 98620. Phone 509-773-3733.) Perhaps the most unusual building in the Gorge, Maryhill Museum was built by eccentric railroad lawyer Sam Hill. In 1926, his friend, Queen Marie of Roumania, dedicated it and described it as a "curious and interesting building." It now houses a collection of art pieces and historic artifacts that can only be described as eclectic, including memorabilia of Queen Marie and Sam Hill, more than 100 chess sets, sculpture by Auguste Rodin, and a large collection of American Indian artifacts. The museum and grounds are open from March 15 to November 15. An admission fee is charged at the museum, but the grounds are open for picnicking free of charge. A small cafe is also open in the museum.

Stonehenge Memorial. (Hwy 14, milepost 102.5, 1 mile east of US 97.) As if building a castle high on a bluff overlooking a remote section of the Columbia were not enough, Hill also constructed a replica of Stonehenge as a monument to the futility of war, and to the thirteen soldiers of Klickitat County who died in World War I. Although the replica is made of cement rather than stone, it is the same size as the original, and can be used to observe several interesting astronomical alignments, particularly at the summer solstice sunrise and the winter solstice sunset. On the south

Maryhill Museum

side of the monument, a short path leads to a crypt where Sam Hill's remains now rest. The monument is open daily.

Klickitat County Travel Information Center. (2 Maryhill Highway, P.O. Box 1220, Goldendale, WA 98620. Phone 509-773-4395.) This information center at the entrance to Maryhill State Park provides information on accommodations and sightseeing.

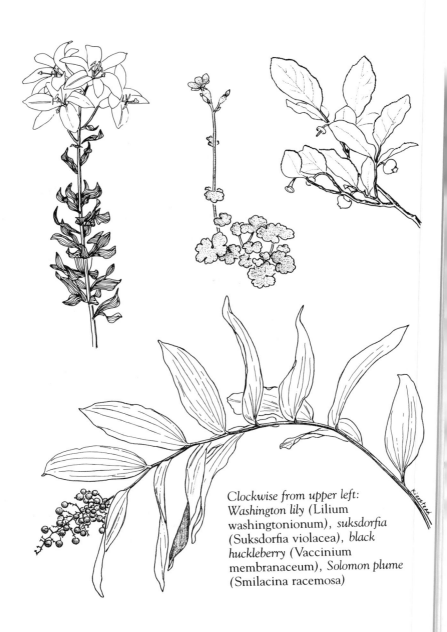

Clockwise from upper left:
Washington lily (Lilium
washingtonionum), *suksdorfia*
(Suksdorfia violacea), *black
huckleberry* (Vaccinium
membranaceum), *Solomon plume*
(Smilacina racemosa)

Hamilton Mountain

APPENDICES

APPENDIX A

Federal and State Agencies

Most of the activities described in this guide are located in the Columbia River Gorge National Scenic Area, which is administered by the Columbia River Gorge Commission (a bistate agency created by the Columbia River Gorge National Scenic Area Act to oversee land-use planning decisions in the Gorge) and by the U.S. Forest Service. For more information concerning the ongoing planning process, contact the Commission or the Forest Service at:

Columbia River Gorge Commission
288 E Jewett Boulevard
P.O. Box 730
White Salmon, Washington 98672
509-493-3323

U.S. Forest Service
Columbia River Gorge National Scenic Area
902 Wasco Avenue, Suite 200
Hood River, Oregon 97031
503-386-2333

Much of the land within the National Scenic Area is within national forests, which are administered by the Forest Service. On the Oregon side of the Gorge, the Forest Service land is part of the Mount Hood National Forest, headquartered in Gresham:

Mount Hood National Forest
2955 NW Division Street
Gresham, Oregon 97030
503-666-0700

The portion of Mount Hood National Forest located within the Gorge is administered through two Forest Service ranger stations, one in the west end of the Gorge and one in the east end:

Columbia Gorge Ranger Station
U.S. Forest Service
31520 SE Woodard Road
Troutdale, Oregon 97230
503-695-2276

Hood River Ranger Station
U.S. Forest Service
6780 Highway 35
Mount Hood–Parkdale, Oregon 97041
503-352-6002; in Portland 666-0701

On the Washington side of the Gorge, the Forest Service land is within the Gifford Pinchot National Forest, with headquarters at:

Gifford Pinchot National Forest
500 W 12th Street
Vancouver, Washington 98660
206-696-7500 or 503-285-9823

The portion of the Gorge located within the Gifford Pinchot National Forest is in either the Wind River Ranger District or the Mount Adams Ranger District:

Wind River Ranger Station
Carson, Washington 98610
509-427-5645

Mount Adams Ranger Station
Trout Lake, Washington 98650
509-395-2501

For information on state parks on the Oregon side of the Gorge, contact either:

Oregon State Parks
525 Trade Street SE
Salem, Oregon 97310
503-378-6305

State Parks Portland Office
3554 SE 82nd Ave.
Portland, OR 97266
503-238-7488

For information on state parks on the Washington side of the Gorge, contact:

Washington State Parks and Recreation Commission
7150 Cleanwater Lane
Olympia, WA 98504-5711
206-753-5755

APPENDIX B

Exits from Interstate 84

Interstate 84, which follows the Oregon shore of the Columbia River through the Gorge, is a limited-access interstate freeway. Along its 86-mile length in the Gorge, exits and entrances occur at only thirty-seven locations. Most of those locations permit both access and exits for both eastbound and westbound travelers, but some offer access only, or exit only, or are available only to vehicles traveling in one direction.

All of the access and exit points are listed below. Most are official numbered freeway exits, but a few are simply wayside rest areas, some less developed than others. All are numbered according to the closest mile-post, those small, green, numbered signs seen at every mile of the freeway. The mileposts appear in ascending order from Lewis and Clark State Park (exit 18, 18 miles east of Portland) to Biggs Junction (exit 104).

Except as noted to the contrary, all offer four-way access, meaning that both access and exits are available to both eastbound and westbound traffic.

18 Lewis and Clark State Park.
22 Corbett.
23 Viewpoint (westbound only).
25 Rooster Rock State Park.
28 Bridal Veil (no access eastbound or exit westbound).
29 Dalton Point boat ramp (westbound only).
30 Benson State Park (eastbound only).
31 Multnomah Falls Rest Area.
35 Dodson/Ainsworth State Park.
37 Warrendale (no exit eastbound or access westbound).
40 Bonneville Dam and Fish Hatchery.
41 Eagle Creek (eastbound only).
44 Cascade Locks/Bridge of the Gods.
47 Columbia Gorge Work Center (no exit eastbound or access westbound).
51 Wyeth.
55 Starvation Creek State Park (eastbound only).
56 Viento State Park.
58 Rest Area (Mitchell Point) (eastbound only).
60 Wygant/Lausmann/Seneca Fouts State Park (no exit eastbound).
61 Ruthton Point (westbound only).
62 West Hood River.
63 Hood River City Center.

64 Port of Hood River/Hood River Bridge.
66 Stanley Rock Rest Area (westbound only).
67 Koberg Beach Wayside (westbound only; undeveloped).
69 Mosier.
73 Memaloose State Park/Wayside (park/wayside access and exit westbound only; rest area, on south side of freeway, access and exit eastbound only).
76 Rowena.
82 The Dalles (no exit westbound or access eastbound).
83 The Dalles (no exit westbound).
84 The Dalles (exit only; no access).
85 The Dalles City Center.
87 The Dalles Bridge.
88 The Dalles Dam.
97 Celilo Park.
104 Biggs Junction.

INDEX

The Contributors

Dr. John Eliot Allen is emeritus professor of geology at Portland State University, where he taught for nearly twenty years. A noted authority on the geology of the Gorge, he is the author of *The Magnificent Gateway: A Layman's Guide to the Geology of the Columbia River Gorge*, first published in 1979 by Timber Press (second edition 1984) and co-author of *Cataclysms on the Columbia* (Timber Press, second edition, 1991). His latter book describes the geologic features produced by the catastrophic Bretz floods that swept through the Columbia Gorge. Allen wrote the weekly geology column "Time Travel" for the Portland *Oregonian* from 1983 to 1987.

Bowen Blair, Jr., a Portland attorney, served as executive director of The Friends of the Columbia Gorge for several years. The Friends of the Columbia Gorge was among those responsible for passage of the Columbia River Gorge National Scenic Area Act in 1986, and Blair was its primary spokesman and lobbyist while the legislation was winding its way through Congress. He is presently employed as the Oregon representative for the Trust for Public Land. In his spare time, he is an avid windsurfer in the Gorge and on other waters of the Northwest.

Stewart Harvey is a Portland photographer and photography instructor. In addition to his work as a commercial, portrait, and wedding photographer, Harvey operates Portland Photographic Workshop, a school for fine art photography, and was one of the founders of the Portland Photographers Forum.

Mike Houck is employed by the Portland Audubon Society as their urban naturalist, where he is responsible for conservation issues pertaining to the preservation of wildlife habitat in the metropolitan region. He is also editor and a primary author of *The Urban Naturalist*, a quarterly publication of the Portland Audubon Society.

Russ Jolley is active with the Native Plant Society of Oregon, the Friends of the Columbia Gorge, and the Oregon Environmental Council. He has been studying the wildflowers of the Gorge since 1976. In 1988, the Oregon Historical Society Press published his comprehensive field guide *Wildflowers of the Columbia Gorge*.

Philip N. Jones is the author of *Canoe Routes: Northwest Oregon* and *Bicycling the Backroads of Northwest Oregon*, both published by The Mountaineers Books. He is an avid cyclist, paddler, and photographer, and is an active member of several outdoor organizations in the Northwest. He practices law in Portland.

Julie Kierstead Nelson is the Forest Botanist for the Shasta-Trinity National Forests in northern California. She was formerly employed by the Berry Botanic Garden in Portland as the curator of the Garden's Seed Bank for Rare and Endangered Plants of the Pacific Northwest, and has served as newsletter editor and conservation chairwoman for the Native Plant Society of Oregon. Her drawings have appeared in *Madroño, The Public Garden,* and other periodicals.

Ed Newville, a former expeditionary climber and Northwest Outward Bound instructor, has explored many of Oregon's waters by raft, sea kayak, and whitewater kayak. His climbing exploits have taken him up new routes in the Northwest, Canada, and Alaska. While this book was in preparation, he moved to New Mexico, where he is employed by the state supreme court.

Richard N. Ross is the transportation planner for the city of Gresham, Oregon, and has served as chair of the Ladds Addition Historic District Advisory Council in Portland, where he lives. Since 1980, he has been a leader of efforts to preserve and reuse the historic Columbia River Highway on behalf of the Historic Preservation League of Oregon and other organizations. He also serves on Portland's Urban Forestry Commission. He formerly taught American and Northwest history, which he studied at Reed College. He is an enthusiastic hiker and cyclist.

Jeff Thomas has been active on the Oregon climbing scene since 1970, and has climbed throughout North America and Europe. He has served as chairman of the Oregon section of the American Alpine Club and as a regional vice-president of the NADS Alpine Club. He is the author of *Oregon Rock,* a rock climbing guide to the state, and of *Oregon High,* a climbing guide to the high peaks of Oregon, published in 1991 by Keep Climbing Press. He operates a tree service in Portland.

Kathleen Tyau has been involved in a number of environmental issues on behalf of The Friends of the Columbia Gorge and the Oregon chapter of the Sierra Club. She is a member of the Oregon Natural Heritage Advisory Council. An active member of the Oregon Nordic Club, Tyau is a free-lance writer in Portland.

Joe Walicki has been exploring the Columbia Gorge and other wild areas of the Northwest for nearly two decades. In addition to leading hikes for the Oregon chapter of the Sierra Club and other groups, Walicki has played an active role in many environmental issues. He is employed as an admissions counselor at Marylhurst College near Portland.

Bill Wantz was a meteorologist for 22 years with the Bonneville Power Administration after graduating from the University of Washington. In addition to several professional papers, Wantz wrote articles for lay audiences and a pamphlet on weather for the Portland Parks Bureau. He died in 1985 at the age of 45.

Chuck Williams is the author of *Bridge of the Gods, Mountains of Fire: A Return to the Columbia Gorge,* published in 1980 by Friends of the Earth and Elephant Mountain Arts. Other works of his writing and photography include *Mount St. Helens: A Changing Landscape* and a guide to the Mount St. Helens National Monument. A former national parks specialist for Friends of the Earth, Williams is co-founder of the Columbia Gorge Coalition, one of several groups that worked for passage of the Columbia River Gorge National Scenic Area legislation. He is descended from Cascade Indians, and is a member of the Confederated Grand Ronde Tribes. He lives in Mosier, Oregon, and works for the Columbia River Inter-Tribal Fish Commission.

THE MOUNTAINEERS, founded in 1906, is a non-profit outdoor activity and conservation club, whose mission is "to explore, study, preserve and enjoy the natural beauty of the outdoors. . . ." Based in Seattle, Washington, the club is now the third largest such organization in the United States, with 12,000 members and four branches throughout Washington State.

The Mountaineers sponsors both classes and year-round outdoor activities in the Pacific Northwest, which include hiking, mountain climbing, skitouring, snowshoeing, bicycling, camping, kayaking and canoeing, nature study, sailing, and adventure travel. The club's conservation division supports environmental causes through educational activities, sponsoring legislation, and presenting informational programs. All club activities are led by skilled, experienced volunteers, who are dedicated to promoting safe and responsible enjoyment and preservation of the outdoors.

The Mountaineers Books, an active, non-profit publishing program of the club, produces guidebooks, instructional texts, historical works, natural history guides, and works on environmental conservation. All books produced by The Mountaineers are aimed at fulfilling the club's mission.

If you would like to participate in these organized outdoor activities or the club's programs, consider a membership in The Mountaineers. For information and an application, write or call The Mountaineers, Club Headquarters, 300 Third Avenue West, Seattle, Washington 98119; (206) 284-6310.

Other titles you may enjoy from The Mountaineers:

Exploring Oregon's Wild Areas: A Guide for Hikers, Backpackers, X-C Skiers & Paddlers, Sullivan.
Detail-stuffed guidebook to Oregon's 65 wilderness areas, wildlife refuges, nature preserves, and state parks.

Washington's Wild Rivers: The Unfinished Work, McNulty & O'Hara.
Beautiful, full-color celebration of state's rivers. Prose and photographs explain the place of rivers in the Northwest, existing systems for protecting them.

50 Hikes in Oregon's Coast Range and Siskiyous, Ostertag.
Hikes in mountain corridor between I-5 and Highway 101, from 1/2 mile walks to 47 mile backpacks.

Best Hikes With Children in Western and Central Oregon, Henderson.
100 easily-accessible hikes, many lesser-known, with detailed trail information Tips on hiking with kids, safety, and wilderness ethics.

Day Hikes From Oregon's Campgrounds, Ostertag.
Guide to campgrounds that access the best hikes and nature walks in Oregon. Facilities, hike descriptions, more.

Bicycling the Backroads of Northwest Oregon, Jones.
Descriptions, maps, mileage logs for 40 trips in Willamette Valley, from Portland south to Eugene.

A Pedestrian's Portland, Whitehill.
Features 1- to 5-mile walks in and around forty Portland, Oregon parks and neighborhoods.

The 100 Hikes Series
Washington's Alpine Lakes, Spring, Manning & Spring.
Washington's North Cascades: Glacier Peak Region, Spring & Manning.
Washington's North Cascades: Mount Baker Region, Spring & Manning.
Washington's South Cascades and Olympics, Spring & Manning.
Inland Northwest, Landers & Dolphin.

50 Hikes in Mount Rainier National Park, Spring & Manning

Available from your local book or outdoor store, or from The Mountaineers Books, 1011 SW Klickitat Way, Suite 107, Seattle, WA 98134. Or call for a catalog of over 200 outdoor books: 1-800-553-4453.